THE UNIVERSITY OF
WINCHESTER

Unstable universalities

Manchester University Press

Simon Tormey and Jon Simons · series editors

The times we live in are troubling, and as always theory struggles
to keep pace with events in its efforts to analyse and assess
society, culture and politics. Many of the 'contemporary' political
theories emerged and developed in the twentieth century
or earlier, but how well do they work at the start
of the twenty-first century?

Reappraising the Political realigns political theory with its
contemporary context. The series is interdisciplinary in approach,
seeking new inspiration from both traditional sister disciplines,
and from more recent neighbours such as literary theory and
cultural studies. It encompasses an international range,
recognising both the diffusion and adaptation of Western political
thought in the rest of the world, and the impact of global
processes and non-Western ideas on Western politics.

already published

Rehinking equality: the challenge of equal citizenship
Chris Armstrong
Radical democracy: politics between abundance and lack
Lars Tønder and Lasse Thomassen (eds)
*The biopolitics of the war on terror: life struggles, liberal modernity
and the defence of logistical societies*
Julian Reid

Saul Newman

UNSTABLE UNIVERSALITIES

Poststructuralism and radical politics

Manchester University Press
Manchester and New York

distributed exclusively in the USA by Palgrave

Published by Manchester University Press
Oxford Road, Manchester M13 9NR, UK
and Room 400, 175 Fifth Avenue, New York, NY 10010, USA
www.manchesteruniversitypress.co.uk

Distributed exclusively in the USA by
Palgrave, 175 Fifth Avenue, New York,
NY 10010, USA

Distributed exclusively in Canada by
UBC Press, University of British Columbia, 2029 West Mall,
Vancouver, BC, Canada V6T 1Z2

British Library Cataloguing-in-Publication Data
A catalogue record for this book is available from the British Library

Library of Congress Cataloging-in-Publication Data applied for

ISBN 978 0 7190 7128 7 *hardback*

First published 2007

16 15 14 13 12 11 10 09 08 07   10 9 8 7 6 5 4 3 2 1

Typeset
by Action Publishing Technology Ltd, Gloucester
Printed in Great Britain
by MPG Books Ltd, Bodmin, Cornwall

To my Dad, who always urged me to cut down on my use of the word 'posit'

Contents

Acknowledgements

There are a number of people I would like to thank, whose help was crucial in writing this book. Thanks must go to the 'Reappraising the Political' series editors who encouraged me to go ahead with this project – and particularly to Simon Tormey for his invaluable comments on my first draft. Here I must also mention Ben Noys and Michael Levine for their insightful suggestions and comments on several chapters. I would also like to acknowledge the assistance and support of Bruce Stone and the Department of Political Science and International Relations at UWA in allowing me generous use of its facilities while writing this book.

Introduction

IF, AS MARX believed, the role of philosophy was not to interpret the world but to change it, then radical political philosophy is doubly charged with this task. Yet ever since the spectacular collapse of the Communist systems nearly two decades ago, and indeed for some time before, the radical political imaginary of the Left had been in a state of crisis. Even socialists today embrace capitalism and the global free market, and devote their energies to fighting 'cultural wars' against ever more minute forms of discrimination. The so-called Third Way, which originally sought a 'middle road' between capitalism and socialism, has become no more than a New Age neo-liberalism coupled with a socially conservative discourse of 'responsibility' and 'community protection'. Moreover, not only has the Left been unable to counter the recent resurgence of the Far Right, particularly in Europe, but many social democratic parties have actually adopted, in a disguised form, much of its anti-immigrant ideology and rhetoric – if not its actual policies.

So what is the future for radical left politics in an age that proclaims itself to be not only post-ideological but post-political as well? How can one define what a radical position is at a time when it is virtually unthinkable to question global capitalism, and when the very idea of emancipation is looked upon suspiciously, even by many on the Left? More specifically, what is the role of radical political theory today in addressing these concerns? This latter question is the one that most concerns this book.

This crisis in the radical political imaginary is often seen as being an aspect of the 'postmodern condition' in politics. Postmodernity is a term that for some time now has been widely and somewhat extravagantly applied in both academic and cultural discourse. Generally speaking, postmodernity refers to a cultural condition symptomatic of late post-industrial capitalist societies and which is characterised by, as Jean-François Lyotard put it, an *incredulity towards metanarratives*. In other words, the 'postmodern condition' is one of a fundamental questioning of the grand ideals and universal discourses that had defined our social, political and cultural reality since the Enlightenment. The Enlightenment, whose bright beam of reason had for centuries illuminated our lives, liberating us from the dark world of religious and ideological obscurantism, was now coming to be seen as itself an ideology, one that was no longer central to our social existence and which, moreover, masked a distinctly Eurocentric and 'logocentric' perspective. Our faith in progress, science and modernity had been misplaced, since these discourses now merely obscured the plurality and incommensurability of different epistemological and moral perspectives that make up contemporary society. Theorists of postmodernity contend, in other words, that life in post-industrial societies is too complex, diverse and heterogeneous to be explained within the rational and moral categories of the Enlightenment paradigm, and that therefore these categories can no longer serve as the foundation for social and political consensus.

However, it is too simplistic to see postmodernity as an actual historical stage beyond modernity. Even if this were the case, it would be impossible to agree on a date for the dawning of the 'postmodern age' – did it not begin, paradoxically, at the height of modernity? For instance, did Freud's anatomy of a dream mark the triumph of science over the dark regions of the unconscious, or did it highlight the very limits of man's rational self-transparency? While the 'postmodern condition' has its conditions in technological, cultural and social transformations endemic to late twentieth-century capitalism, nevertheless philosophical perspectives that could be described as 'postmodern' were around long before then. Therefore, postmodernity may be seen as referring to a critical engagement with the discourses of the Enlightenment and an ongoing questioning of its universal assumptions, rather than a specific period in history.

This 'paradigm' of postmodernity has had an enormous impact on radical political theory. For the past two hundred or so years, radical political thought – from socialism to anarchism – has been founded on the epistemological and normative discourses of the Enlightenment, discourses which are now being questioned. From the utopian societies dreamt up by the early socialists like Saint-Simon and Fourier, to the revolutionary projects of Marx and Lenin, and even to the later sexual rebellions of Marcuse – all of these aspirations had been largely motivated by an Enlightenment way of thinking. This included: a concept of society and social reality as transparent, scientifically observable and determined by historical forces; a faith in rationality to both overcome social antagonisms and to liberate the individual from the obfuscating veils of religion and ideology; a belief in the universal liberation of all humanity from oppressive social and political arrangements; and a notion of the human subject with essential moral and rational characteristics which could flourish given the right social conditions.

Now it is precisely some of these ideas that have been challenged within the paradigm of postmodernity. They are seen as 'metanarratives' which can no longer be sustained in the contemporary world of multiple perspectives, heterogeneous identities and ever-shifting and 'virtual' realities. For instance, how can the idea of human emancipation any longer apply to a world in which there are not only differing notions of what emancipation means, but also differing notions of what it means to be human? Did not Foucault predict that the figure of Man would disappear like a face drawn in sand at the edge of the sea? Many have suggested that this has already happened, and that we are seeing the

dawning of a new post-human and cyborg age.[1] Moreover, how can we assume
that rational ideas and discourses would be universally understood and accepted
when they are not only a reflection of a particular European epistemological
perspective, but have also been used in the past to legitimise European colonial
domination? Furthermore, has not Nietzschean genealogy undermined history
and the dialectic? Has not 'paganism' supplanted science?

These challenges have had important consequences for radical politics, and
have led to a general displacement of its conceptual categories. Instead of the
essentially rational human subject who was to be emancipated from power and
ideology, we have a subject who is dispersed amongst a multiplicity of desires
and intensities, and whose identity is deeply interwoven into discursive and
power structures. Related to this also is the displacement of the category of
class from the summit of radical politics: the proletariat is no longer the essential radical subject, and political struggles are no longer overdetermined by
'class struggles' as they were in the Marxist schema. Instead, many have pointed
to the emergence over the past few decades of new radical political subjectivities and forms of activism – blacks and ethnic minorities against racism,
feminists against patriarchy, gays against homophobia, and so on. These are
the 'new social movements' that have coloured the postmodern political
terrain.

There is no doubt that many aspects of the postmodern critique of the
universal radical politics of emancipation are valid and relevant. For Foucault,
for instance, the conservative role played by the French Communist Party (PCF)
in the May '68 insurrections in Paris was indicative of the inability of Marxist
theory to see radical politics in any other terms but class struggle as determined
by economic conditions, and its blindness to new forms of activism that were
emerging around questions of power, authority, subjectivity and autonomy.
Indeed, May '68 was the defining moment of the New Left, a political and theoretical tradition associated with, and influenced by, poststructuralism. I shall
define poststructuralism later, as well as explore its nuances and political implications in more depth – as it is the central theoretical problematic of this book.
However thinkers in this tradition – including Foucault, Lyotard and Deleuze –
were all deeply influenced by the political experience of May '68, and they
became critical of what they saw as the totalising and universalising logic of
Marxist theory. Indeed, Foucault believed that by focussing on the broad aspects
of economic and class domination, Marxism neglected more localised practices
of power and domination, and the struggles that sought to contest them – a
phenomenon that was highlighted by the experience of May '68 itself. He said in
an interview:

> Where Soviet socialist power was in question, its opponents called it totalitar-
> ianism; power in Western capitalism was denounced by Marxists as class
> domination; but the mechanics of power in themselves were never analysed.

This task could only begin after 1968; that is to say on the basis of daily struggles at a grass roots level among those whose fight was located in the fine mesh of the web of power.[2]

For Foucault, the nature of radical politics had changed from one of universal emancipation and social transformation, to one of particular and differentiated struggles against particular and differentiated forms of domination. Moreover, the role of the intellectual had changed from the Sartrean notion of articulating the universal interests of the masses, to a much more limited function of applying one's technical expertise to a specific area. Deleuze, and his collaborator Guattari, similarly emphasised politics occurring at the 'micro' rather than 'macro' level – in other words, at the level of differentiated and heterogeneous struggles.[3] Lyotard advocated an approach to politics that remained open to what he called the *differend* – that is, the incommensurable differences between discourses and perspectives. To try to occlude these differences through a more universal political position was seen by Lyotard as 'terroristic': rather, the goal of politics was simply to testify to these differences themselves, to allow them to be heard.[4]

What is rejected in these various approaches is therefore a universal emancipatory politics in favour of a politics that is localised, specific and differentiated. Universal political positions and strategies are seen as inherently authoritarian because they not only fail to confront more diffuse, hidden forms of domination – at the level of discourses, social practices and institutions – but also because they are based on essentialist conceptions of subjectivity and rationality, and they therefore deny perspectives and forms of subjectivity that do not fit into this paradigm.

However there is a problem: with this dismissal of 'totalising' Enlightenment-based political discourses, is there not the danger of radical politics losing a universal emancipative dimension upon which its critique of domination is based? In other words, has not poststructuralism, with its valorisation of difference, specificity and incommensurability, not deprived radical politics of a universal ontological ground upon which collective identities and movements could be formed? Is poststructuralism not therefore confined to a localised politics of resistance – the lonely struggle of the prisoner in his cell, or of the homosexual against his discursive 'incarceration'? It is true that the thinkers mentioned above have all, at various times, discussed collective forms of resistance: for instance, Foucault was interested in the emergence of a collective political 'spirituality' during the 1979 Iranian Revolution; Lyotard was interested in the anti-imperialist struggle against the French in Algeria, and the way it could be seen as a form of resistance to a totalitarian imposition of French culture, values and institutions upon the Algerian people. However, the problem is that without a universal emancipative dimension, these events appear to be singular occurrences which could not serve as a basis for thinking about broader political and social struggles. I see this theme of universality as central to radical politics, and the main question that I will be dealing with in this book is to what extent this theme is thinkable within the discourse of post-structuralism.

There are a number of central issues emerging today that present fundamental challenges to the way we think about radical politics and which call into question this perhaps over-hasty dismissal of a universal idea of emancipation. The first is the so-called 'war on terror' and the new forms of power, domination and ideology that are emerging with it. The second is what is broadly termed the 'anti-globalisation' movement, which is still in its nascent state, and which already represents a significant political challenge to global capitalism. The third issue – perhaps less concrete than the previous too, yet just as crucial – is what is referred to by various theorists as the new 'non-politics'. That is, that politics in general today is characterised by an overwhelming sense of stagnation, by a turning away from the idea of progressive social transformation more towards notions of the 'middle road', free market 'consensus' and technocratic government. This condition in a way forms the background to the previous two issues, and signifies a fundamental mutation of traditional political structures, institutions and values. Any discussion of radical politics today must take into account these three developments. Moreover, the ability of radical political theory to address these concerns will depend on its ability to theorise a new universal and collective dimension of emancipation.

The global 'war on terror' is the new dominant ideological paradigm that we are all living in today. It is the discourse on everyone's lips: we are told by repeatedly by every politician and every media outlet that we are now in a state of war with global terrorism, and that this war will last a generation. With almost astonishing alacrity and uniformity, governments tell us that the world has changed since September 11 and that we now face an invisible, faceless enemy who can strike anywhere at any time. A new climate of fear and paranoia has pervaded political and social life – to the extent that the principle of 'security' has now become the dominant, overriding feature of contemporary politics.[5]

It is also important to examine the way that the 'war on terror' has become the reigning ideology today, and is being used by the modern state as a pretext for perpetuating its power. Apart from the more obvious abuses of the discourse on terror – cynically using it to justify the invasion of Iraq – there has been a general intensification, to unprecedented levels, of surveillance and control. Agamben talks about a 'state of exception' in which normal legal protections no longer apply and the state acts with impunity. Paradoxically, rather than this being an extraordinary or anomalous situation, it is the moment when sovereignty reveals its true face. Moreover, it is when this state of exception becomes the rule, when it becomes indistinguishable from everyday life, that the situation becomes truly dangerous.

The problem is that the 'state of exception' *is* becoming the rule. What is perhaps surprising, however, is that there has not generally been a serious, critical analysis of the new techniques of surveillance and control that have emerged with the 'war on terror'. The expansion of the power of the state and its increasing incursion into social life should alarm radical political theorists and activists as much as it might liberals and libertarians, especially at a time when the ideological terrain appears to have shifted to such an extent that to be radical these days is precisely to insist on things like the rule of law and the protection of civil liberties and human rights. It may be, however, that the traditional liberal discourse of rights and freedoms is now meaningless in the face of this new form of domination. Agamben has argued that all politics is now 'biopolitics' – that, in other words, state control now functions at the level of the regulation of biological life itself (something that is all too apparent today with widespread DNA surveillance), and that this forms the nexus that underpins both authoritarian and liberal-democratic regimes. However, this should at least suggest that what is needed is an extensive analysis and critique of the new forms of power that are emerging today, especially as questions of power and autonomy are central to contemporary radical political theory.

However, perhaps the most important question posed by the 'war on terror' and the aggressive reassertion of state sovereignty, is that of the contours of radical politics itself. That is to say, the increasing expansion of state power is something that concerns humanity as a whole. Ordinary people – not just minority groups – are now subjected to these new techniques of surveillance and control. This is perhaps the most crucial feature of biopolitics – it takes as its target human existence itself. In other words, the implications of the 'war on terror' are universal, but not in the sense that its advocates suggest: it is rather that everyone is being caught up in a strange new network of power, and inscribed on a new ideological terrain where the only choice that appears to be available is that between an authoritarian state and a fundamentalist dogma, and between the violence and terror inflicted by both. Humanity itself is caught between these forces. Radical left politics must urgently address this polarisation of the political and social field. However, the only way it can do this is through the inclusion of a universal category of 'the people'. In other words, radical politics must devise a more universal and collective approach to this problem – and this requires a rethinking and re-inclusion of the very idea of universality itself, as well as the development of new collective identities of resistance. It would seem that theoretical perspectives that valorise only difference and incommensurability, and construct a politics and ethics around these terms, have limited relevance to this project. In other words, there has been a general shift in the political terrain to much broader concerns, concerns which go beyond the politics of difference and identity and which relate to humanity as a whole. If radical politics fails to construct a new collective political imaginary, then it risks being pushed aside entirely by an ideological conservatism which is pervading Western societies, where any form of political dissent is now in danger of being branded with the convenient term 'terrorism'.

However, a glimpse of a new form of radical political universality might be seen in what is generally referred to as the 'anti-globalisation' movement. In recent years, notwithstanding the current climate of repression, we have seen the emergence of an entirely new political and social movement that calls into question the neo-liberal vision of capitalist globalisation which seems to form the very parameters of our age. This is a movement that has exploded across our horizons, and has generally been directed against the more visible symbols of global capitalism – WTO and IMF meetings and large multinational corporations – as well as having intersected with the global anti-war movement since 2003. What makes this movement interesting from the perspective of contemporary radical politics, is the new form of political universality that it embodies. On the one hand, it goes beyond the narrow and particularistic identity politics that had prevailed for some time in Western societies. It is much more universal in its makeup and its aspirations. It seeks to challenge the hegemony of global capitalism by highlighting the different forms of exploitation and domination that are inherent in it – from the dispossession of indigenous people, to the exploitation of sweatshop workers, to environmental degradation, to the power of multinational companies. However, the anti-globalisation struggle also goes beyond the traditional class politics of Marxism. Firstly, it does not confine itself strictly to economic issues, but also highlights, for instance, environmental concerns, and issues of autonomy and exclusion. Secondly, it does not limit itself to the struggle of the industrial working class, nor does it regard other struggles as being of secondary importance to that of workers. It is much more heterogeneous than that, and includes the campaigns of environmentalists, labour rights activists, refugee groups, and so on. Thirdly, it also rejects centralist and authoritarian structures, structures that characterised many forms of Marxist politics: there is no one political party or identity at its helm. Rather, the movement is entirely decentralised and based on autonomous, self-governing groups and democratic principles.

One of the aims of this book will be to explore the political practices, structures and identities that characterise the anti-globalisation movement in order to show how a new radical political universality might be constructed from contemporary conditions. In other words, perhaps the anti-globalisation movement might serve as a practical model for radical politics today. The emergence of this movement is one of the most important developments in radical politics in recent years. It suggests entirely new forms of collective identity, political organisation and activism. It is perhaps surprising, then, that there has been a general reticence about it on the part of many radical political theorists. One reason for this reticence might be a reluctance or even inability to think beyond the parameters of the present. What is unique about the anti-globalisation movement is that it does what is almost unthinkable today from the perspective of dominant political and ideological paradigms – that is, to question the very legitimacy of global capitalism.

This ideological impasse, in which radical social projects are seen as no longer possible or legitimate, is part of a technocratic approach to politics that has prevailed for some time in modern Western societies, and which, I suggest, constitutes the third condition that radical political theory today must address. For some time now – at least since the fall of the Berlin Wall and the hegemony of neo-liberal economics – political discourse, even, and, indeed especially, that of social democratic parties, has shied away from any reference to a possible alternative to global capitalism, or even to the possibility of significantly reforming its conditions. Such aspirations are now regarded with a vague sense of embarrassment, even astonishment, as though one were a remnant of an ideological dinosaur age. Indeed, we are told we live in a 'post-ideological' age where 'good governance' and 'sensible policies' have supposedly replaced the ideological struggles of the past. Responsible economic management is now the dominant signifier of contemporary politics. Notwithstanding the blatantly ideological position from which the end of ideology is trumpeted – one which has revealed itself in New Labour's steady shift to the right in the UK, culminating in Blair's decision to join the ignominious 'coalition of the willing' in Iraq – the point is that this new governmental rationality has for some time been the paradigm in which parties from both sides of the political spectrum in Western democracies now operate.

This paradigm has a number of key characteristics: an obsession with spin and media profile; a fetishism of opinion polls; constant appeals to the 'political mainstream'; and, most particularly, an increasing social conservatism, marked by the competition between political parties to outdo each other in 'law and order' and anti-immigrant policies.[6] This last characteristic has of course been intensified in recent years, intersecting with the 'war on terror'; but already for some time it has been a convenient way for politicians to divert attention away from the social dislocations wrought by neo-liberal capitalist economic policies. Society always needs its enemies as Foucault would say, and these enemies now take the form of criminals, illegal migrants, asylum seekers and 'enemy combatants'. Moreover, because governments today like to claim to be 'reformist' and have therefore always to be seen to be doing *something*, they engage in a kind of feverish false activity which disguises their very inability to make any significant social changes. Thus, in the name of reform, hard fought for democratic rights and civil liberties are done away with at the stroke of a pen. We are told that they are remnants of an outdated legal system that is no longer relevant. More subtly, this paradigm seeks to vitiate potentially radical political demands by responding to them in a technocratic manner. Thus, they become incorporated into an institutional discourse which isolates them from other demands.

So we have three fundamental and, in some ways, contradictory conditions that radical political theory must contend with today: the so-called 'War on terror' with its new and dangerous articulations of state power and social control; the 'anti-globalisation' movement which seems to be inventing its own conditions and radical possibilities; and the stifling atmosphere of consensus and centrism that so dominates modern democratic politics, and which itself leads to the explosion of racist, nationalist and fundamentalist forms of politics as a kind of 'return of the repressed'. These concerns are central to the future of radical politics: the 'war on terror' not only imposes an ideological straightjacket on radical political activities, but constitutes a significant threat to individual freedom; the 'anti-globalisation' movement, in the new forms of politics it encompasses, suggests a need to revitalise radical political theory through a rethinking of its conditions; while the paradigm of 'non-politics' implies a need to re-examine democracy and its importance for radical politics. Moreover, they all touch, in different ways, on the question of political universality central to this book: the 'war on terror', while it claims to be targeting tiny extremist minorities, is actually much more universal in its scope and aims at the total surveillance and control of society; the anti-globalisation protests invoke the idea of a universal struggle against the state and capitalism; while the contemporary managerial approach to politics, while it claims to serve the interests of the 'Centre', is actually a way of excluding the dimension of universality from the symbolic register of democracy.

For these reasons, radical political theory must rethink the question of universality. However, the problem is that if we are to take the political implications of postmodernism seriously – and I think we should, at least to some extent – then upon what theoretical basis can the idea of universality be conceived? Many have argued that postmodernism simply equates with a politics of difference which no longer represents any threat to hegemonic political, economic and social structures. Frederic Jameson, for instance, has seen postmodernism as the 'cultural logic' of late capitalism. In other words, postmodernism embraces certain motifs such as simulacra, heterogeneity and the absence of depth, and these are precisely the cultural forms adopted by contemporary capitalism.[7] Terry Eagleton has criticised postmodern cultural theory on similar grounds – that both postmodernism and capitalism share a contempt for stable identities, unity and permanent ground; both valorise difference, flux and heterogeneity.[8] Indeed, the folly of postmodern cultural theory, according to Eagleton, lies in its claims to be radical by transgressing fixed boundaries and limits – whereas this transgression is exactly what capitalism itself, in its endless pursuit of profit, thrives on. In the same vein, Slavoj Žižek has criticised the postmodern politics of difference, pointing to the way in which the differential demands of minority groups are effortlessly accommodated within the liberal multicultural framework of capitalism.[9] Liberal multiculturalism, according to Žižek, presupposes a sort of menagerie of differences, each of which must be maintained in its particularity, and that this is precisely the outcome of a postmodern politics which demands 'respect' for otherness and difference.

These insights suggest that radical politics is currently in crisis, and that any consideration of the importance of postmodern theory for radical politics must be tempered with the sober realisation that dominant political, social and economic structures have themselves become postmodern*ised*, and have in a sense incorporated the very strategies that sought to transgress them. So the fundamental dilemma for radical political theory is *which way to turn?* There are a number of possible responses here. We could simply turn our backs on postmodernity, reject its political implications, and return to traditional Marxist categories – such as the dialectic and the political primacy of the working class. This would be the strategy of someone like Alex Callinicos, who explicitly repudiates postmodernism as a conservative discourse that fits hand in glove with global capitalism.[10] Alternatively, one could embrace postmodernism uncritically, revelling nihilistically and resignedly in the universe of endless flux and multiple 'subject positions'. Those who celebrate the 'subversive' and 'transgressive' potential of the cyber, and indeed, cyborg, age, with its cynical manipulations of the human experience – the bonding of man and machine – and the cold perversions of the 'fully liberated' and 'hybrid' sexual subject, might be indicative of this latter position. However, I would suggest that both enterprises are ultimately misguided and self-defeating: the former seeks refuge in the hallowed identities and concepts of the past; while the latter not only lacks the commitment to rigorous political and ethical critique of contemporary conditions, but seems to provide a kind of fetishised ideological supplement to these very conditions. In this way, both positions are conservative, but for different reasons.

My contention, however, is that there is a middle road, a sort of theoretical 'third way' for radical politics to take. This would be to take a kind of critical distance from, or at least a measured attitude towards, postmodernity, while at the same time taking account of its very significant implications for politics today. This would also involve a much more qualified stance towards the Enlightenment and the discourse of humanism – neither an outright rejection nor a simple reaffirmation – but rather a rethinking of them in the light of contemporary political conditions, and a re-consideration of their critical potential. In other words, one should ask: what is there in the Enlightenment and humanism that still speaks to us today, that allows us to critically engage with political challenges, and that is therefore worthwhile salvaging and indeed building upon? What is worth preserving, I would argue, *is* a notion of universality – an idea of a common political imaginary that transcends particular political perspectives and identities, and that speaks – perhaps in different ways, but nevertheless *speaks* – to all those who today are oppressed, excluded, exploited, dominated, marginalised and deprived. Radical politics simply cannot continue without some sort of idea of emancipation – from poverty, from state oppression, from racism, from violence, and so on.

However, the question then becomes *how* exactly to theorise this universal dimension if, at the same time, we are taking seriously poststructuralism's challenge to humanism, rationalism and essentialism? How should the universal dimension be constituted, for instance, if not on the basis of a universal notion of the human subject, or on assumptions about a universal rationality or a set of values that everyone supposedly shares? If we were liberals or communitarians we could simply appeal to shared norms or to a communicative rationality. Rawls' 'original position' might serve as the ultimate rational foundation for establishing a notion of universal equality and freedom. From a poststructuralist perspective, however, we would be forced to question the assumptions that Rawls makes about the rational choice behaviour of subjects.

So, in other words, if we are to take account of this critique, we can no longer rely on assumptions about an essential human rationality or morality to form the foundation for universal political action. Indeed, we cannot rely on firm foundations at all. We therefore have to investigate other ways in which this ambiguous universality might be theorised. And this is precisely the task of this book – to rethink the concept of universality in light of postmodernity, or at least, in light of the poststructuralist critique of essentialist identities and fixed moral and rational norms.

In doing so, the book will examine and critically appraise the ideas of a number of key thinkers who have all had a strong impact on radical political theory, having forced us to rethink the very political categories and concepts we have hitherto taken for granted. Some of these thinkers cannot accurately be described as 'poststructuralist' – some indeed would vigorously reject the label. However, they all engage – albeit in very different ways – with the postmodern condition: some are more critical and sceptical of it, others less so. But the point is that they all take its implications seriously, and try to find ways of responding to it. That is, they all work within a 'paradigm' that tends to reject essentialist identities and universal rational and moral norms. They might be seen, then, as being part of the Continental, rather than Anglo-American or analytical tradition of philosophy and political thought. Moreover, their theoretical trajectories could be broadly described as post-Althusserian and post-Saussurian, implying a move beyond structuralism in both politics and linguistics.

Amongst those that I will be discussing, then, are: Foucault, Lacan, Derrida, Deleuze, Lyotard, Žižek, Rancière, Agamben, Laclau, Mouffe, Badiou, Connolly and Hardt and Negri. They represent a broad range of theoretical perspectives:

poststructuralism, psychoanalysis, deconstruction, post-Marxism, autonomism – while others would not come under any of these categories. So it has to be emphasised, firstly, that these thinkers are very different, despite a certain theoretical heritage that some might share. They engage with different political questions in very different ways, some more obliquely than others. Moreover, their differences are just as important, for the purposes of this study, as their similarities. Indeed, it is through the tensions, debates and disagreements between these thinkers – both actual and potential – that new insights for politics can be developed. So this book will examine the points of intersection and divergence amongst these various thinkers on questions that are central to radical political theory today: power and ideology, subjectivity, ethics, democracy and collective action. Forming a background to these debates and issues will be the question of universality, and the extent to which these various interventions allow for some sort of universal, emancipative dimension to be realised. It is clearly the case, for instance, that while certain thinkers, like Laclau, Badiou and Žižek engage with this universal political dimension directly, others such as Foucault, Deleuze and Lyotard tend to place more emphasis on the politics of the local and particular. However, what they do share, as I have said, is a desire to rethink politics beyond the traditional normative questions, rational choice models of behaviour and essentialist identities that have generally characterised it, at least in the Anglo-American world.

The second point to emphasise is that this book is not intended as simply a survey of ideas and thinkers. The treatment of these thinkers is by no means systematic, and certainly not comprehensive. It is, rather, intended as an exploration of certain key themes and issues in radical politics today, seeking to shed light on them and address them in some way through the application and development of these thinkers' ideas. More precisely, it is the elaboration of a central position about the continued importance of universality in radical politics today, and an attempt to develop a theory of universality that does not rely on essentialist identities and concepts.

Chapter outline

In the first chapter, I outline some of the characteristics of the 'postmodern condition' as defined by Lyotard. The cultural condition of postmodernity, which emerges with late capitalism, has led to a dislocation of our accepted political reality. Instead of the universal discourses and 'metanarratives' of the past, which were founded on the rational certainties of the Enlightenment, there is a severing of the social bond and a general sense of fragmentation in the fields of knowledge, culture and social relations. Here I examine the two main responses to the decline of the metanarrative: the 'foundationalist' approach – exemplified by Habermas – which seeks to re-establish firm rational foundations for political action; and the anti-foundationalist or broadly termed 'post-structuralist' strategy, which seeks to question these foundations, showing their contingent and unstable character. These two conflicting strategies present us with a theoretical and political dilemma: if we accept the postmodern condition – that is, if we acknowledge the absence of absolute foundations and essential identities – then how do we theorise radical politics today?

Chapter 2 examines the concept of power. I argue that an understanding of modern power relationships and the new forms of 'postmodern' social control and surveillance that are emerging today – particularly in the 'war on terror' – is vital to the development of new radical political strategies. Here, I take as my point of departure Foucault's notion of power. However, while recognising its radical innovation, I also point out certain limitations here: its general focus on 'micro-political' relations tends to imply a kind of localised politics of resistance and, moreover, neglects to some extent the 'broader picture' of political domination, including the problem of state sovereignty itself. Furthermore, I also argue for a reconsideration of the concept of ideology which, far from having been surpassed, as Foucault had suggested, seems to be never more relevant today in our so-called 'post-ideological' world.

The following chapter (3) takes as its point of departure the condition of the subject under power, exploring the problem of self-domination or self-subjection: the way that the subject, rather than simply being coerced or repressed, often willingly conforms to the very identities and subject 'positions' that have been constructed for him. This creates certain problems for radical politics, however: there is no longer a universal human subject to be emancipated or a completely autonomous conception of human agency. Here I explore a number of different responses to this crisis of the 'death of Man': Foucault's strategies of self-mastery and autonomy through the ethic of 'care'; Deleuze and Guattari's attack on Oedipal subjectivity, and their Nietzschean dispersal of the very category of subject into a multitude of forces, potentialities and moments of flux. Neither approach, I argue, is adequate. Instead, we must seek a new approach to the question of subjectivity – one which retains the central category of the subject, yet which is no longer defined through a stable, essential identity. Using Lacanian psychoanalytic theory, I try to develop from this a new understanding of political subjectification – one that involves at the same time a rupturing of existing identities and subject positions.

In examining the conditions for radical political subjectification, one inevitably encounters the question of ethics: to what extent should radical politics be guided by a notion of ethics? In Chapter 4, I examine the place of ethics in radical politics today, suggesting that the postmodern condition is characterised, on the one hand, by the breakdown of the Kantian notions of ethics, and on the other, by the uncanny return of conservative 'values' and moral fundamentalism. Moreover, ethics today increasingly takes the form of an ideology which is perpetuated by different institutions, and often serves as a guise for political domination and Western imperialism. We must therefore chart a course here between these simulacra, and develop a new radical politico-ethics. Here I consider various contemporary approaches to the question of ethics: Habermas' notion of 'discourse ethics'; Lyotard's ethics of incommensurability; Rorty's liberal ethics of 'postmodern irony'; Lacan's ethics of psychoanalysis; and Derrida's ethics of deconstruction.

And what of democracy? Is democracy the only ethical form of polity, or has the term become so corrupted and impoverished today, so much associated with the US imperialist project, that we must abandon it altogether and develop a new form of politics? This is the central question that I consider in Chapter 5. Here I explore the crisis of democracy today – the way that, in the conditions of the 'war on terror' and with the ideological consensus that has emerged around the 'free market' and 'security', the term 'democracy' has become largely meaningless. However, rather than simply abandoning democracy, I suggest that democracy contains a radical and emancipative potential that can be reactivated today. Here I explore a number of different attempts to revive democracy: Connolly's democratic ethos of pluralism; Habermas' and Benhabib's notions of 'deliberative democracy'; Lefort's concept of the democratic revolution; and Mouffe's pluralistic approach to radical democracy. In pointing out the benefits and limitations of these different approaches, I arrive at the conclusion that for democracy to be taken seriously today – for its principle of liberty and equality to be realised – then it must be detached from the concept of state sovereignty.

The final chapter (6) draws these various themes, strands and arguments together and applies them to an analysis of radical politics today. Taking postmodernity as its *theoretical* background, and globalisation as its *political* background, this chapter focuses on the 'anti-globalisation' movement. I argue that the movement highlights new forms of political practice and articulation, as well as a new relationship to political identity. Moreover, in taking global anti-capitalism as its political and ethical horizon, I show how this movement can be seen as an expression of a new form of political universality, one that can be understood through a poststructuralist 'paradigm'. Here I take issue with a number of contemporary thinkers for their reticence about the anti-globalisation movement, showing how their approaches to radical politics correspond, in certain important ways, to the strategies, identities and forms of discursive articulation evident in contemporary anti-globalisation politics. Here I try to develop an understanding of anti-globalisation politics as based around the concept of 'the people' and the demand for rights.

In engaging with these questions, I will attempt to outline briefly a theory of post-anarchism. Anarchism, or left libertarianism, forms the underlying ethical and political referent for this study. This is for a number of reasons. Firstly, the new radical politics today – that which is symbolised by the anti-globalisation movement – can be seen as an 'anarchist' form of politics: it is a politics without a leader or centralised party, and in which there are decentralised and non-hierarchical forms of organisation and collective mobilisation; it is also a politics which fundamentally challenges not only the hegemony of global capitalism, but also the sovereignty of the state. Secondly, I see poststructuralism as implying an anti-authoritarian *ethos* – that is, a political and ethical commitment to question and interrogate the authority of institutions, discourses and practices that we tend to see as being legitimate and rational. I therefore see a kind of ethical continuum between anarchism and poststructuralism, notwithstanding the significant differences between these discourses.[11] Thirdly, given the theoretical and political decline of Marxism, the central problem that confronts radical political theory and practice today is how to retain a strong commitment to universal emancipation, equality and social transformation, without falling back into authoritarian politics – centralised party apparatuses, libidinal attachments to a leader, terroristic and violent pragmatics, and totalitarian political institutions – with all the oppression, misery and death that they imply. While I cannot hope to satisfactorily answer such a pressing question, I will attempt to devise new ways of thinking through this quandary, trying to find a middle road between the recognition of pluralism and the need to remain faithful to universal ideas of equality and emancipation. Anarchism and *postanarchism* are important here because they seek to combine the principles of individual freedom and autonomy, and social and economic equality, to their fullest possible extent. In doing so, they provide a political and ethical point of departure for the project I have embarked upon.

Notes

1 See D. Haraway, 'A cyborg manifesto: science, technology, and socialist-feminism in the late twentieth century', in *Simians, Cyborgs and Women: The Reinvention of Nature* (New York: Routledge, 1991), pp. 149–181.

2 M. Foucault, 'Truth and power', in *Power/Knowledge: Selected Interviews and Other Writings 1972–77*, ed. Colin Gordon (New York: Harvester Press, 1980), pp. 109–133, p. 116.

3 See G. Deleuze and F. Guattari, *A Thousand Plateaus: Capitalism and Schizophrenia*, trans. Brian Massumi (Minneapolis: University of Minnesota Press, 1987), p. 33.

4 J.-F. Lyotard, *The Differend: Phrases in Dispute*, trans. G. Van Den Abeele (Manchester: Manchester University Press, 1988), p. 13.

5 See G. Agamben, 'Security and terror', trans. Carolin Emcke, *Theory and Event* 5 (2002): <http://muse.jhu.edu/journals/theory_and_event/v0005/5.4agamben.html>.

6 The former British Home Secretary David Blunkett was particularly notorious here, having introduced extremely draconian 'law and order' and anti-immigrant policies, including the Criminal Justice Bill in 2003 which seeks to limit even basic legal safeguards such as trial by jury. The decision to bring in a compulsory national ID card is only the latest development in this process. Was there not a strange kind of irony here

in a blind man being at the helm of one of the most extensive state surveillance systems on earth, one whose all-seeing Cyclops eye relentlessly roams the interiors of British society?

7 F. Jameson, *Postmodernism, Or the Cultural Logic of Late Capitalism* (London: Verso, 1991).

8 T. Eagleton, *After Theory* (London: Allen Lane, 2003), p. 118.

9 See S. Žižek, *The Ticklish Subject: the Absent Centre of Political Ontology* (London: Verso, 2000), pp. 215–221.

10 See A. Callinicos, *An Anti-Capitalist Manifesto* (Oxford: Polity Press, 2003), p. 13.

11 For an extensive analysis of the relationship between anarchism and poststructuralism, see S. Newman, *From Bakunin to Lacan: Anti-authoritarianism and the Dislocation of Power* (Lanham, MD: Lexington Books, 2001).

1

The politics of postmodernity

POSTMODERNISM is something that we have heard a lot about for some time now. However its meaning remains ambiguous and open to different interpretations. Moreover, it is a term that appears in a number of different contexts: art, architecture, cultural studies, literature and social theory all bear reference to the 'postmodern condition'. Indeed, some thinkers, like Žižek and Eagleton, see postmodernism as now the dominant discourse in many academic disciplines – although perhaps this institutionalisation indicates not the prestige of postmodernism but rather its very ossification and immanent decline. It is possible that we are now living in a *post*-postmodern age where, tired of the motifs of difference, heterogeneity and displacement, we cling once again to established identities and firm moral grounds. Religion, family values, neo-conservative doctrines and market fundamentalism seem to be the dominant ideological referents of today. Does this signify a turning away from the implications of postmodernity? Perhaps instead, we could say that this uncanny return of social and moral conservatism is actually *symptomatic* of postmodernity itself; perhaps it emerges as a reaction to the uncertainty associated with the postmodern condition.

This sense of uncertainty and dislocation is best characterised by Nietzsche's motif of the premature death of God. The madman in Nietzsche's *The Gay Science*, on hearing of God's death, runs into the crowded market place and cries:

> But how did we do this? How could we drink up the sea? Who gave us the sponge to wipe away the entire horizon? What were we doing when we unchained this earth form its sun? Whither is it moving now? Whither are we moving? Away from all suns? Are we not plunging continually? Backward, sideward, forward, in all directions? Is there still any up or down? Are we not straying as through an infinite nothing?[1]

The postmodern world is a world that seems to have lost its bearings, that is directionless, without future or past, plunging giddily in all directions. Therefore, perhaps God had to be reinvented in order to counter this unbearable sense of crisis and dislocation. It was with great surprise that we, who had believed for many years that God was dead, witnessed his sudden global reappearance: from the religious ecstasies of the suicide bomber to the fervid convictions of the powerful in our 'secular' Western democracies, the name of God is once again on everyone's lips. It remains to be seen if the postmodern God – the God of Bin Laden, Bush and the televangelists – can restore the world to its proper moral position.[2] We might recall, however, that when Nietzsche's madman announces the portentous event of God's death, no one believes him anyway – they simply stare at him in astonishment and incredulity. The madman realises then that he has 'come too early'. Postmodernism always arrives either too early or too late. Indeed, this sense of the untimely is central to the postmodern experience.

In this chapter, I shall explore and try to define the postmodern condition, as well as investigate its implications for politics in particular. I shall suggest that postmodernism has had fundamental implications for the way we think about politics, leading to a displacement of traditional narratives, identities and institutions and to the emergence of new political discourses and practices. I will then examine two major contrasting responses to the postmodern condition in the dispute between Jürgen Habermas and Jean-François Lyotard. Habermas seeks to reinvent strong foundations for political and ethical action through the idea of a universal consensus achieved through rational speech acts and established rules of communication and deliberation; whereas Lyotard denies the possibility of achieving any sort of consensus, affirming instead the heterogeneity and incommensurability of different language games and 'genres'. I will argue that the approach taken by Habermas is untenable because it seeks to establish a firm moral and rational ground where there can be none. Taking, instead, Lyotard's 'poststructuralist' approach as my starting point, I will nevertheless explore its limitations for political analysis and will suggest that we need to go beyond this thematic of incommensurability.

The collapse of the 'metanarrative'

The postmodern condition has been most famously and succinctly summed up by Lyotard's definition: *an incredulity toward metanarratives*.[3] The metanarrative might be understood as a universal idea or discourse that is central to the experience of modernity. This might be found in the notion of objective truth, and the idea that the world is becoming rationally intelligible through advances in science. Or it might be seen in the Hegelian dialectic, whose unfolding determines historical developments. Here we might also think of the Marxist discourse of proletarian emancipation. All these ideas derive from the Enlightenment, and they imply a truth that is absolute and universal, and which will be rationally grasped by everyone. Moreover, the metanarrative implies a certain knowledge about society: society is understood either as an integrated whole or as internally divided, as in the Marxist imagery of class struggle. Indeed, these two opposed understandings of society are really reverse mirror images of one another; they are united by the common assumption that social reality is wholly transparent and intelligible.

So why are these metanarratives breaking down; why do we no longer believe in them? Lyotard explores the reasons for their dissolution in an examination of the condition of knowledge in contemporary post-industrial society. According to Lyotard, scientific knowledge is experiencing a crisis of legitimation. Legitimation refers to the rules of truth which determine which statements can be admitted to a 'scientific' body of statements – which statements are scientifically verifiable according to these rules, in other words – and which statements are to be excluded and thereby rendered illegitimate or untrue.[4] Lyotard argues that because of certain transformations that knowledge is undergoing in the post-industrial age, this process of legitimation has become ever more questionable and unstable: the contingency and arbitrariness of its operation – the fact that it is ultimately based on acts of power and exclusion – is becoming apparent, thus producing a crisis of representation. In short, it is increasingly difficult for *scientific* knowledge to claim a privileged status as being the only arbiter of truth.

Knowledge in the post-industrial age is being transformed through the proliferation of new computer and information technologies.[5] What happens to the prestige of scientific knowledge, then, when it becomes just another commodity to be bought and sold on the capitalist marketplace; or when it becomes a tool of technocratic governments or is put into the hands of the military-scientific machine or multinational companies? Does this not displace the universal position of scientific knowledge; does science not become, under the conditions of commodification and bureaucratisation, just another form of knowledge, another narrative? Moreover, Lyotard points to a breakdown of the knowledge about society: society can no longer be adequately represented by knowledge – either as a unified whole or as a class-divided body. The social bonds which gave a consistency of representation to society are themselves being redefined through the language games that constitute it. There is, according to Lyotard, an '"atomization" of the social into flexible networks of language games …'.[6] This does not mean that the social bond is dissolving altogether – merely that there is no longer one dominant, coherent understanding of society but, rather, a plurality of different narratives or perspectives. Here we might think of the multiplicity of heterogeneous discourses, ideological perspectives, religious sensibilities, moral positions and social identities that make up contemporary societies.

These changes lead to the conclusion that scientific knowledge is not the only (legitimate) form of knowledge, and that alongside it we have to consider other narratives and language games which have an equal claim to legitimacy. Central to the 'postmodern condition', then, is the acknowledgement that all forms of knowledge have to be seen as particular narratives with their own 'stories' and internal structures which organise their statements and utterances. What defines the status of knowledge, then, in the condition of postmodernity, is no longer the universal position of truth, but rather a 'pragmatics' of storytelling – a series of specific rules for the authorisation of statements. The desire for legitimation on the basis of this universal position of truth had in the past led only to the denigration of other narratives and discourses as 'obscurantist', and thus to a Western cultural imperialism. Postmodernity puts paid to this illusion of a universal, absolute truth, thereby creating a crisis of legitimation for science: science is increasingly aware of its own limits, of the contingency of its language games, and of its inability to legitimate the truth of its own statements. Science, in other words, becomes increasingly aware of the shakiness of its own foundations – of the absence of any absolute bedrock of truth upon which it can ground its own statements. The only source of legitimation for science today is institutional power: science has become dependent for its legitimacy on the symbolic authority of institutions such as universities, research institutes, government bureaucracies and private corporations, which regulate and transmit scientific knowledge, and subject it to new 'performance criteria' of technological and economic efficiency.[7]

Postmodernity can therefore be seen as a process of unmasking the scientific and positivist discourses of the Enlightenment. This critique is not only epistemological but also *ethical*. The ethical argument here is that such discourses, in their desire for legitimation through universal truth, are totalising discourses. They are hostile to any form of questioning, to any difference, and they marginalise and denigrate other forms of knowledge. Indeed, as many thinkers – including Lyotard, and Adorno and Horkheimer – point out, scientific knowledge has often been placed in the service of totalitarian political regimes, with the Holocaust symbolising the murderous and barbaric ends that scientific rationality – coupled with the bureaucratic mentality – can be put towards. Moreover, totalitarian regimes have always invoked metanarratives – whether in the form of a 'historical destiny' or the dialectic. It is important to emphasise, of course, that science does not always put itself in the hands of the state, and that on many occasions it has provided an important critical voice against the actions of governments. However, the point here is that there is a parallel between totalising metanarratives which ruthlessly organise their statements according to universal notions of truth, and totalitarian regimes which repress differences and heterogeneities in the name of a social whole and a universal truth. Indeed, as Lyotard argues, attempts to restore this social whole lead only to terror: 'By terror I mean the efficiency gained by eliminating, or threatening to eliminate, a player from a language game one shares with him.'[8] Perhaps contemporary terrorism – both in its state and non-state forms – can be seen in this way, as the attempt to restore the social bond that has been ruptured and fragmented by postmodernity. Perhaps the dream of absolute commensurability can only appear today in the figures of fundamentalist Islam and the neo-conservative 'security' state, whose incoherent attempts to eliminate difference and heterogeneity in the name of some universal truth or rationality lead only to a paranoid and terrorist violence.

The obsessive and terroristic desire for commensurability is thus one possible response to the present crisis of legitimation and the decline of the metanarrative. Quite simply, grand narratives have lost their credibility. Postmodernity is characterised not by grand narratives, but by what Lyotard calls 'little narratives' (*petit recit*). Moreover, there is no possibility of a universal consensus being established between these narratives; rather, they are incommensurable. Postmodernity consists in the recognition of this incommensurability, and in emphasising difference, heterogeneity and *dissension*, rather than consensus.

Lyotard's assessment of the 'postmodern condition' is somewhat ambiguous in tone. While he recognises and, to some extent, celebrates the decline of the metanarrative and the crisis in legitimation of scientific knowledge, he recognises at the same time the way that the postmodern motifs of finitude, multiplicity and differences can be co-opted by the capitalist system. Even the political system tolerates the quiet revolution that is taking place at the level of language games, because of the economic and performative efficiencies that these finite, plural language games allow. Postmodernism is caught between, on the one hand, a conservative reaction against it in the name of restoring the social bond, and on the other, the brutal realism and nihilism of the capitalist system which ruthlessly commodifies and co-opts it. Here postmodernism can function as a sort of cultural vector of capitalism:

> When power is that of capital and not that of a party, the 'trans-avantgardist' or 'postmodern' solution proves to be better adapted than the antimodern solution. Eclecticism is the degree zero of contemporary general culture: one listens to reggae, watches a western, eats McDonald's food for lunch and local cuisine for dinner, wears Paris perfume in Tokyo and 'retro' clothes in Hong Kong; knowledge is a matter for TV games.[9]

Thus for Lyotard, postmodernism is in danger of becoming (or indeed it has already become) a cultural index of capitalist globalisation: its central themes of fragmentation, multiplicity and heterogeneity become so many aesthetic elements, 'tastes', modes of subjectivity that can be marketed to and turned into commodities. Postmodernism, then, is not necessarily always subversive; or perhaps it might be more accurate to say that its very subversion – its transgression of stable identities, universal truths and grand narratives – can become part of the 'system', of an economic, cultural and social logic which itself thrives on the constant proliferation of differences. However, rather than conclude from this, as Žižek does, that postmodernism's transgression is a false or pseudo transgression, or, Habermas does, that it is inherently conservative, I would suggest that it is always ambivalent and can have both radical and conservative implications.

In order to explore these implications – and it is the *political* implications that I am most interested in here – we must define postmodernism more precisely. Postmodernism, it must be made clear, does not refer to any historical period. Despite the glib pronouncements that we now all live in a 'postmodern age', postmodernity is not an actual period after modernity. While Lyotard, for instance, talks about contemporary post-industrial transformations in technology and knowledge, he sees the postmodern condition more as a critical reflection on these transformations rather than as a period that we now all live in. Indeed, he says that postmodernity is 'undoubtably part of the modern'.[10] In other words, we have not gone beyond modernity – something that would be impossible in any case, because modernity is not so much a temporal notion as a certain way of experiencing the world that builds into itself even the notion of its own overcoming. Rather, postmodernity has to be seen as a critical response to modernity itself and an interrogation of its discursive limits. In other words, postmodernism is something that, as Heller and Feher suggest, is 'parasitic' upon modernity itself.[11] It may be seen, then, as a reflection upon the limits of modernity, unmasking its inconsistencies, contradictions and aporias, rather than as a stage beyond modernity. The postmodern 'sensibility' would be the experience of living in the present – that is, living in the period that we call modernity – while at the same time *being after* or *post-histoire*.[12] In this sense, then, postmodernity is both inside and outside modernity at the same time, always working at the limits of modernity and exposing those elements and tendencies which, while they are spawned by modernity, do not fit into its discourses. Postmodernism thus reveals the heterogeneity of modernism itself – the multitude of different language games and possibilities inherent in it, yet disavowed by, its rationalist metanarratives.

The postmodern approach therefore reveals a split in the Enlightenment and modernity itself, and seeks to use their very tools – those of rational and critical inquiry – in order to expose their limitations and tensions. In this sense, because it is animated by the critical spirit of modernity, it remains indebted to and a part of modernity. It is incorrect to claim, as many do, that postmodernism equates with irrationalism or relativism. On the contrary, it is eminently rational in the sense that it demands that reason live up to its own expectations – that it apply its own critical spirit towards itself and recognise the limits and precariousness of its own claims to universality.

The centrality of reason – and the ability of the individual to use reason critically – is a fundamental characteristic of modernity, and is what separates it from the pre-modern world of religious obscurantism and political tyranny. Modernity instigated a radical break with this world, rending apart its opaque universe of divine right and social hierarchy. Modernity, whose high point was the Enlightenment, brought about a new understanding of the individual and his place in the world – one that was no longer cemented by a traditional cosmic order based on divine authority. Instead, the individual was seen as autonomous and self-determining, and as having essential moral and rational capacities that would emancipate him from arbitrary political authority and religious mystification. The metaphysical foundationalism that characterised the pre-modern era gave way to a belief in the universality of reason and the unlimited capacities of humanity. Man replaced God, and reason and morality supplanted religion.

However, a number of nineteenth-century thinkers – including Stirner and Nietzsche – remained sceptical about this secular emancipation. Nietzsche claimed that while God was dead, we were not at all ready for this event, as the untimely announcement of the madman showed. Instead of affirming the radical consequences of this break, we continued to cling to the remnants of Christianity, now dressed up in the garb of humanism. Max Stirner showed, too, that God had simply returned in the guise of Man, and that the humanist secular revolution had not overthrown religious mystification and superstition as it had claimed, but had simply reinvented it in the form of human essence and the universal moral and rational ideals that accompany it. The humanist figure of Man, according to Stirner, was simply another version of God – another superstitious ideal that the individual has once again become enthralled to: 'Man, your head is haunted ... You imagine great things, and depict to yourself a whole world of gods that has an existence for you, a spirit-realm to which you suppose yourself to be called, an ideal that beckons to you.'[13] The modern world that now confronts the individual is just as alienating and mystifying as the premodern Christian world. The discourse of Enlightenment humanism is just as totalising and absolutist – just as dominating in its own way – as religion.

This diagnosis of Enlightenment humanism as still being beset by the remnants of religion, is part of a postmodern sense of dissatisfaction with modernity. Modernity, it is argued, has simply found a new form of metaphysical foundationalism – no longer in God and religion, but in Man and rationalist humanism. For the work of modernity to be completed – for modernity to live up to its radical promises – it must abandon these foundations altogether. It must reject, for instance, the notion of a human essence which is seen to form the basis of the subject; there is no a-historical rational 'species being' or essential humanity behind the subject. Rather, as thinkers like Foucault have shown, the subject is written through and through by history, and is a construct of external social factors such as power relations and discourses. Postmodernism also interrogates the universal notions of reason, truth and morality that are the central metadiscourses of modernity and the Enlightenment. These discourses are based on a certain Western cultural context which cannot be universally applicable, and are constructed, as we have seen, through a series of arbitrary and violent exclusions of heterogeneous elements. The central narrative of modernity – that of a universal subject who is liberated through Reason – is rejected, or at least, radically destabilised in a postmodern critique. Postmodernism invites us to consider a world without firm foundations or an absolute moral and rational ground.

The postmodern political condition

Postmodernism can be seen, then, as destabilising and rending modernity, opening up fissures in its edifice and revealing its limits and inconsistencies. What are the political implications, then, of this postmodern critique? Postmodernity involves the rejection of the political grand narrative – found in the idea, for instance, of proletarian emancipation, or in the universal liberal notions of natural rights and freedoms. These are seen as 'stories' which rely for their legitimation on questionable ideas such as universal Reason or the dialectic. This critique of political metanarratives is associated with a number of conditions. Firstly, there is the abandonment of the notion of the universal rational subject who could act as an autonomous and self-willed agent in the political sphere. Rather, as someone like Freud showed, the subject remains opaque even to himself, rather than transparent and unified as the Cartesian model would suggest. Moreover, the subject is shown to be affected and, indeed, constituted by conditions that are often outside his control, there being no possibility of a strict separation between the subject and the objective world. Secondly, rationality and morality can no longer serve as the absolute foundations that guide the subject's political and ethical judgement and decision making.[14] Thirdly, the postmodern political condition is characterised by the breaking down of traditional sites of collective decision making, such as those based on the nation state, as well as a general fragmentation of the political and social field into a multitude of incommensurable identities and ideological perspectives. This has had an impact on radical politics in particular, where new social movements and identities have mobilised around issues such as gender, ethnicity and sexual identity, as well as environmental causes, and have to some extent taken the place of Marxist class struggles over economic issues.

Let us examine, then, some of the political identities that have emerged against the background of postmodernity. Feminism, of course, is not a new discourse or political identity – having its roots in modernity – and it has often been in tension with postmodernity. Nevertheless, postmodernism has had significant implications for feminist theory and politics. As Diana Coole shows, central to this often uneasy relationship between feminism and postmodernism is the question of whether feminism should abandon its universalism and its gendered oppositional politics, both of which are expressed in its central narrative about the universal emancipation of women from patriarchal oppression. Postmodernism destabilises this narrative in a number of ways. Firstly, it questions and deconstructs essentialist identities and binary oppositions, thus throwing into doubt the idea of a biologically-determined and morally-privileged female identity. Postmodernism breaks the link between biology and gender, showing that identity – both male and female – is heterogeneous, unstable and indeterminate. As Coole suggests, a postmodern feminism would consist of a number of theoretical strategies, following Lyotard's motif of agonistic and heterogeneous language games.[15] *Theorising the game* would involve deconstructing the conceptual categories of feminist politics: instead of positing a binary division between men and women and a relationship of oppression and domination of the former over the latter, a postmodern approach would emphasise a strategic and agonistic model of language games. In this understanding, power would not be a zero-sum game between men and women, but rather would be seen, along the lines of Foucault, as a series of fluid and unstable power relationships in which there are multiple sites of resistance and political invention rather than a universal confrontation. *Playing the game* concerns the subversion of dominant cultural representations of women, the displacement of the structures of meaning and the gaze, and the invention of new and unpredictable meanings. Lastly, *exploding the game* involves the interrogation of the gendered structures of modernity itself – in particular the discourse of rationality which is central to it – and instead evoking the *unrepresentable*, that which is outside the rational order of representation. Here Coole calls for a feminist form of avant-garde transgression.[16] Therefore, while there may not be a coherent postmodern feminism, postmodernism nevertheless presents feminism with a number of interesting challenges and possibilities. Through an interrogation of the grand narratives, essential identities and binary oppositions upon which feminism – along with other radical political discourses – has relied, postmodernism allows for a radical renewal of feminist projects.

However, we should not imagine that postmodernism is always associated with a progressive politics. As I have suggested, postmodernism is fundamentally ambiguous in its effects, and it can not only be co-opted by capitalism itself, but can even rise to reactionary forms of politics. Even though postmodernism resists totalising narratives and political institutions, and emphasises instead heterogeneity, difference and flux, it also spawns new forms of authoritarianism and violence that emerge as a reaction to it, and yet, paradoxically, draw upon its implications. Today we are seeing the preponderance of violent, intolerant (neo)conservative forces and religious fundamentalisms – resembling a kind of 'return of the repressed'. With the collapse of the Communist systems and the general decline of the ideological apparatus of Marxism, far from seeing the promised universal reign of a liberal utopia we instead saw the uncanny return of ethnic violence, virulent nationalism and religious conservatism. As Jacques Rancière says: 'The territory of "posthistorical" and peaceful humanity proved to be the territory of new figures of the Inhuman.'[17] These forces have been intensified and invigorated by September 11. What we are seeing today is a global proliferation of religious fundamentalism – of both the Islamic and Judeo-Christian kinds – with all the violence, intolerance and paranoia that it entails. Religious fundamentalism can be seen as a reaction to postmodernism in the sense that it is threatened by difference and heterogeneity, and seeks to eliminate or violently disavow what does not fit in with its narrow worldview. What religious fundamentalists find unbearable is the moral uncertainty and the instability of identity that comes with postmodernity; and they seek to restore the social bond through the assertion of a non-negotiable moral ground. Because such ideologies retain the fantasy of a lost social bond, they can also be seen as symptomatic of the postmodern condition, which, as we have seen, posits the fragmentation of the social bond, or at least its transformation through multiple language games.

Moreover, what perversely connects these reactionary tendencies to post-modernism is a common critique of the Enlightenment and modernity. The politico-ideological climate, in recent times, has been characterised by a general hostility towards the Enlightenment, particularly in the areas of secularism, universality and human rights. Everything from the acceptance – or at least covert toleration – of the use of torture and other barbaric practices in the 'war on terror', to the resurgence of the religious Right in the United States and the open questioning of the separation of Church and State, suggests that the Enlightenment is in danger of being rolled back. Of course, religious funda-mentalism/neo-conservatism and postmodernism are critical of the Enlightenment and modernity for entirely different reasons: the former harkens back to some imaginary pre-modern life-world which modernity has disrupted, while the latter wants to radicalise modernity and the Enlightenment and reveal its latent emancipative potential. Thus, the former looks to the past, while the latter looks towards the future, not wanting to turn back the project of moder-nity but rather mobilise its radical potential by deconstructing its categories and premises. I utterly reject here Habermas' allegation that postmodernism is a neo-conservative discourse and that it seeks to 'turn back the clock' on moder-nity and the Enlightenment. I shall examine Habermas' critique of postmodernity later. However, it is nevertheless important to point out here the way that modernity and the Enlightenment are contested sites, from which both postmodern theory and reactionary ideologies take their critical point of depar-ture. Postmodernity – as a general cultural and epistemological condition – is as much associated with the emergence of violent fundamentalisms as it is with innocuous New Age spiritual cults.

Furthermore, we could also point to new forms of racism and xenophobia that have become more prevalent in recent times, and have been intensified by the 'war on terror'. Here we might take as an example the anti-immigrant racism that has been prominent throughout Western Europe, and which is particularly directed towards Muslim minorities. Such prejudices are not confined to marginal groups but have become part of the political mainstream – witness the rise of the Far Right in France, and, more insidiously, the adoption by the moderate 'centre' parties of both the Left *and* Right of these racist senti-ments in the veiled form of policies designed to 'protect our communities from terrorism' or to 'get tough on illegal migration'. This form of racism is different from the biological racism of the Nazi type, or from more traditional forms of racism. It may be described as a kind of cultural xenophobia or a postmodern neo-racism. It draws upon, in an extremely perverse way, the postmodern thematic of difference to insist on a separation of different cultural and ethnic communities. Balibar characterises this new racism as a 'racism without race':

> A racism whose dominant theme is not biological heredity but the insur-mountability of cultural differences, a racism which, at first sight, does not postulate the superiority of certain groups or peoples in relation to others but 'only' the harmfulness of abolishing frontiers, the incompatibility of life-styles and traditions.[18]

In other words, it is the sort of racist discourse that wants to assert and reinforce cultural and ethnic differences, and that says: *We Europeans have our own culture, which is based on Judeo-Christian traditions, and you Muslims have your own culture, which is based on your own traditions. We are not denigrating your culture, and we are not claiming that our culture is superior – simply that it is different and ultimately incompatible with yours. These differences are incommen-surable, and we want merely to have nothing to do with your culture (or you).* There is something akin here to Freud's notion of the narcissism of minor differences, where the insistence upon differences between groups becomes more intense the closer in proximity these groups are to one another. Can we not see here, in a very paradoxical sense, a reflection of Lyotard's notion of different and incommensurable language games – for which any sort of attempt at consensus and reconciliation is ultimately impossible?

Lastly we might speak of a resurgence of violence within our cities and suburbs, a violence that might take the form of racist violence, but is more often than not simply *nihilistic* – a violence with purpose or even an identifiable moti-vation. Balibar talks about forms of ultra-violence that contain an excessive dimension of *jouissance*, or enjoyment, that is *unmediated*. This would be a mode of violence that is beyond utilitarian or even ideological considerations, corresponding more to the ravages of the pre-Oedipal Id.[19] Žižek also talks about this nihilistic violence, bringing up the example of the skinhead who engages in meaningless acts of violence, and who, when questioned as to his motivations, starts talking like a social worker or social psychologist, quoting unemployment statistics and spouting well-worn theories of social alienation and marginalisation.[20] There is a strange self-reflexivity going on here, where the individual in question is aware of all the apparent socio-economic reasons for his sporadic outbursts of violence, and yet continues to engage in them. In other words, what is really behind this violence is something that cannot be grasped by socio-economic explanations, which is precisely inexplicable and nihilistic. Can we see this as a 'postmodern' violence, a violence for its own sake; a violence that simply exists on the surface and that defies 'deeper' socio-economic explanations? There is something of this in the riots that took place in France in November 2005. While there were no doubt profound socio-economic reasons why this violence occurred, and while the young men and women were expressing their legitimate sense of suffering and frustration at the high levels of unemployment, marginalisation, racism and police victimisation – was there not also at the same time an element here of this postmodern nihilistic violence, which could be seen in the blind destruction the rioters engaged in? There was little attempt at political articulation, little desire to turn the anger and frustration into some sort of social or political movement.

Could it be that these riots were a sign of a new form of 'politics' – a violence that, while it is directed at identifiable targets of authority (the rioters' confrontation with the state and its police apparatus was magnificent in its sheer audacity and effrontery) has no real aim or purpose? Can they be seen perhaps as the violent version of the new phenomenon of 'flash mobbing', where masses of people, upon receiving a mobile phone text message, gather together spontaneously in a public place, make some unintelligible gesture or utterance and then leave? Is postmodern politics, in other words, limited to simply the nihilism of the empty symbolic gesture (or the empty act of violence) without any distinct ethico-political content? This is the allegation that many critics have made against postmodernism, and the remainder of this chapter will be devoted to exploring this question.

Postmodernism and nihilism

I have explored some of the new social and ideological forces that have emerged with postmodernism, as well as the implications of postmodern theory for radical political identities such as feminism. I have suggested that postmodernism is highly ambiguous in its effects, and that its emphasis on difference, heterogeneity and the instability of identity can produce both progressive and reactionary forms of politics – although the latter is largely a reaction to the postmodern fragmentation of social bonds and identities. For this reason, postmodern theory has been criticised by many on the Left – particularly by thinkers from the critical theory, Left-liberal and Marxist traditions – who argue that postmodernism is politically and ethically vacuous. In other words, they suggest that because postmodernism questions Enlightenment discourses of rational truth and morality, and because it is sceptical of the grand narrative of human emancipation, it undermines the progressive and radical implications of modernity and leaves politics floundering in an ethical no-man's land, without firm normative and epistemological criteria to guide it. Postmodernism, it is alleged, amounts to a nihilism and irrationalism that condemns radical politics to a dead-end – thus only contributing to the general malaise that radical politics has been in since the collapse of Communism.

Perhaps the most strident of these critical voices has been that of Habermas, whose long-term project has been to defend and renew the legacy of the Enlightenment and modernity. He has argued that postmodern theory, because it questions many of the fundamental categories of the Enlightenment – in particular its notions of progress and universal emancipation – equates with what is ultimately a conservatism. In his lecture series *The Philosophical Discourse of Modernity*, Habermas argued that 'counter-Enlightenment' thinkers like Foucault and Lyotard are the modern heirs to a sceptical romantic tradition – represented by figures like Nietzsche, Schlegel and Holderlin – which harkens back to a mythicised pre-modern era.[21] Habermas seeks to defend the legacy of the Enlightenment and modernity against this 'abandonment', and to renew what he sees as the emancipative, progressive and democratic potential of these forces.

Habermas seeks to re-establish the social bonds of modernity, and to salvage modernity's discourse of universal rationality by basing it, no longer in the autonomous subject, but in a notion of intersubjectivity. He outlines a theory of rational communication based on established rules of conduct, where the subject is required to speak the truth and to believe in the truth of what he says. According to these rules, a rational consensus can be established between participants in these interactions: 'I call interactions communicative when the participants coordinate their plans of action consensually, with the agreement reached at any point being evaluated in terms of the intersubjective recognition of validity claims.' This is what Habermas refers to as the 'ideal speech situation': there is a potential agreement or consensus reached by participants, which is based on a mutual recognition of the claims to validity of their speech acts. Such claims to validity consist of claims to truth, rightness and truthfulness,

> according to whether the speaker refers to something in the objective world (as the totality of existing states of affairs), to something in the shared social world (as the totality of the legitimately regulated interpersonal relationships of a social group), or to something in his own subjective world (as the totality of experiences to which one has privileged access).[22]

This ideal speech situation presupposes, in other words, a potential rational consensus being achieved on the basis of a kind of a shared intersubjective 'life-world' of experiences, as well as commonly agreed rules for speech acts. It is on this basis, according to Habermas, that disagreements can be resolved and decisions reached in the political and social spheres.

Thus we see the major difference between Habermas and Lyotard. For Habermas, a rational consensus between different subject positions, narratives and language games is possible, provided that certain basic rules of communication can be agreed upon. For Lyotard, on the other hand, there is no intersubjectively shared 'lifeworld' or common social bonds upon which such communication could take place; there is only a multiplicity of different and incommensurable language games with no possibility of a consensus being established between them. He says:

> There is no reason to think that it would be possible to determine metaprescriptives common to all these language games or that a revisable consensus like the one in force at a given moment in the scientific community could embrace the totality of metaprescriptions regulating the totality of statements circulating in the social collectivity ... For this reason, it seems neither possible, not even prudent, to follow Habermas in orienting our treatment of the problem of legitimation in the direction of a search for universal consensus through what he calls *Diskurs*, in other words, a dialogue of argumentation.[23]

Indeed, Habermas' notion of rational consensus has the potential to lead to a kind of terror, according to Lyotard, because it would entail a marginalisation or elimination of alternative language games.

Habermas' notion of the 'ideal speech' situation is more of a regulative ideal – a model of communication to aspire to – rather than an actual concrete situation present in communication acts. However, even as a regulative ideal it still presupposes the possibility – a possibility present in all speech acts – of an unbroken, transparent and rational communication between interlocutors. However, what if we were to suggest that not only is such a fantasy of perfect communication impossible, but also that distortions in speech acts and meaning are the structural condition of *any* communication? In other words, what if it were the case that communication is structurally distorted – that there is always a misunderstanding between interlocutors – and that this distortion is the constitutive condition necessary for communication to take place? According to Jacques Lacan, the subject becomes a speaking being – a subject of language – through a fundamental distortion or misrecognition (*meconnaissance*), where he is only partially represented by signifiers in the symbolic order. This *partial* signification is created by a void within the symbolic order itself – what Lacan refers to as the real (*du reel*); something which cannot be signified, which is outside representation, and yet which, paradoxically, allows signification to take place. This means that all acts of signification take place on the basis of an element that is missing from the structure of signification itself, thus at the same time disrupting the process of communication. Try as we might, we can never entirely say exactly what we want to say or in the way we want to say it, not because we are inarticulate or lack the capacities of clear communication, but because of a flaw or void within the structure of communication itself. This, however, is a necessary void: because we are always trying to overcome this void, to represent the unrepresentable, we continue to signify, to talk, to communicate. If there was perfect communication – if the ideal speech situation prevailed and we could say it all without any distortions – then we would eventually cease to communicate. Having *said it all*, we would stop talking altogether. As Paul Verhaeghe says, Lacan 'starts from the assumption that communication is always a failure: moreover, that it has to be a failure, and that's the reason we keep on talking'.[24] The point here is that Habermas' theory of rational communication is untenable because it is not aware of its own limits: it does not recognise that the distortions and dissimulations that are present in communication are not aberrations from an ideal mode of communication, but rather are inherent to communication and the very conditions under which it takes place.

The differend

Both Habermas and Lyotard represent two different responses to the postmodern condition. Habermas, as we have seen, tries to counter postmodernity by seeking to restore the universal rational ground of modernity through the notion of an intersubjectively achieved rational consensus. Lyotard, on the other hand, celebrates postmodernity's fragmentation of the social bond by affirming incommensurability of language games. This is what he refers to as *le differend*.

The differend is a conflict between two parties that cannot be adequately resolved because there is no judgment that can apply equally to both parties. When one tries to adopt a universal position of judgement above these parties in dispute – when one tries to make a judgment that would be universally applicable – one commits a wrong, an injustice, because one enforces certain rules upon a discourse that are not part of that discourse: 'A wrong results from the fact that the rules of the genre of discourse by which one judges are not those of the judged genre or genres of discourse.'[25] Let us take as an example of this 'wrong' a situation that occurred recently in Australia: a member of an Aboriginal tribe was tried and convicted under Anglo-Australian law for having (consensual) sex with an underage girl, even though the two were legitimately married according to traditional Aboriginal custom. Here we have a conflict between different sets of laws and cultural norms – two genres of discourse in Lyotard's terms – in which something that was perfectly legal and legitimate according to one genre was a crime according to another. How does one fairly judge a situation like this; which set of legal norms, which genre, should prevail here? How can one impose a judgement without at the same time imposing a certain genre upon another to which it is entirely alien or inappropriate, thus causing a wrong to be done to that other? Such a situation would appear to be irresolvable, and this points to the limits of any universal position or rule according to which judgements are made. Judgements, if they must be made, will always be singular, finite and involve some sort of wrong. According to Lyotard, there is an irresolvable differend of this kind at the basis of all phrases and language games, a differend that undermines any possibility of a consensus being achieved without a wrong being done to a particular genre. Phrases are heterogeneous and have their own rules, which make them incommensurable and therefore always potentially in dispute with one another. There is no universal genre of phrases to regulate such conflicts.

Lyotard's point, however, is not that we should give up on making judgements or on making links between different phrases – this is an inevitable part of any social existence – but simply that any kind of judgement, or any attempt to find agreement between certain phrases, is always contingent and, thus, always a question of politics.[26] In other words, there is no natural or 'essential' relation between discourses; any agreement between them will be a problematic and undecidable relation that always is contestable and unstable. The task of philosophy and politics is to respect the heterogeneity of genres and to not seek to absorb them into a totalising discourse. Indeed, politics itself is not a genre but rather a multiplicity of different genres: it is the name for this heterogeneity. As such, it points towards a certain void or emptiness: 'Politics ... is the threat of the differend. It is not a genre, it is the multiplicity of genres, the diversity of ends, and par excellence the question of linkage.'[27] Moreover, politics must eschew the myth of the social contract or the notion of a shared commonality upon which traditional conceptions of politics are based. Such conceptions imply that the social is a wholly intelligible dimension that can be grasped within a single political discourse. However, the social is composed of this multiplicity of heterogeneous phrases which undermine any singular sense of the 'social' as such. That is why, according to Lyotard, a poststructuralist politics must remain sceptical of universal political metanarratives, such as was symbolised by the revolutionary Declaration of 1789. Such discourses, while they invoke a universal dimension – that of universal equality and the rights of all men – are nevertheless articulated from a particular position (the French nation) and are thus addressed to a particular subject (the French citizen). Therefore, a poststructuralist politics – that is, a politics appropriate to the postmodern condition – should question the collective 'we' of such universal political narratives. In this sense, politics can only attempt to construct a temporary hegemony out of different genres. Lyotard's politics of the differend is not nihilistic – it still allows for, and indeed endorses, certain forms of politics and ethics: however, for Lyotard, the only 'ethical' position is to respect hetero-geneities and differences between genres, and to remain sceptical of all collective projects.

Poststructuralism

The political and ethical position being outlined here might be said to be post-structuralist. Poststructuralism can be seen as a theoretical response – or series of responses – to the postmodern condition: a response that recognises and *cautiously* affirms the breakdown of metanarratives and the pluralisation of language games. It should be made clear here that poststructuralism is not the same as postmodernism – it is a theoretical, political and ethical response to postmodernism as a general cultural condition.

Poststructuralism refers to a series of thinkers and theoretical approaches that emerged out of structuralism. Structuralism maintains that relations of language – the relation between signifiers – fundamentally structure our social reality. In other words, we perceive ourselves and the world around us only through an external linguistic structure that determines meaning. Ferdinand de Saussure, for instance, saw language in terms of a system of linguistic signs composed of signifier (the material sign itself) and signified (the object to which it referred). However, for Saussure there is no necessary or essential relation between the two – it is only a matter of convention that we use a particular signi-fier to refer to a particular object. What really determines the signifier is not the object that is arbitrarily attached to it, but rather its relation to other signifiers in a fixed system of differences. Louis Althusser applied structuralism to an understanding of the political and social field, seeing it as a symbolic dimension in which identities were fixed – or *overdetermined* – within an ideological system that bestowed meaning upon them.

The strength of structuralism was that it avoided essentialist understandings, in which identity and experience were seen as being grounded in an objective intelligible 'substance' or 'reality' that was internal to it – the 'thing in itself'. Structuralism showed that there was no such thing as the 'thing in itself', and that what really mattered was the way that identity and experience were deter-mined by an external structure. However, the problem with this was that because the structure was so totalising and determining, it came to be seen as a kind of essence in itself. In other words, structuralism came increasingly to be seen as a new form of essentialism or foundationalism, in which identity was once again founded on an absolute ground.[28] Structuralism, in this sense, had merely replaced the absolute ground of metaphysics with the absolute ground of the structure itself. This could be seen in Althusserian structuralist Marxism, where the capitalist economy determined *in the last instance* the entire field of social and political relations and symbolic identifications. Post-structuralism does not, however, reject structuralism per se but, rather, radicalises it. In other words, it does not call into question the fundamental insight of structuralism that identities are constructed discursively through external relations of language; it does not return to a pre-structuralist essentialism. Rather, we could say that poststructuralism takes structuralism to its logical conclusion: in order to avoid the implication of essentialism and foundationalism, the unity, consistency and stability of the structure itself had to be questioned.

This 'deconstruction' of the structure has taken two basic forms in post-structuralist thought. The *first* position – exemplified by thinkers like Lyotard, Deleuze and, with certain exceptions, Foucault – contends that rather than there being a single, centralised structure, there are instead multiple and heterogeneous discourses, power relations or 'assemblages of desire' that are constitutive of identity and are immanent throughout the social field. The *second* position – exemplified by thinkers like Derrida and Lacan – places more emphasis on the structure itself, but sees it as indeterminate, incomplete and unstable. One way to think about this is through Gödel's 'incompleteness theorem', which states that in any given branch of mathematics there will always be certain propositions that cannot be verified using the axioms of that particular branch, and which require going outside the system, thus creating ever larger systems. Simply put, there can be no closed, complete or self-contained system or structure, because there will always be elements within this system whose identity can only be established by something outside it. The structure can therefore only be sustained by a structural element that stands outside it and is incommensurable with it. However, this excluded element is not an essential identity or a metaphysical point of departure that emerges from beyond the structure: rather it has to be seen as the *internal limit* of the structure itself. It is something that is, paradoxically, inside and outside the structure simultaneously, and it is the point around which identity is both constituted and destabilised.

There is a certain tension in poststructuralist theory between these two 'positions' – a tension that will be brought out in this book. We must be careful, though, in drawing too distinct a line between these two approaches; they overlap in many ways, and, moreover, a thinker like Foucault would perhaps fall into both 'camps' (or none of them). Furthermore, this book will also discuss a number of thinkers – like Jacques Rancière, Ernesto Laclau, Slavoj Žižek and Alain Badiou – who cannot satisfactorily be classified as 'poststructuralist' (certainly not according to the first approach) and would be more appropriately termed 'post-Althusserian'. In this sense, they would be more closely aligned with the second poststructuralist position (that of Derrida and Lacan), and yet they also go beyond this in the sense that they articulate a more consciously political position. However, they do bear some relation to poststructuralism, not only in their debt to Lacanian psychoanalysis (although here Žižek would insist on a non-poststructuralist reading of Lacan) but also in the way that they see politics as a contingent enterprise, taking place on a ground that is unstable and indeterminate. They point to a certain void of the political – a void that ruptures and dislocates stable political and social identities. If they accept that politics has an ontological ground, it would be one that is conditioned by the unpredictable *event* rather than by stable grand narratives. Perhaps we might see these thinkers as developing a *post*-poststructuralist position, not in the sense that they come after poststructuralism, but in the sense that they extend a number of its implications to a more sustained exploration of the political.

The approach taken in this book will itself be more closely aligned with the second poststructuralist position, without of course discounting the insights of the first. I accept – albeit with reservations – the implications of Lyotard's analysis of the postmodern condition[29] – the fragmentation of the social bond, the contemporary incredulity toward metanarratives and the pluralisation of language games and discourses. Moreover, I also accept that politics must at least acknowledge the differend – the heterogeneity of different genres and the difficulties encountered in trying to develop a coherent political position on this basis. Where I differ from Lyotard is in my wariness about his insistence that genres and language games are incommensurable – that they are, in other words, radically different, and that their differences make it virtually impossible to reach an agreement between them. This notion of absolute difference or absolute incommensurably could be seen, paradoxically, as implying another form of essentialism – an essentialism of difference itself. In other words, by insisting upon the absolute difference of an identity, there is a risk of turning this difference into an essential feature of that identity, and this presupposes that this identity is somehow closed and self-contained in its difference. However, identities and language games are never simply self-enclosed in this way: their borders and limits are always unstable and are constituted by an undecidable element that at the same time threatens these limits. Discourse analysis, in this way, points to the instability of any identity – not only the identity of grand narratives but also the identity of the little narratives as well. Rather than incommensurability, then, I would suggest an alternative motif – one of *contamination*. Identities are never secure in their difference, and are always contaminated by what is outside them, by the other identities and discourses that are beyond their borders. In this sense, perhaps heterogeneity may be understood as operating *against* the notion of pure difference. Heterogeneity is what contaminates identities internally, what opens them up to the other beyond their own difference, what opens them even to the possibilities of the Same.

This attempt to think the heterogeneity of identity through the notion of contamination rather than pure difference, has important political implications – implications that will be explored throughout this book. Briefly, though, it would mean that a pure politics of identity is impossible. That is to say, it would be possible for a certain particular group to assert a purely differential identity because this identity can only be established against a background of universality – say the demand for equal recognition or rights – that at the same time contaminates this identity and destabilises its purely differential position. Put simply, if a certain political identity – an ethnic or cultural minority for instance – demands to be recognised in its particularity, this demand can only be made in reference to some sort of universal demand for equality or equal rights; and, moreover, it can only be articulated in the context of relations with other groups. As Ernesto Laclau's theory of hegemony shows, for a particular identity to participate in politics, its endeavours will be limited and ultimately self-defeating unless it can form 'chains of equivalence' with other identities against a common 'enemy'.[30] In other words, there can be no pure 'politics of difference'.

Universality and the event

Central here is this notion of universality and the role it plays in radical politics. Many have claimed that postmodernism leads to the abandonment of any idea of universality and, with it, the relinquishment of radical projects of emancipation and social and political transformation. My response will be to suggest that universality is still thinkable within the conditions of postmodernity and indeed that postmodernity can lead to a renewal of radical and emancipatory politics; but that in order for this to happen, universality must itself be rethought. Poststructuralist theory, I would suggest – because it rejects the idea of absolute foundations and points instead to the contingency of political identities – provides the theoretical conditions under which universality may be rethought. It would be a mistake to conclude that because poststructuralist theory acknowledges the instability of identity it leaves no place for universality in politics. As I have suggested, this acknowledgement does not amount to a simple recognition of self-enclosed differences; nor does it equate with an individualism which eschews collective political projects. Rather than the 'respect for difference' with which it is commonly associated, perhaps poststructuralism might be more accurately and fruitfully characterised as a respect for *singularity*. Singularity is not simple difference, but refers rather to an *event* – the emergence of something unpredictable, other; an event that dislocates our pre-existing frameworks of representation and political and social structures. Here I would suggest that, paradoxically, the event of singularity is always at the same time the *event of universality*. Indeed, there is no simple opposition between singularity and universality, but rather a relationship of undecidability between them, one always invoking the other. In this book, I will attempt to show the various instances where the singularity of the event opens up onto a universal dimension of unconditional equality and freedom. These instances of universality would be found in the fields of subjectivity, ethics and, of course, radical politics itself.

The elaboration of a new radical politics of universality must begin, however, with an examination of the conditions currently opposing and constraining it. The following chapter will therefore analyse the workings of power and ideology today.

Notes

1 F. Nietzsche, *The Gay Science*, trans. W. Kaufmann (New York: Vintage Books, 1974), p. 181.
2 In an interview, Alain Badiou insists that God is dead – even for George Bush and Osama Bin Laden: 'I think that even for them He is dead. It's a dead God's action, He is dead and still acts. A dead God is being removed.' 'A conversation with Alain Badiou' (interview with Mario Goldenberg, 2004) <www.lacan.com/lacinkXXIII6.htm>.
3 J.-F. Lyotard, *The Postmodern Condition: a Report on Knowledge*, trans. G. Bennington and B. Massumi (Manchester: Manchester University Press, 1991), p. xxiv.
4 Foucault, of course, also highlighted the ultimately arbitrary nature of the discursive divisions between 'true' and 'untrue', between statements that were included with a certain scientific discourse or body of knowledge, and those that were excluded from it; as well as the institutional rationalities and coercive practices in which these determinations of truth were situated – thus pointing to the intimate connection between power and knowledge (see Foucault, 'Truth and Power').
5 Lyotard, *The Postmodern Condition*, p. 5.
6 Lyotard, *The Postmodern Condition*, p. 17.
7 Lyotard, *The Postmodern Condition*, p. 47.
8 Lyotard, *The Postmodern Condition*, p. 63.
9 Lyotard, *The Postmodern Condition*, p. 76.
10 Lyotard, *The Postmodern Condition*, p. 79.
11 A. Heller and F. Feher, *The Postmodern Political Condition* (Cambridge: Polity Press, 1988), p. 11.
12 Heller and Feher, *The Postmodern Political Condition*, p. 1.
13 M. Stirner, *The Ego and Its Own*, ed. D. Leopold (Cambridge: Cambridge University Press, 1995), p. 43.
14 J. Torfing, *New Theories of Discourse: Laclau, Mouffe and Žižek* (Oxford: Blackwell, 1999), p. 61.
15 See D. Coole, 'Master narratives and feminist subversions', in J. Good and I. Velody (eds), *The Politics of Postmodernity* (Cambridge: Cambridge University Press, 1998), pp. 107–125.
16 Coole, 'Master narratives and feminist subversions', pp. 122–123.
17 J. Rancière, 'Who is the subject of the Rights of Man?', *South Atlantic Quarterly*, 103.2/3 (2004): 297–310.
18 E. Balibar, 'Is there a "neo-racism"?', in E. Balibar and I. Wallerstein (eds), *Race, Nation, Class: Ambiguous Identities*, (London: Verso, 2002), pp. 17–28. See also Balibar's essay 'Is there a European Racism?', in E. Balibar, *Politics and the Other Scene*, trans. C. Jones et al. (London: Verso, 2002), pp. 40–55.
19 Balibar, *Politics and the Other Scene*, p. 143.
20 See S. Žižek, 'You may', *London Review of Books*, 18 March 1999: <www.lacan.com/zizek-youmay.htm>.
21 See J. Habermas, *The Philosophical Discourse of Modernity: Twelve Lectures*, trans. F. Lawrence (Cambridge, MA: MIT Press, 1990), p. 309.

22 J. Habermas, *Moral Consciousness and Communicative Action*, trans. C. Lenhardt and S. Weber Nicholsen (Cambridge, MA: MIT Press, 1990), p. 58. See also J. Habermas, *The Theory of Communicative Action: vols I–II* (Cambridge: Polity Press, 1984–1987).

23 Lyotard, *The Postmodern Condition*, p. 65.

24 Paul Verhaeghe, 'From impossibility to inability: Lacan's theory of the Four Discourses', *The Letter*, 3: 76–99, p. 81. Cited in Yannis Stavrakakis, *Lacan and the Political* (London: Routledge, 1999), p. 115.

25 Lyotard, *The Differend*, p. xi.

26 Lyotard, *The Differend*, p. xiii.

27 Lyotard, *The Differend*, p. 138.

28 See M. Peters, 'What is poststructuralism? The French reception of Nietzsche', *Political Theory Newsletter* 8:2 (1997): 39–55.

29 Here I think it is important to consider Badiou's powerful critique of the concept of postmodernity, which he refers to as the 'age of the poets'. He suggests that the postmodern discourse of the collapse of the metanarrative is itself another metanarrative, another totalising discourse: 'The announcement of the "End of Grand Narratives" is as immodest as the Grand Narrative itself, the certainty of "the end of metaphysics" proceeds within the metaphysical element of certainty ...'. Badiou's critique here serves as a valuable corrective to the tendency of philosophy to unthinkingly accept and revel in the notion of the 'end of modernity'. See A. Badiou, *Manifesto for Philosophy*, trans. and ed. N. Madarasz (Albany, NY: State University of New York Press, 1999), pp. 30–31.

30 See E. Laclau with J. Butler and S. Žižek, in *Contingency, Hegemony, Universality: Contemporary Dialogues on the Left* (London: Verso, 2000), p. 56.

2

Power

THE PREVIOUS chapter explored the 'postmodern condition' and, particularly, its implications for politics. I suggested that postmodernity is fundamentally ambiguous in its effects, and can give rise to different forms of politics, whether progressive, reactionary or simply nihilistic. Its motifs of difference, fragmentation and flux, and its questioning of the 'metanarrative' can, on the one hand, lead to either a radical displacement of social identities, institutions and discourses, and on the other, to a paranoid desire to cling to them ever more firmly – or worse, to a conservative mania that seeks to resurrect some sort of imagined pre-modern 'lifeword' with all its attendant obscurantisms and authoritarianism. Moreover, while postmodernity can create the conditions for a sustained critique of existing power relations and ideologies, it can lead to the production of new and equally pernicious forms of domination. A 'postmodern' radical politics must diagnose and confront these new modalities of power.

Indeed, the question of power has always been central to radical politics, which has sought an emancipation of the subject from various forms of domination, coercion and exclusion, whether they be in the form of authoritarian political institutions, unequal and hierarchical social relations, or exploitative economic arrangements. However, should the theorisation of radical politics begin with the problem of power? Should power, and the question of resistance against it, be the point of departure for the consideration of radical politics today? Alain Badiou does not seem to think so. In an interview he said:

> In particular, you begin thinking politics through consideration of the forms of power. I think this is completely wrong. If you enter politics by thinking the forms of power then you will always end up with the state (in the general sense of the word) as your referent.[1]

Here Badiou is criticising, in particular, the Foucauldian idea that resistance is the other side of power, that power presupposes resistance, in other words. For Badiou, seeing resistance and power as part of the same dynamic only ties the politics to the power that it resists, thus extinguishing its emancipative potential. For a politics to be truly emancipative, according to Badiou, it must go beyond the problem of power and seek a *separation* from it: in other words, it must be thought on its own terms, as something which emerges outside the problematic of power.

My argument here will be somewhat different: that while radical politics must be more than simply a politics of resistance, while it must, in other words, go beyond the forms of power that it resists, any discussion of radical politics cannot proceed without at least an understanding of the contemporary forms of power that it seeks to emancipate itself from. However, this does not mean that radical politics will be always enthralled by the power it seeks to free itself from – simply that in order to devise strategies, to develop analytical weapons, the functioning and operation of power must be effectively grasped. The problem with 'postmodern' power – and indeed this was the very ambiguity of power that Foucault pointed to – was that it always has the potential to incorporate into its own structures that which seeks to resist and transgress it. Contrary to what Badiou maintains, the attempt to see resistance and power as subsisting in a relationship of undecidability where the line between them was blurred, was not to somehow bind resistance to power, but rather to point out the dangers inherent in any politics of resistance – that there is always the potential for it to become incorporated into the very power structure it resists, and that, consequently, it must remain *one step ahead* of power.

However, my analysis will also address some of the limitations and problems with Foucault's own notion of power. Firstly, while Foucault's well-known 'micro-analysis' of power radicalised the concept, taking it beyond the staid behavioural and structuralist debates, it also to some extent neglected the operation of power at the 'macro' level. Foucault's fragmentary analyses of the points of intersection between the functioning of 'everyday' power relations (as a 'mode of action upon actions') and the functioning of large institutions and structures of domination, was incomplete and marked with ambiguity. What was lacking here was an analysis of sovereignty, which, rather than having been displaced by disciplinary and bio-power, as Foucault suggested, continues to work in conjunction with these more dispersed forms of power. Indeed, what we have seen in recent years is the aggressive and brutal reassertion of state sovereignty. The 'war on terror' has provided the rationalisation for the expansion of the power of the state and its transformation into a 'security state', a paradigm whose dangerous potential we are only just beginning to grasp. And what about those transnational structures of power – like the IMF and WTO – whose activities, in collaboration with states and multinational corporations, form, as Hardt and Negri claim, the contours of a new postmodern global empire?[2] My argument would be, then, that any consideration of power must take into account these larger and more global structures of domination. Therefore, any understanding of power is incomplete without an understanding of sovereignty. State sovereignty does not, unfortunately, look like disappearing any time soon – on the contrary, new forms of sovereignty are proliferating, and therefore the problem of sovereignty requires careful and patient examination.

Secondly, Foucault's account of power explicitly repudiates the problematic of ideology, seeing it as a hangover from an outdated critical theory/Marxist approach, and as presupposing an essentialist concept of the subject whose 'real interests' are supposedly distorted by its operation. However, I would suggest that we cannot do without a concept of ideology today: we live in a time when, despite the protestations of those in power that the age of ideologies is over, we seem to be surrounded by all sorts of neoconservative and fundamentalist ideologies; and, moreover, we are increasingly caught up in a new global and totalitarian ideology – whose key features are the need for security and the inevitability of the free market. The 'war on terror' has to be seen as an ideological apparatus – one that has concrete political effects, which is obscurantist and fundamentalist, and which positions us as 'subjects'. Therefore, the concept of ideology is indispensable today. However, we need to reformulate the notion of ideology in ways that avoid essentialist assumptions about the subject and 'objective' reality.

Postmodern power

Postmodernity, as a logic of differentiation, heterogeneity and flux not only gives impetus to new struggles of emancipation, but, perversely, also defines a new field of power and domination which these struggles must contend with. We can say, broadly, that postmodern power operates increasingly through localised and decentred points, is productive rather than purely repressive and prohibitive, and constitutes a system of free-floating control and surveillance, working in conjunction with the 'old' system of prohibition and law. Moreover, it is a system of power which is made possible through the expansion of the market, and the shift from industrial to post-industrial modes of production. In particular, the 'information age' and the development of new communications technologies, virtual reality, and new forms of biotechnology, have allowed for new and much more pervasive forms of power to be exercised over individuals in contemporary society. We might speak here of a generalised form of 'biopolitical' control. Bio-power/biopolitics will be examined in greater detail later; but, simply put, it is a form of power which is exercised at the level of biological life itself, and which acts not to destroy life – although this is always its lethal and permanent underside – but rather to sustain, control and regulate it, to direct its energies and productive powers. Indeed, Hardt and Negri, in their analysis of postmodern Empire, speak of a biopolitical form of sovereignty which has proliferated globally, and which operates through structures of differentiation, hybrid networks and fragmented notions of subjectivity. Therefore, the postmodern motifs of difference, fragmentation and flux are no longer necessarily radical or subversive – indeed, in some sense they are the emblems of this new system of domination.

In his short piece 'Postscript on the Societies of Control', Gilles Deleuze describes a new form of power that has superseded, to some extent, the disciplinary mode of power whose emergence was observed by Foucault. This was a mode of power based on a kind of free-floating and modulated control, rather than on the model of the prison and the enclosure of the individual within certain spaces. In other words, in contrast to disciplinary societies, where the movements of the individual were regulated within the confined spaces of the school, prison, hospital or factory, societies of control extend this regulation beyond the walls of institution through new techniques such as electronic surveillance, DNA monitoring, information technology and even marketing strategies.[3] Thus, control, as opposed to disciplinary power, presupposes a certain freedom of movement and choice – a freedom which is, at the same time, minutely regulated and policed so that the 'right' choices are made. Can we deny that today the most insidious forms of control come in the guise of a certain 'freedom of choice', where we as consumers are confronted in the marketplace with an endless series of products and 'lifestyles' to choose from. This multitude of choices is reflected in a certain fragmentation of our daily experience and, indeed, our very identity. The 'postmodern' individual, it is said, consists of a series of different and even inconsistent identities existing in the one person – corporate warrior during the day, transvestite hooker by night, environmentalist at the weekends, etc. This idea of life as flux, as a proliferation of identities, as constant becoming is not necessarily something to be celebrated or fetishised. It does not necessarily equate with liberation – on the contrary it not only fits hand in glove with the capitalist market, which always looks for different lifestyle niches, but also allows for the functioning of complex and pervasive systems of control. As Deleuze shows, while the subject of disciplinary societies was the individual incarcerated in his own identity, the subject of control societies is the *dividual* – in other words, the divided, fragmented self, the person who is not even able to form a coherent identity, and who does not have time to *finish anything*.

The loss and fragmentation of the self, as an effect of contemporary forms of power, is also a phenomenon observed by Paul Virilio. In his analyses of societies of 'speed', Virilio shows the way that new information technologies which allow instantaneous flows of communication and media coverage, are contributing to an experience of life that is increasingly virtualised and 'unreal'. In particular, the intervention of technology into nearly every aspect of our lives

– from computer gadgets to 'smart' houses to new developments in bio- and nano-technology – is leading to a general displacement of man by machine, and a blurring of the distinction between human and non-human.[4] Again, these developments should not be fetishised or seen as a form of liberation, as those harbingers of the 'post-human' cyber age are wont to do. There is nothing emancipating, necessarily, about the disappearance of man or the loss of reality, especially if what replaces them are only media-manipulated virtual reality or corporate-controlled consumerist existence. The important point made by Virilio is that technology always has a dark side, amongst other things, the potential – already being realised – to produce the most extreme measures of surveillance and control. We live in a society that is more closely and minutely monitored, regulated and policed than ever before; where personal privacy is more or less non-existent; where information about our whereabouts, our personal details, our spending habits is ceaselessly collected; where biometric data must be exhibited on passports and ID cards; and where our DNA rather than, as Foucault believed, our sexuality, is now seen as the absolute secret of our being. We are seeing the installation of a kind of global surveillance system – a 'globalitarianism' as Virilio calls it – where electronic communications can be monitored through satellite and personal information made available to governments.

However, while 'postmodern' power is a 'soft' form of control, functioning through the techniques and measures just described, it also operates in conjunction with more traditional forms of juridical power. Indeed, we might say that 'postmodern' techniques of surveillance and control have intersected with a legal and police system that is becoming increasingly repressive. We live in what may now be called, not exaggeratedly, a 'zero-tolerance' society, a police state, in which we see the proliferation of increasingly restrictive laws which are designed to regulate, police and 'normalise' every aspect of our lives. One thinks here, for instance, of the extremely draconian legislation against what is considered as 'anti-social' behaviour, which gives police powers to detain people, impose curfews, break up crowds and gatherings, and restrict people's activities and movements.[5] The idea that society or the 'community' must be protected from certain sorts of behaviour that are considered 'offensive' or 'dangerous' indicates the way that the law is increasingly being used to enforce some sort of social norm. Indeed, Foucault recognised that even in disciplinary societies of the nineteenth century, the law started to be seen as something that could be used increasingly to enforce certain norms of behaviour:

> There also appeared the idea of a penalty that was not meant to be a response to an infraction but had the function of correcting individuals at the level of their behaviour, their attitudes, their dispositions, the danger they represented – at the level of their supposed potentialities.[6]

One thinks here, in this context, of current laws designed to monitor and incarcerate the mentally ill, delinquent or 'problem' children, 'potential sex offenders', before they have even committed any offence, precisely because of the potential danger they supposedly represent. And what of those draconian laws against smoking in public places; or the myriad of laws, rules, infringements, infractions designed to prevent 'sexual harassment' and regulate conduct between men and women, adults and children? Of course, we should not ignore the way that people, whipped up into a hysteria by the media about paedophiles and violent crime, and manipulated by governments, clamour for these new laws and regulations that dominate them. But there is a sense in which, in contemporary societies, our lives are becoming increasingly policed, beset by an abundance of useless and petty laws and rules. The tyranny of the norm and the tyranny of the law combine and intersect with one another, producing a generalised system of social domination where power is exercised through social networks and government institutions, and administered by the courts, the police, doctors, psychiatrists, counsellors and social workers. Foucault referred to nineteenth-century disciplinary societies as inaugurating the 'age of social control'.[7] This would apply even more so today.

What is interesting, though, is that this ceaseless proliferation of laws – with governments working tirelessly on new 'legislative agendas', their frenetic activity disguising the complete absence of any sort of progressive politics – signifies at the same time the very *impotence* of the law. That is to say, the law ceases to be able to protect us from the sovereign power of governments, as the proponents of classical liberalism had hoped. Indeed, with the new forms of power and domination that have been given to the executive under 'anti-terrorist legislation' – in which extra-judicial detention without trial features most prominently – perhaps it no longer makes sense to talk about liberalism or liberal democracy. Liberal democracies stand on the threshold of a new form of power that is defined, as we shall see later on, through the notion of the *exception* – and which makes them all but indistinguishable from the authoritarian regimes they like to claim they are so distant from. Perhaps it may be more accurate to say that liberalism, as a political rationality, has always had a paradoxical relationship with sovereign power, only being able to be articulated through a repressive police and law-and-order regime. Yes, policing is the truth of liberalism. However, the point is that the liberal discourse of the rule of law, of individual rights and liberties, of rule by consent, no longer has any force today: the law no longer functions to curb the power of the sovereign, but is simply a tool, a vector through which excessive forms of sovereign power are articulated.

So, postmodern power – or the form of power that functions in 'postmodern societies' – has three general characteristics. Firstly, it is a power that operates in loose networks, and constitutes, through the use of all sorts of surveillance technology, a form of seamless monitoring and free-floating control. Secondly, this 'soft' form of control works in tandem with more coercive forms of juridical power: an endless array of laws designed to regulate and normalise behaviour and punish transgression. Lastly, there is the sovereign state of exception, in which the two previous forms of 'governing' reach their ultimate conclusion. It is sovereignty, in other words, which coordinates all the decentralised techniques and forms of control; moreover, it is sovereignty which makes the law serve its ends, so that ultimately the law itself is suspended through 'states of emergency' and extra-juridical forms of control. It is through sovereignty, in other words, that law becomes control and control becomes law. For instance, the use of the infamous 'control orders' to monitor and detain terrorist suspects without trial – which can range from electronic tagging right through to house arrest – signifies this point of *indistinction* between control and law. That *extra-judicial* detention and control is at the same time authorised *by* the law – through legislation, acts of parliament – shows what the law itself has become in the face of an aggressive new form of sovereignty. Another example can be used to illustrate this strange new world of power: technology is currently being developed that will apparently allow surveillance cameras to recognise 'suspicious' or potentially 'dangerous' activity in public places – on buses and trains for instance – by matching footage of passengers against computer files on 'abnormal' behaviour and automatically raising an alarm when these coincide. Thus, we see that abnormal or 'anti-social' behaviour is not only determined by police, magistrates and social workers, but now also by computers. Such technology is, of course, being feted as not only an effective tool in fighting crime and curbing 'anti-social behaviour', but also as a weapon in the 'war on terror'. At the same time, a recent law was passed by the Italian parliament – again in the name of 'security' – which prohibits the covering of one's face in public, whether by the Islamic veil or even simply a mask. So it is between the sophistication of new surveillance technology, and the extremity and crudeness of the law, that we are increasingly trapped.

The 'micro-physics' of power: Michel Foucault

The developments and transformations of power, from the classical age to modernity and beyond, have been extensively analysed by Foucault. Foucault charted, during the eighteenth and nineteenth centuries, the emergence of the 'disciplines' – a new network of power relations, discourses and institutional practices – that had as their aim, function and effect the normalisation of the individual. Moreover, this was a power that was exercised infinitesimally at the level of the body, as well as the individual psyche, controlling its movements, supervising its behaviours, policing its desires. Disciplinary power emerges, moreover, at the point when Enlightenment humanist ideals and liberal political rationalities began to gain ascendancy, showing the fundamental complicity between the 'rights of man' and new forms of power: 'The "Enlightenment", which discovered the liberties, also invented the disciplines.'[8]

The radical innovation of Foucault's 'micro-analysis' of power was that it tried to go beyond what he termed the 'juridico-discursive' or 'juridico-sovereign' paradigm: that which saw power as being based, symbolically, on the figure of the sovereign. From this 'juridico-sovereign' perspective, power was seen as emanating from centralised institutions, namely the sovereign state; as being based on notions of juridical right and the social contract; and as taking the form, largely, of laws that prohibit, repress and restrict certain freedoms. Foucault's critique of this paradigm questions these central assumptions about power: rather than power being based on the central symbol of the sovereign, and radiating downwards from centralised institutions, it often functions in a diffuse, decentralised form, emanating from a multitude of points within the social body; rather than power being defined and legitimised through notions of juridical authority and consent, it has to be seen instead as a violent form of domination; and, lastly, rather than power being simply repressive and prohibitive, it is also productive – it *produces and incites*.[9] The problem, according to Foucault, is that most theories of power still remain within the traditional paradigm of sovereignty, and have not caught up with developments and transformations in the functioning of power that have taken place since the early nineteenth century. The analysis of power therefore needs to abandon this symbolic figure of the sovereign. As he said, famously: 'What we need is a political philosophy that isn't erected around the problem of sovereignty ... We need to cut off the King's head.'[10]

War and biopolitics

Foucault's anti-sovereign reformulation of power is perhaps most extensively explored in his lecture series at the College de France from 1975–1976, organised around the title 'Il faut defendre la société' or 'Society must be defended'. Here he seeks to develop a new understanding of power – one that is based no longer on sovereign notions of juridical right, nor even on the Marxist economic model of repression, but rather on the metaphor of war. War serves as a methodological tool for deciphering power relations: 'Can we find in bellicose relations, in the model of war, in the schema of struggle or struggles a principle that can help us understand and analyze political power, to interpret political power in terms of war, struggles, and confrontations?'[11] In other words, in Foucault's analysis, war serves as a 'grid of intelligibility' through which to observe power relations: power is seen, from this perspective, as being based on violent conquest and an antagonistic clash of hostile social forces, discourses and modes of representation. War, moreover, is a kind of ontological essential condition raging behind social relations, political institutions and legal structures. According to Foucault, there is a constant state of warfare that finds its way into discourses, political rationalities and laws, and it is the task of a new form of political analysis – which he terms 'historico-political' and which operates as an alternative to the 'philosophico-juridical' discourse of sovereignty – to unmask this antagonism, to 'awaken beneath the form of institutions and legislations the forgotten past of real struggles, of masked victories or defeats, the blood that has dried on the codes of law'.[12]

The conceptual apparatus of power/war that Foucault develops here suggests a radical new way of understanding the political field, one that, I would argue, is close to an anarchist political analysis. It seeks to overturn the very discourse of sovereignty itself, in which sovereign power is legitimated through the social contract and some notion of juridical right – through its ability, essentially, to put a stop to the permanent state of antagonism and violence that characterises the state of nature. However, as this anti-sovereign analysis shows, sovereignty is simply the continuation and extension of war and conquest, and is based not on the consent of the people but rather on their violent subjugation.

This 'strategic' analysis of power is interesting for a number of reasons. For instance, in pointing to the nexus between war and power, perhaps it allows us to explain why the discourse of warfare is so easily called upon today. The discourse of the 'war on terror' for instance, deliberately deploys and mobilises the language of war: the 'terrorist' is not seen as a criminal, to whom would be applied police actions, judicial procedures and legal sanctions, but rather as an enemy who must be destroyed, even through military means.[13] Moreover, the 'war on terror' signifies the collapse of any sort of conceptual distinction between war and politics: now politics has become a kind of warfare – 'the war on terror' and the 'need for security' becoming the sole prerogative of political life and the standard of legitimacy for any government. Furthermore, this can be seen as a war that is fought both externally and internally, constructing enemies beyond and within national borders. Indeed, one could see the 'war on terror' as a struggle that has as its real aim the total surveillance, regulation and control of populations. The excessive and hitherto unimaginable powers that the state has given itself in the name of guaranteeing our security – the unprecedented powers of surveillance and detention, of search and arrest, the power to restrict public gatherings and protests, to suspend civil liberties and habeas corpus, etc – suggest that this is really a war waged by governments against their own people, even in our esteemed 'Western democracies'. There is little doubt that the state has a vested interest in making this war last as long as possible.

Moreover, this convergence between war and politics also defines a new field of power: according to Foucault, during the eighteenth century, disciplinary power begins to overlap with what he calls he calls 'bio-power'. Unlike disciplinary power, which operates at the level of the individual and his body, bio-power functions at the level of the population, seeking to regulate its movements, monitor its trends and coordinate its productive powers. Foucault shows the way, for instance, that during the late eighteenth century the figure of the population started to appear in political discourses, governments for the first time taking an interest in birth and death rates, longevity, sexual and biological health, epidemics etc. The emergence of these new biopolitical rationalities of government is only made possible through the exercising of a new technology of power over biological life itself. This form of power is contrasted in dramatic terms, in Foucault's analysis, with older forms of sovereign power: the power of the sovereign is defined by the right to take life or to let live, whereas bio-power is defined by the right to *make live and to let die*.[14] In other words, the power of the sovereign is defined by the right to kill, to take life – one remembers the horrible torture and execution of the regicide Damiens, upon whose body this sovereign right was vividly inscribed; while bio-power seeks to *sustain* life, thus controlling it much more effectively – its violence consisting in a withdrawal, upon which life collapses. One might think of the humanitarian relief operation as an example of bio-power: the biological life of the starving people is entirely dependent upon those Western governments feeding them, which surely produces a situation of total domination. It is perhaps no wonder today that humanitarian relief operations are increasingly carried out by military forces, and are simply the other side of military interventions.

More broadly, however, we might say that we live today in a 'bio-culture', particularly in the wealthy West where we have a kind of cultural obsession with 'lifestyle', with 'quality of life' issues, as well as with those forms of behaviour – such as smoking, binge drinking and over-eating – which threaten this 'quality of life'. There is almost a super-ego injunction to be healthy, to exercise regularly, to not be depressed – messages imbued with all the ferocity of moral strictures. Governments involve themselves in these issues, promoting strategies of well-being, expressing concern at the high incidence of obesity, and generally seeking to regulate behaviour according to a series of biological norms. Moreover, we see in medical discourse the attribution of every personality defect, every pathology, every psychological deficiency – even 'unstable emotions' – to some genetic abnormality, some disturbance in our DNA, some hereditary factor; eugenics, it would seem, has made a comeback. These might all be seen as instances of the kind of power that Foucault is describing: a power that seizes hold of life, sustaining and regulating it.

Methodological considerations

Foucault's theorisation of power can be seen as 'postmodern': power is seen here not as a one-sided, monolithic and repressive force, but rather as a fluid and dynamic relationship that emerges from a multitude of points, that is coextensive with the social body, and that can give rise to all sorts of strategic reversals and possibilities of resistance. Power, for Foucault, involves a heterogeneous series of antagonistic forces, each vying for supremacy.

Moreover, power is *productive* as well as simply repressive and prohibitive. Here Foucault has taken the analysis of power beyond what he sees as the 'repressive hypothesis' – which is an aspect of the 'juridico-sovereign' model of power – and which sees power as that which represses the freedoms and capacities of the subject and distorts the objective truth of social relations. This understanding of power as repression has been central to radical politics in particular: classical radical political theory, from Marxism to anarchism, has depended on a certain discourse of emancipation, in which the subject is liberated from the forms of power – whether the institution of the state or the capitalist economic relations – that deny his subjectivity and thwart his creative potential as a human being. However, the problem with this 'metanarrative' is that, according to Foucault, the subject who is to be liberated from power, 'the man described for us, whom we are invited to free, is already in himself the effect of a subjection much more profound than himself'.[15] In other words, the subject is always already fully implicated in power relations, the effects of power constituting the very core of his being. The identity of the subject is constructed discursively through relations of power/knowledge and 'regimes of truth' which, through their power effects, require the subject to speak the 'truth' about himself and his identity. Even our sexual desire – that which we consider to be most natural to us, the secret of who we are – is, as Foucault has shown, a construct of power relations, institutional practices and discourses about sexuality. Bio-power, in particular, concerns itself with sex, no longer simply for the purposes of promoting 'normal' heterosexual identities and thus ensuring the reproduction of life, but also, increasingly, in an experimentation with divergent sexualities and sexual practices. Here perhaps Foucault was wrong in his belief that 'bodies and pleasures' could serve as a site of resistance to this sexualising bio-power:[16] 'bodies and pleasures' have simply become a threshold *of* bio-power, a power that elicits a proliferation of *jouissances* ('enjoyments'). In any case, power today encourages the subject to talk incessantly about sex, to reveal the 'truth' of his desires: however, instead of the promised liberation from sexual repression, we are subordinated to a new 'monarchy of sex', and tied to a certain constructed sexual identity. This is the 'ruse of power' according to Foucault: we are tricked into thinking that there is an essential subject that is repressed, whereas, in fact, this subjectivity is itself an effect of power, and the assertion of this identity as an attempt to transgress power plays right into its hands. Power is therefore 'subjectifying' – it produces the subject as a site of his own domination.

The advantage of this postmodern theory of power developed by Foucault is that it avoids essentialist understandings of the subject: the subject is not an essential identity outside power, but rather an identity already complicit in power relationships, and, in part, an 'effect' of power. While this raises certain problems for resistance – there is no pure outside, 'no single locus of great Refusal, no soul of revolt, source of all rebellions, or pure law of the revolutionary'[17] – it does not make it impossible, as many have alleged: resistance is something that takes place within the field of power, working at its interstices, looking for cracks, openings and points of rupture which might allow for unpredictable and dramatic shifts and reversals. Moreover, while society can never hope to free itself entirely from power – while power is, to some extent, inevitable in any social formation – political struggles can nevertheless transform and radicalise power relations, making them more egalitarian, reciprocal and less dominating.

However, I would argue that there are certain aspects of Foucault's theory of power that are more problematic, both conceptually and practically, and which impose serious constraints on radical politics. Firstly, Foucault's understanding of power as dispersed and heterogeneous seems to lead to a certain fragmentation of the political field, thus limiting it to localised political struggles that take place around specific sites of domination. Foucault sees power in terms of an almost Nietzschean struggle of forces and affects, a struggle that produces an absolute differentiation, making it impossible for any common ground to form between them. In other words, there is an absolute incommensurability between the different forces engaged in power struggles. The clash of forces that Foucault describes occurs in a 'nonplace' – a purely differentiated relation of antagonism, without the stable political identities that would otherwise unify the political field: indeed, Foucault speaks of a struggle of differences and representations that takes place in 'a pure distance, which indicates that the adversaries do not belong to a common space'.[18] We must recognise here that Foucault is not necessarily talking about actual political identities and struggles, but rather to a clash of representations and forces that lie behind power relationships. Nevertheless, this genealogical motif of difference, particularity and incommensurability does suggest a kind of fragmentation of the socio-political field and therefore the loss of a universal political dimension. The problem with Foucault's understanding of power, then, is that it in some ways reflects and even contributes to this loss of a universal horizon of emancipation. The localised struggles of resistance that Foucault speaks of, which emerge around specific sites of power – those of prisoners, the mentally ill, homosexuals, etc – are very important. However, there is little sense in Foucault's writings of any real possibility of a collective ground emerging between these disparate struggles and identities; there is little possibility, it would seem, of a universal politics being constructed.

The second problem I have with Foucault's account of power is that there is no symbolic place of power as such. This displacement of power is central to

Foucault's critique of the sovereign model of power. However, this notion of power as dispersed and plural is, I would argue, incomplete. Or perhaps, it would be more accurate to say that there is a certain inconsistency or ambiguity in Foucault's work on the question of sovereignty, and the points where power relations crystallise into central institutions like the state. Foucault does not exactly reject the notion of sovereignty – indeed there is a lengthy discussion of state racism in the College de France lectures. But he seems to suggest that modern forms of disciplinary and bio-power have largely superseded it: in other words, the problem of sovereignty is no longer all that important in his analysis of the power. Furthermore, Foucault has also questioned the relevance of the concept of the state. The state

> no more probably today that at any other time in its history, does not have this unity, this individuality, this rigorous functionality, nor, to speak frankly, this importance; maybe, after all, the state is no more than a composite reality and a mythicised abstraction, whose importance is a lot more limited than many of us think.[19]

Instead of the state as a conceptual unity, as an instance of domination, Foucault suggests that it may be more productive to think in terms of strategies and rationalities of 'government'. However, I would suggest that the problem of the state – and indeed of sovereignty itself – cannot be so easily dismissed. While power today is certainly more diffuse, while it circulates through a multitude of different institutions, practices, discourses and governmental rationalities, there is still what can be considered a state, a central structure of authority – even if this is undergoing a permanent transformation as a result of globalisation. Indeed, with the 'war on terror', as I have suggested, we are seeing a kind of aggressive reassertion of the state: we see a state that more closely regulates and controls its populations, that subjects people to detention, that tortures and humiliates detainees in off-shore prison camps and so on. We have seen the re-emergence of a violent and lawless sovereignty which no longer even pretends to be democratically accountable. So I think there is something lacking in Foucault's analysis of power: a reflection on the more globalising institutions and forms of sovereignty, and on structures of domination that are not so easily reversed. There is a sort of disconnection in Foucault's analysis between his notion of power functioning at an everyday level – which is simply a way of *acting on the actions of others*, presupposing a reciprocity and freedom of move-ment[20] – and the larger structures of domination, which allow for little or no reciprocity or freedom. This is a point that is also made by Étienne Balibar, who argues that Foucault's analysis of power – in which power relations are seen as fluid, reversible and reciprocal – cannot adequately account for the instances where power seems completely *asymmetrical*, where it allows for no reversibil-ity, and where its effects are felt as the most violent of dominations. Here he points to what he calls 'extreme situations' – such as exterminations, ethnic cleansing and mass slaughters – where the exercise of power is excessive, violent and entirely one-sided, and where, moreover, it is conditioned by a kind of *jouissance* that is found in its cruelty and sadism:

> I call it ultra-subjective violence because such actions are undoubtedly intentional and have a determinate goal. They also have a face – that of the persecutors who are all too human, cruel and cowardly, cunning and stupid – but the will which gives rise to them can only be described, ultimately, as the expression of a 'thing' (to use Freud's term, picked up on by Lacan) of which the subject is the mere instrument of that identity which is (which he 'believes' to be) in him, an identity totally exclusive of any other, one which imperiously commands its self-realization through the elimination of any trace of otherness in the 'we' and the 'self'.[21]

So I would argue that Foucault's analysis of power, while it constitutes a major contribution to postmodern political theory, has a number of conceptual limits and blind spots – particularly when it comes to dealing with instances of power that are not only dominating, but also excessively violent and cruel, and where the notion of reciprocity and strategic reversal simply has no relevance. For Foucault, the precondition of power is that the subject on whom it is exercised has a certain degree of freedom. However, the victims of ethnic cleansing, mass pauperisation or radical abandonment (refugees for instance) – the people upon whom an *excessive* power is exercised – not only have little or no possibility of resistance, but cannot even see themselves as 'subjects' in this sense. The cruelty and violence of institutional power arrangements – the viciousness with which asylum seekers are treated by governments, for instance, or the cold calculations of global capitalist institutions which leave millions to their unbearable poverty and exclusion (the fundamentalism of the market is just as much of a mania as that nationalist fervour which intoxicates the hearts of ethnic cleansers) – needs to be taken into account here.

What we need, then, is a new understanding of institutional violence and sovereign power. One might see sovereignty as a principle of exception – as a point of authority that stands outside the law, thereby providing its foundation and defining its limits but always at the same time invoking a violence that is beyond the law. As Derrida shows in 'Force of Law', the law itself is ultimately grounded on something that is, strictly speaking, non-legal because it had to exist prior to law. The original act of instantiating the law is structurally outside the limits of the law: it is prior to the law and therefore has no legal authority. It would be an illegitimate act of discursive violence: '... a violence without ground'.[22] The mystery of authority, the secret of its being, is a lawlessness and violence that forms its ontological ground. Sovereignty can be seen, then, as a kind of authority that cannot be grounded on anything other than itself: it takes itself as its own authority in a tautological sense that says *I am because I am*. This is no longer the power conditioned by reciprocal relations and strategies of freedom – in the Foucauldian sense – but rather a kind of irrational, mystical 'voice' of authority. Sovereignty is that which gives itself its own law.[23]

The sovereign state of exception

How then should we rethink the problem of sovereignty, the problem that was perhaps too hastily dismissed in Foucault's theory of power? According to Agamben, sovereignty is actually the missing link in Foucault's account between the techniques of individualisation – in which the individual constructs his identity through a certain negotiation with power – and the broader, more total-ising strategies of bio-power/biopolitics, through which these individualising technologies are coordinated.[24] What is important in Agamben's theorisation of power is that, unlike Foucault who sees bio-power as superseding sovereign power, Agamben sees sovereignty and bio-power converging into what he calls a *zone of indistinction*. The ground upon which this convergence takes place is precisely that of 'life' itself. According to Agamben, sovereignty – which we know from Foucault is based on the right to kill – refers to a certain relationship in which life is held in a kind of no-man's land beyond the protection of the law: *homo sacer* is the dimension of the subject which is reduced to bare life – life stripped to its biological substratum, without political or symbolic significance, and which is completely at the mercy of a sovereign power that operates with more or less total impunity. *Homo sacer*, as Agamben shows, refers to an ancient Roman punishment where a person would not be killed directly, but instead would be stripped of all legal protections, so that he could be killed by anyone with complete impunity. What is interesting here is that *homo sacer* refers to a certain space or relation – *the ban* – which is reproduced by sovereign power: those consigned to this 'no man's land' have simply been abandoned by the law and are no longer afforded its protections. Agamben's point is that this void beyond the law and its relationship to 'bare life' is the essence of sovereignty – its hidden secret.

Emblematic of this sovereign power would be the concentration camp, which is, according to Agamben, the exemplary biopolitical space. The camp is an extra-judicial space in which sovereign power can be unrestrictedly exercised over the body and biological life of the detainee: 'this is the principle according to which "everything is possible"'.[25] It is the camp, rather than, as Foucault believed, the prison which therefore serves as the appropriate paradigm of modern life. It is the ultimate point of convergence between the bio-power that regulates life – the minute control exercised over the bodies of those detained, right up to barbaric human experiments – and the sovereign power that presides over death. Can we not also find this sovereign power at work in other spaces of detention today: such as refugee detention camps or the secret CIA prisons, in which the detainees there are *homo sacer*, having no legal status whatsoever, and where the power that is exercised over them is absolute?

Perhaps the clearest example today of this sovereign space that Agamben speaks of would be the off-shore detention camps run by the United States military in Guantanamo Bay, Cuba. The sight of the detainees clad in orange overalls being held in cages behind masses of barbed wire, has become emblematic of this 'war on terror' and the strange new world of power and violence that has emerged with it. Again this camp represents a kind of exception – it is controlled and administered by the US government and yet is deliberately placed outside the jurisdiction of the US court system. Detainees are incarcerated there without having been tried or even charged with any specific offence. They have no legal status, which means that they are subject to an unrestricted, unlimited sovereign power. Literally *anything* could happen to them because the camps are not subject to judicial oversight.

Moreover, in such camps, as Judith Butler argues, a new micro-politics is operating, in which Foucault's theory of governmentality and bio-power coincides with a re-emergence of the apparition of sovereignty.[26] This is, moreover, a violent and lawless sovereignty that haunts these secretive spaces – a sovereignty that has the absolute power over life and death. It is also a sovereignty which is diffuse, fragmented, and embodied in those who administer the camps – the bureaucrats, guards, military judges, officials and private contractors who have the power to decide on the fate of the detainees: the power to interrogate, humiliate, torture and kill more or less with impunity.[27] These are the 'petty sovereigns' who administer a power that they are also at the same time caught up in and do not fully understand or control. Did we not see an example of this lawless power – this power run amok – in that other infamous place of detention, Abu Ghraib? There we saw a power that, as Baudrillard says, 'no longer knows what to do with itself, and cannot stand itself'.[28] This is no longer the old sovereign power resplendent in its glory, but rather the sovereign power of dirty little secrets and perverse rituals – a power that heaps as much humiliation on itself as it does on those subjected to it.

The importance and originality of Agamben's and Butler's interventions lies in showing that the problem of sovereignty is still with is, and that sovereignty is even more dangerous because it now works in collaboration with modern techniques of power and control. Moreover, sovereignty can no longer be entirely understood in terms of a single individual, or an actual institution or series of institutions, but rather as a certain *relationship* – between the sovereign and *homo sacer*, defined by violence and the suspension of the law; and a certain *space* – the space of exception, as exhibited in the model of the camp. In this way the camp is symbolic of the state of exception that defines the very condition of sovereignty. Indeed, as Agamben says, '*The camp is the space that is opened when the state of exception begins to become the rule.*'[29] So what is meant by the state of exception? According to Agamben, the sovereign is defined by the ability to stand outside the law, and to suspend it at critical moments through the act of unilateral decision – in other words to *decide on the state of exception*, as Carl Schmitt said.[30] However, it is not simply that the sovereign rules outside the law; the sovereign stands inside and outside the law simultaneously. This is the paradox of sovereignty: the sovereign guarantees the authority of the juridical order (the power to enforce laws, essentially) and, precisely because of this, also stands outside the limits of this order. The condition of sovereignty, in other words, is marked by a radical *indistinction* between law and lawlessness.

This moment of exception which the sovereign has the power to declare is made possible, according to Agamben, by a certain ambiguity or *aporia* in the law itself. In an examination of different constitutions and legal systems, Agamben shows that they always contain a certain provision which allows them to be suspended during moments of national crisis. Here the law seems to embody its own lack, a central void which both constitutes its limits and fundamentally destabilises it. This lack or aporia is precisely what is meant by the state of exception. For Agamben, then, there is a sort of grey zone or no-man's-land between law and lawlessness – between the rule of law and its abrogation. When the law *is* abrogated and a 'state of emergency' is declared, sovereign power can be exercised without legal restriction. However, the point that Agamben makes is that this legal 'no-man's land' – this lonely and destitute terrain that has been abandoned by the law – is the permanent condition of sovereignty itself. Sovereignty might be understood as the point where violence and law intersect, one becoming indistinguishable from the other: 'the sovereign is the point of indistinction between violence and law, the threshold in which violence passes over into law, and law passes over into violence'.[31]

Through this notion of the state of exception, Agamben explores what he sees as a new paradigm of government emerging today. Increasingly, in the name of fighting the 'war on terror', we see governments invoking the idea of the exception or an 'extraordinary situation' in order to justify the implementation of extraordinary measures: the suspension of civil liberties and habeas corpus, and the general accrual of powers of surveillance and detention without trial. What is emerging is a situation of rule by emergency decree which is becoming, at the same time, normalised: that is to say, this emergency situation is increasingly coming to be seen as the normal state of things, and the measures that are invoked in its name are coming to be seen as the legitimate and normal powers that a 'liberal democracy' must have in order to protect itself. For instance, in 2005 the British government voted itself the power to suspend Parliament in the case of a national emergency, specifically, a terrorist strike – and this was not even regarded at the time as all that controversial. The state of exception has become the rule: the permanent condition of political life. Moreover, we already see the 'state of emergency' being extended to other areas such as law and order and policing: a state of emergency was declared, for instance, during the Paris riots in November 2005 and remained in place for some time afterwards, giving local governments the power to impose curfews, and giving the police extraordinary powers of search and arrest. It is worth noting that this state of emergency was not initially opposed by the Socialist opposition in the French National Assembly: thus we see a new political consensus forming around the idea of 'security'.

The global 'security' state

With these developments the very distinction between liberal democratic and authoritarian regimes seems to be losing its clarity. A new paradigm is emerging, in which the liberal democratic state passes imperceptibly into tyranny without any apparent contradiction – this is the paradigm of the 'security state'. The 'security state' takes the idea of 'security' as its fundamental condition and *raison d'être*. However, the problem with this security function is that, as Agamben says, 'it can always be provoked by terrorism to become terroristic'.[32] In other words, if the state now defines itself solely through its ability to provide security from terrorism, then it *needs* terrorism in order to legitimate itself. That is why the function of the 'security state' lies not so much in the prevention of terrorist attacks – if this was the case, then Iraq would never have been invaded – but rather in their production and management. The ultimate conclusion of this obsession with security will be the complete eclipse of politics – already politics is being reduced to policing – and the formation, as Agamben says, of a 'single deadly system' in which security and terrorism depend on each other for their legitimation.

I would suggest that this 'security' state is becoming a kind of global paradigm. Here, though, we must consider the logic of security in relation to the processes of globalisation itself. The relationship between globalisation and the state itself is paradoxical: on the one hand, transnational movements of capital and technology – facilitated by free trade agreements and global financial institutions – are undermining and weakening the traditional functions of the state: its ability, for instance, to regulate its national economy or to provide social welfare. On the other hand, globalisation seems to produce a counter-dynamic in which the state asserts its control ever more forcefully. However the only area of authority really left to the state is that of policing and 'national security'; thus we see the state increasing its powers of surveillance and control, and more ruthlessly policing its national borders. Therefore, 'security' is a mode through which the state can reassert its authority by intervening in and more closely regulating social relations. However, the emergence of the 'security' state signifies at the same time a fundamental crisis in the concept of the *nation* state. Instead of an international order composed of autonomous nation states, what we are seeing increasingly is a kind of blurring of the borders of nation states, and the folding between inside and outside through the expansion of this idea of security. I am not talking about the traditional notion of 'collective security' that defined the United Nations, but rather a kind of a globalisation of the very 'security' paradigm itself. The 'security' paradigm is increasingly articulated through both formal and covert networks and structures that go beyond national state borders: this can be seen in the sharing of intelligence between national security agencies, and the collaboration in 'counter-insurgency' efforts, as well as in the secret prisons which the CIA has apparently been operating in Europe. The existence of these prisons symbolises this sort of blurring of national borders that I am talking about; they form a *zone of indistinction*, not only between sovereignty and law, but now between two or more sets of sovereignties and laws – those of the United States and the countries who house these prisons – thus indicating a *double exception*. Such developments suggest the eventual emergence of a global security 'state' which would most likely be led by the United States but not confined to it, and whose underside would be those shadowy terrorist networks with whom it is already so intimately linked. Here the concept of national sovereignty will only exist in a depleted and superficial form, as new forms of fragmented sovereignty will be unleashed throughout the social space and a global 'state of emergency' – or, as Agamben refers to it, a 'planetary civil war' – descends upon us.

The question of the state

In light of this rethinking of sovereign power – first through the notion of the state of exception, and then through the paradigm of 'security' – how should we approach the general problem of the state? What does the concept of the 'state' mean today, and what sort of relevance does it have for radical politics? According to Badiou, the state has been, and continues to be, the central problem for radical politics and the rock against which its hopes of emancipation have been repeatedly dashed:

> More precisely, we must ask the question that, without a doubt, constitutes the great enigma of the century: why does the subsumption of politics, either through the form of the immediate bond (the masses), or the mediate bond (the party) ultimately give rise to bureaucratic submission and the cult of the State?[33]

This is the problem that I have termed elsewhere the 'place of power': in other words, the structural logic of power that is central to the state, and which seems to lead to its reaffirmation precisely at those moments of revolution which sought emancipation from it.[34] Revolutions in the past have attempted to seize state power with the view to its eventual 'withering away'; however, the result has often been a strengthening and expansion of the state, and with it a repression of the very revolutionary forces that sought to control it.

Moreover, the problems encountered in classical revolutionary strategy when addressing the state have been exacerbated by the fact that today the state is infinitely more complex, multilayered and ubiquitous. It cannot be simply identified, nor can it be easily overthrown. Perhaps this indefinability and ubiquity is the very essence of the state today. Badiou argues, for instance, that the power of the state lies in its 'errant' nature, in its excessive superpower which is, at the same time, everywhere and nowhere. That is to say, the power of the state today resides in the fact that we do not really know how powerful it is: we have no way of measuring its power, and we therefore feel powerless in its massive and ubiquitous presence. It is only truly identifiable when it responds with excessive force to those movements that resist its authority: one might simply observe here the massive security arrangements and oppressive police presence that accompany meetings of the G8 or the WTO. Indeed, although Badiou would disagree that the anti-capitalist protests that have often interrupted these gatherings present any real threat to the state or to global capitalism – an issue that I shall take up with him later in the book – one could say that the function of such radical politics is to, as Badiou says, 'place the state at a distance'. In other words, by inventing a form of politics that goes beyond the state, thus resisting it, radical movements have the virtue of, at the same time, 'measuring' the state's power, of identifying its limits, limits which are otherwise so opaque. As Badiou says: 'whenever there is a genuine political event, the State reveals itself. It reveals the excess of its power, its repressive dimension'.[35]

This excessive power, which is revealed through the state's response to radical political movements, signifies at the same time its fundamental instability and impotence. Even though the state is a mode of domination, defined through an excessive and ubiquitous power, we should not imagine that the state is invulnerable. While power relationships may not be as fluid and reciprocal as Foucault imagined, and while there are terrible asymmetries of power and the most overwhelming of dominations, we should not think that this power cannot be challenged, resisted or undermined in all sorts of ways. While I have argued here for retaining the notion of a 'structure' of power and a relationship of sovereignty, however loosely defined, we should not necessarily see this structure as always stable, absolute or impervious to challenge. If power is a structure, it is a structure that is at the same time deficient and subject to symbolic breakdowns.[36] Such an account of power as *lacking* would allow us to understand resistance as emerging from its points of dislocation. As Žižek says: 'every power structure is necessarily split, inconsistent; there is a crack in the very foundation of its edifice – and this crack can be used as a lever for the effective subversion of the power structure ...'.[37] This notion of power as structurally deficient – as an unstable structure which is subject to moments of inconsistency – might be seen as part of a 'post-structuralist' critique or deconstruction of power, one that conforms more closely to the second reading of poststructuralism that I have outlined in the previous chapter. Rather than power being understood in Foucauldian terms of pure proliferation and differentiation – as a diffuse series of force relationships which are fluid and reversible, without any symbolic centre or structural logic – perhaps power can be seen as in terms of a decentred 'centre', a structure which is at the same time unstable and ambiguous, and subject to moments of symbolic crisis.

Ideology

These symbolic crises of power refer to the question of ideology. Ideology can be seen as a dominant system of beliefs, discourses and practices which sustains hierarchies of power, which gives power a symbolic consistency and allows it to be extended. However, poststructuralism has had an ambiguous relationship with the problematic of ideology, particularly as it has taken its distance from the last great theorist of ideology, Althusser. Here I would like to briefly address the question of ideology, and consider what relevance the concept has today.

Althusser's structuralist account of ideology radicalised the concept, taking it beyond the classical Marxist theory in which ideology was understood as the ruling bourgeois system of ideas which deceived the working class as to its 'true' interests. Ideology was thus seen as having a distorting effect on the subject. However, the problem here was that this presupposed an essential notion of the subject as having objective interests. Here ideology conforms to an Enlightenment model, in which rational truth cuts through the layers of ideological distortion and reveals the truth about society and the subject. By contrast, the Althusserian theory of ideology dismisses this idea of the essential subject: the subject is already an 'effect' of ideology, as he is completely implicated in ideological mechanisms which form his very identity. In other words, ideology was no longer about the subject who was deceived, but rather the structures or 'ideological state apparatuses' through which people were interpellated *as* 'subjects'.[38] Ideology was not something that could be overcome: ideological 'distortion' was all around us, at the level of our social relations and daily practices, and was constitutive of the subject as such.

However, Foucault's poststructuralist critique of ideology went even further than this. If ideology is, as Althusser contends, so closely implicated with daily practices, social relations and the very identity of the subject itself, then why not simply abandon the whole problematic of ideology altogether? According to Foucault, the problematic of ideology still rests on the question of truth – a truth which is distorted in some way: however, 'the political question . . . is not error, illusion, alienated consciousness or ideology; it is truth itself'.[39] In other words, for Foucault, power no longer functions to distort, conceal or repress truth, but operates through 'regimes' in which truth is *produced*. So what is at issue here is not the distortion or misrepresentation of truth itself but, rather, its epistemological status. Thus, according to Foucault, the whole problematic of ideology simply loses its relevance, and it is much more productive to see the subject as constituted, not through ideological interpellation, but rather through material mechanisms and relations of power which operate at the level of his body and movements.

However, can the concept of ideology be abandoned so readily? Could not *our* time – more so than perhaps previous times – be characterised as the 'age of ideologies'? We seem to be beset today by a proliferation of all sorts of neo-conservative and religious fundamentalist ideologies that have uncannily returned from the past, particularly in the wake of September 11. The 'end of ideologies' and the triumph of liberal democracy, which was so loudly trumpeted by Fukuyama and others, now seems an almost laughable proposition. We live in a strange new ideological universe, in which God has made a comeback and in which people are prepared to die for their religious beliefs – a new obscurantism of the most deadly kind.

Moreover, I would suggest that the 'war on terror' has itself become a dominant ideology – a belief system in which we are all implicated and bound up. The 'war on terror' is the discourse on everyone's lips today, spouted from every politician and media outlet; a new global belief system which is held up as an incontrovertible and absolute truth. This is an ideological system, moreover, with concrete political effects – providing the pretext for the growing authoritarianism of the 'security' state, as well as for an extremely aggressive phase in US foreign policy. It could be argued that the 'war on terror' is the ideology which allows the global capitalist project to become hegemonic. While the existence of fundamentalist terrorism is portrayed as a threat to the global market, it is really the limit which, paradoxically, allows it to accelerate and expand. Capitalism, as Deleuze showed, thrives on contradictions – and today, 'fundamentalist terrorism' or 'violent extremism' has replaced Communism as the contradiction within the global system, and the enemy that must be eliminated. The existence of this 'enemy' not only defines global capitalism, but allows it to be associated with the spread of democracy. One notices here how, in this ideology, democracy and the free market go hand in hand – this extremely tenuous and contingent link is regarded as unquestionable. Moreover, 'fundamentalist terrorism' enables the global capitalist project to articulate itself increasingly through the logic of 'security', which allows the coercive apparatus of the state to be used to defend capitalist institutions. One sees here the way in which 'economic freedom' – economic deregulation and the global spread of free markets – is accompanied by a diminishing level of social and political freedom: 'anti-terrorist' legislation is used increasingly to suppress forms of protest and political militancy, especially the anti-capitalist protests. As Baudrillard points out:

that the idea of freedom, a new and recent idea, is already fading from minds and mores, and liberal globalisation is coming about in precisely the opposite form – a police state globalisation, a total control, a terror based on 'law-and-order' measures. Deregulation ends up in a maximum of constraints and restrictions, akin to a fundamentalist society.[40]

We see that the 'war' against fundamentalist terrorism ends up in a fundamentalism of its own – a fundamentalism of the market and a fundamentalism of 'security'. Indeed, it is not an exaggeration to speak of a new totalitarianism here: the 'war on terror' is a totalitarian ideology, one that brooks no dissent, no contestation, requiring absolute adherence. Can President Bush's warning that *you are either with us, or with the terrorists* be seen as anything other than a totalitarian statement? The 'war on terror' has the effect of reconstructing the totality of the political and social space through the mechanism of fear: we, as subjects, are positioned not only as possible targets of terrorist attacks, but as potential terrorists ourselves (terrorists 'in our midst'): we are encouraged by government advertisements to keep a watchful eye on our neighbours, to report 'suspicious activity'; passing through airport security has become an ordeal designed to inspire fear. What is particularly concerning is that 'anti-terrorist' legislation increasingly seeks to control speech itself: statements which could be seen as inciting, supporting or praising terrorism are now criminal offences in many countries. In the wake of the London bombings in July 2005, Tony Blair met with leaders of the Islamic community and told them that remarks made by Islamic clerics to their congregation condemning US foreign policy could be construed as an incitement to commit terrorist acts. Such is the absolute obedience that this ideology commands; expressions of dissent are coming to be regarded as themselves a threat to security. As Ari Fleischer, the White House Press Secretary at the time warned, shortly after the September 11 attacks, people should 'watch what they do, watch what they say'. The terrorism of this statement is obvious.

The emergence of this new dominant ideology shows us that we must retain the general problematic of ideology. However, in order to avoid the essentialist presuppositions and objective notions of truth that the classical understanding of ideology was based on, we need to revise the concept in light of poststructuralist theory. Here I would draw on Lacan's insight that it is possible to *lie in the guise of truth*, referring to the difference between two orders of truth: the 'objective' truth of statements, and the psychoanalytic truth of the unconscious. In other words, perhaps ideology operates through statements that are objectively true, yet still distorting at the level of their 'deeper' position of enunciation. This idea is summed up by Žižek: 'ideology has nothing to do with "illusion", with a mistaken, distorted representation of its social content. To put it succinctly: a political standpoint can be quite accurate ("true") as to its objective content, yet thoroughly ideological'.[41] In other words, what ideology conceals is not really the objective truth as such, but more so the position of power from which it is articulated. To give an example: when the media singles out the Islamic community, claiming that it poses a terrorist risk, even if this might be objectively 'true' – even if there might be certain people within that community who are sympathetic to terrorism (people who would, at the same time, feel as alienated within their community as they would from other communities) – it is still ideological because it conceals the dominant racist paradigm through which this particular community is being observed. So here we see how the understanding of ideology can go beyond the idea of a simple distortion of truth – rather it conceals a distortion within the truth of its statements.

The function of ideology, then, is to give a kind of symbolic consistency to power, to legitimise and naturalise it, and to conceal its structural incoherence. Just as fantasy in psychoanalytic theory plays the role of concealing or covering over the lack in the Other, ideology conceals the lack in the social symbolisations of power. Power refers to a certain way of organising and structuring the social body, and this implies that society is rationally intelligible. For instance, the governmental strategies that Foucault speaks about try to grasp the totality of society, and are premised therefore on a certain representation of society as a whole. However, from a 'discourse-analysis' perspective, society is not an object that can be represented as whole or unified – any representation of society will always be incomplete because of a radical discontinuity at the heart of social identity. Therefore the role of ideology is to conceal this discontinuity and inconsistency in social representation, and to present an image of fullness and unity. Thus we can perceive the function of the 'war on terror' as an ideology: it uses the figure of the terrorist as a 'suturing point', not only to unify society in opposition to this common enemy but also to sustain a fantasy of a lost 'innocence' or stability which had been disrupted by terrorism. How many times have we heard the refrain that 'times have changed since September 11', the moment when the United States and the world 'lost its innocence'?

Moreover, what is the effect of ideology on the subject? If the subject is interpellated by ideology, then perhaps we could say that this is an interpellation without belief. As Žižek has suggested, ideological messages today are entirely cynical and include within themselves their own cynical distance. One can observe the way that 'ad-busting' or 'culture jamming' – the act of cynically satirising an advertising message, particularly on billboards – is now being increasingly incorporated into the advertising strategy itself, so that we now have advertisements which send themselves up. The 'hidden' message of such advertisements is that the consumer does not have to believe in them, as long as he or she buys the product. Perhaps this can be seen as symbolic of the general functioning of ideology today in postmodern societies: the subject is not supposed to believe in the actual ideological message, as long as he buys the ideological 'product' – in other words, as long as the subject conforms to the hidden message and obeys its hidden commands and injunctions. We do not have to believe as long as we *act* as though we believe. Žižek gives an example of this: 'we all know very well that bureaucracy is not all-powerful, but our "effective" conduct in the presence of bureaucratic machinery is regulated by a belief in its all-powerfulness ...'.[42] It is precisely this action – *action without belief* – that sustains structures and relations of domination. It does not matter if we believe in what the state tells us, as long as we 'obey' at the level of our actions. Can we not see the cynical smiles on the lips of our most powerful as they tell us, for instance, that Iraq had to be invaded in the interests of national security, or that they did not manipulate intelligence on WMDs? Everyone knows these are lies, and the politicians know that we know it – but in a sense it doesn't matter, as long as we continue to obey.

The effect, or, if you like, the 'non-effect' of ideology on the subject – this cynical acceptance of the ideological message without actually believing in it – raises important questions about the subject, in particular his willing complicity in the power that dominates him. This problem will be discussed in the next chapter.

Notes

1 See A. Badiou, 'Beyond formalisation: an interview', with P. Hallward, *Angelaki*, 8:2 (2003): 115–136, p. 125.
2 See M. Hardt and A. Negri, *Empire* (Cambridge, MA: Harvard University Press, 2000).
3 See G. Deleuze, 'Postscript on the societies of control', *October*, 59 (Winter 1992): 3–7.
4 See P. Virilio, 'From sexual perversion to sexual diversion', in S. Redhead (ed.) *The Paul Virilio Reader* (Edinburgh: Edinburgh University Press, 2004), pp. 175–190.
5 'ASBOS', or 'anti-social behaviour orders', are widely used in the United Kingdom, and the scope of offences or potential offences covered by them continues to be expanded.
6 M. Foucault, 'Truth and juridical forms', in *Michel Foucault: Essential Works 1954–1984, Volume Three: Power* (London: Penguin, 2002), pp. 1–89, p. 67.
7 Foucault, 'Truth and juridical forms', p. 57.
8 M. Foucault, *Discipline and Punish: The Birth of the Prison*, trans. A. Sheridan (Penguin: London, 1991), p. 222.
9 Foucault, *Discipline and Punish*, p. 94.
10 Foucault, 'Truth and power', p. 121.
11 M. Foucault, *Society Must Be Defended: Lectures at the Collège De France 1975–76*, trans. D. Macey (London: Allen Lane, 2003), p. 23.
12 M. Foucault, 'War in the filigree of peace: course summary', trans. I. Mcleod, *Oxford Literary Review*, 4:2 (1976): 17–18.
13 In 2005 a very revealing semantic disagreement took place between US Secretary of Defence Donald Rumsfeld and President Bush. Rumsfeld openly questioned the appropriateness of the term 'war on terror', suggesting instead that it might be called

'the struggle against violent extremism'. The very next day, in an obvious rebuttal to Rumsfeld, Bush gave a speech reaffirming the term 'war on terror' and emphasising what he saw as its continuing relevance.

14 Foucault, *Society Must be Defended*, p. 241.
15 Foucault, *Discipline and Punish*, p. 30
16 See M. Foucault, *The History of Sexuality VI: Introduction*, trans. R. Hunter (New York: Vintage Books, 1978), p. 151.
17 Foucault, *History of Sexuality VI*, pp. 95–96.
18 M. Foucault, 'Nietzsche, genealogy, history', in P. Rabinow (ed.) *The Foucault Reader* (New York: Pantheon Books, 1984), p. 85.
19 See M. Foucault, 'Governmentality', in C. Gordon (ed.) *The Foucault Effect: Studies in Governmentality* (Chicago: University of Chicago Press, 1991), pp. 87–104, p. 103.
20 See M. Foucault, 'The subject and power', in *Michel Foucault: Essential Works 1954–1984, Volume Three: Power*, pp. 326–348.
21 Balibar, *Politics and the Other Scene*, pp. 25–26.
22 J. Derrida, 'Force of law: the mystical foundation of authority', in D. Cornell (ed.) *Deconstruction & the Possibility of Justice* (New York: Routledge, 1992), pp. 3–67, p. 14.
23 See J. Derrida, *Rogues: Two Essays on Reason*, trans. Pascale-Anne Brault and Michel Naas. (Stanford, CA: Stanford University Press, 2005), p. 11.
24 Giorgio Agamben, *Homo Sacer: Sovereign Power and Bare Life*, trans. D. Heller-Roazen (Stanford, CA: Stanford University Press, 1998), p. 6.
25 Agamben, *Homo Sacer*, p. 170.
26 See J. Butler, *Precarious Life: The Powers of Mourning and Violence* (London: Verso, 2004), pp. 50–100.
27 Not only have there been constant allegations of torture in US-run facilities like Guantanamo, but the US tacitly endorses a policy of outsourcing torture – in other words, sending detainees and suspects to countries where torture is routinely practised.
28 J. Baudrillard, 'War porn' ('Pornographie de la guerre'), *International Journal of Baudrillard Studies*, 2:5 (2005): <www.ubishops.ca/baudrillardstudies/vol2_1/taylor.htm#_edn1.>
29 Agamben, *Homo Sacer*, pp. 168–169.
30 See C. Schmitt, *Political Theology: Four Chapters on the Concept of Sovereignty*, trans. G. Schwab (Cambridge, MA: MIT Press, 1985).
31 Agamben, *Homo Sacer*, p. 32.
32 Agamben, 'Security and terror'.
33 A. Badiou, *Metapolitics*, trans. J. Barker (London: Verso, 2005), p. 70.
34 See Newman, *From Bakunin to Lacan*.
35 Badiou, *Metapolitics*, p. 145.
36 As Balibar argues: 'I would say against Foucault ... that *there is power*, even a power apparatus, which has several centres, however complex and multiple these "centres" may be ... But, having said this, I shall parody Lacan and add: power cannot be all; in fact, in essence it is "not-all" [*pas-tout*], that is, deficient ...'. *Politics and the Other Scene*, p. 136
37 S. Žižek, *The Indivisible Remainder: An Essay on Schelling and Related Matters* (London: Verso, 1996), p. 3.
38 L. Althusser, *Lenin and Philosophy, and Other Essays*, trans. B. Brewster (New York: Monthly Review Press, 1977), p. 171.
39 Foucault, 'Truth and power', p. 133.

40 J. Baudrillard, *The Spirit of Terrorism*, trans. C. Turner (London: Verso, 2002), p. 32.
41 S. Žižek, 'The spectre of ideology', in E. Wright and E. Wright (eds) *The Žižek Reader* (Oxford: Blackwell, 1999), pp. 55–86, p. 60.
42 S. Žižek, *The Sublime Object of Ideology* (London: Verso, 1989), p. 30.

3

The subject

THE PREVIOUS chapter explored the functioning of power and ideology in postmodern societies. Taking Foucault's analysis of power as its point of departure, it showed that the subject is not only a figure upon whom power is exercised – in ways that are both reciprocal and dominating, both 'soft' and 'hard' – but is also an *effect* of power: that is, the identity of the subject is constructed through a mode of power which operates at the level of biological life, regulating the subject's movements and desires. However, the crucial question raised by the last chapter was: why does the subject fall into this trap of subjection; why does the subject seem to submit to this power which both constructs his identity and, at the same time, dominates him? Power cannot operate without the subject's willing complicity with it at some level. This mystery of self-domination will be the starting point for our discussion about the status of the political subject today.

Many postmodern thinkers have suggested that this complicity of the subject in power means that the category of the subject itself must be discarded. We can no longer accept, it is argued, the classical Cartesian view of the subject as transparent to himself and anchored in rational thought. The subject of the Cogito has been displaced by the proliferation of language games, identities and modes of experience that are said to be characteristic of postmodern societies. Indeed, it is claimed that there is no coherent or unified experience of the Self in postmodernity: rather, the 'self' is seen as a contingent and fragmented entity. Instead of a unified and autonomous subject guided by his rationality, there is the notion of a multitude of fluid and hybrid identities, of life in flux. The celebrated fragmented subject of postmodernity is one who can apparently explore different modes of experience, who can inhabit different and inconsistent identities simultaneously, whose life is an empty canvas in a continual process of becoming. Nietzsche exhorted us to treat our life 'as if it were a work of art' – a project of *self-aestheticisation* taken up by Baudelaire, whose desire to make 'of his body, his behaviour, his feelings and passions, his very existence, a work of art' Foucault saw as emblematic of a new (post)modern sensibility.[1]

I am, however, somewhat more sceptical about this 'heroic' postmodern attitude. The idea of a fragmented and fluid self in a continual process of becoming may not necessarily be all that subversive or liberating. Indeed, in certain respects, it seems to fit perfectly into a multicultural capitalist universe, where difference, diversity and flux, far from being repressed, are actually encouraged, representing simply another 'lifestyle' niche to be marketed to. There is virtually no identity – no matter how seemingly marginal – that cannot be integrated into capitalism, that cannot be constructed as another consumer demand to be satisfied by the market. Capitalism, in other words, *wants* us to experiment with different identities and modes of experience – these simply create more and increasingly diversified consumer demands. One simply has to observe the way that capitalist marketing increasingly emphasises the apparent freedom of the individual to make different 'lifestyle choices', to drop out of the 'rat race', to explore other cultures, to partake in 'eco-tourism' etc. Postmodern themes and motifs of difference, flux, hybridity and self-aestheticisation are reflected in the ideological messages of capitalism. Even divergent sexualities are no longer a threat to this order: not only is 'sexual diversity' celebrated by bureaucracies – university campuses even employ 'sexual diversity officers', an example of the liberation of homosexuality culminating only in its bureaucratisation – but it is also increasingly marketed to: think of 'gay-friendly' tourism or TV advertisements which feature single-sex couples buying new SUVs, for instance. Moreover, the postmodern idea of change, flux and becoming as central to life seems to be the perfect palliative to the instabilities and vicissitudes of the capitalist system: life under capitalism, with sudden job losses, downsizing, fluctuations in the share market, *is* precisely a life in flux, but it is something that is experienced not necessarily as liberating but, rather, as deeply traumatic. One can imagine what 'life in flux' means to a worker who has just lost his or her job, or to a slum-dweller in the Third World whose 'life in flux' amounts to a daily struggle for survival. The instability of their lives is obviously not something that they welcome or celebrate. Such instabilities, moreover, are being intensified due to capitalist globalisation, a process which is leading to the uprooting of traditional communities and ways of life, the destabilisation of national economies and the erosion of the welfare state. We can see the way in which the postmodern motif of flux and destabilisation seems to mirror the shattering impact of 'economic deregulation'. Here Žižek criticises the cynicism behind the celebration of the postmodern globalised 'hybrid' subject:

> It is easy to praise the hybridity of the postmodern migrant subject, no longer attached to specific ethnic roots, floating freely between different cultural circles. Unfortunately, two totally different sociopolitical orders are condensed here: on the one hand the cosmopolitan upper- and upper-middle

class academic, always with the proper visas enabling him to cross borders without any problem in order to carry out his business, and thus able to 'enjoy the difference'; on the other hand the poor (im)migrant worker driven from his home by poverty or (ethnic, religious) violence, for whom the celebrated 'hybridity' designates a very tangible experience of never being able to settle down properly and legalize his status, the subject for whom such a simple task as crossing a border or reuniting with his family can be an experience full of anxiety . . .[2]

The problem, then, with the postmodern figure of the fragmented, hybrid subject is that it all too conveniently reflects the contemporary consumerist experience – the experience of the well-off individual in the capitalist West. Nevertheless, our rejection of this clichéd figure does not mean that we should neglect one of the fundamental insights of postmodern theory: that the idea of the universal Subject – the figure of Man that was central to Enlightenment humanism and the Cogito – can no longer be sustained, at least not in its classical form. Not only was this universal Subject often a mask for a particular Western epistemology, whose imperialistic imposition upon other cultures was accompanied by the worst forms of racism, but, more fundamentally, as Lyotard pointed out, the rationalist 'metanarratives' upon which this concept of Man was based are now in a process of disintegration. What is particularly being questioned from this perspective is the idea of human essence – the notion that behind the subject there are immutable human characteristics, or an inherent morality or rationality that conditions his whole experience. In other words, what postmodernism rejects is the idea that there is a universal essence of humanity – whether an innate characteristic or an immanent potentiality which is dialectically realised – behind the subject. As thinkers like Stirner and Nietzsche showed, the humanist figure of Man – the subject with universal properties – was only a cheap imitation of the God he supposedly supplanted, and that to fully affirm the death of God in all its radical possibility, we must also bury with Him this pale apparition of Man. Indeed, Foucault claimed in *The Order of Things* that Man was only a relatively recent discursive invention – a strange 'empirico-transcendental doublet' which came into existence due to the reordering of language, knowledge and discourse that marked modernity. 'Man', in other words, was a discursive construct, one whose existence was made possible due to the emergence of the human sciences. Moreover, for Foucault, the contemporary experience is marked by Man's finitude and immanent decline – indeed the infamous prediction that haunts our time is that Man will disappear: 'one can certainly wager that man would be erased, like a face drawn in sand at the edge of the sea'.[3]

Whether we can now mourn (or celebrate) the disappearance of Man, or whether Foucault has been too hasty here, will be discussed later in the chapter. However, the challenge remains for us to think the question of subjectivity against the background of Man's finitude. I would suggest that we cannot abandon the problematic of the subject altogether and revel in a postmodern 'utopia' of shifting identities and multiple selves. If there is to be any possibility of radical politics today, we cannot relinquish the idea of a subject who resists power, who seeks to emancipate himself from domination and hierarchy, and who seeks to transform existing social, political and economic relations. The subject has always been central to any politics of emancipation. Moreover, subjectivity is more than simply a socio-economic category in radical politics – it is rather a space for a militant political identification: even in the Marxist theory of proletarian subjectification, for instance, the proletariat goes from being a class 'in itself' – the proletariat as existing in an objective socio-economic sense – to a class 'for itself' – that is, the proletariat politicising its struggle and fully assuming its revolutionary role. However, while we cannot do without some notion of the subjectivity, we have to be able to rethink the subject without relying on essentialist ideas of humanity or 'real interests'. In other words, the challenge is to retain the category of the subject, while at the same time accepting the postmodern critique of essentialism: the subject can no longer be based on the firm foundations provided by Enlightenment humanism; subjectivity can no longer be seen as reflecting the immanent rationality of Man's 'species being'.

To this end, I would like to examine a number of different approaches to the question of subjectivity within poststructuralist theory. These can be roughly divided into two contrasting strategies. The first is the dispersal of the subject into relations of power and desire, typified by thinkers such as Foucault and, to a much greater extent, Deleuze, who, in his early collaborations with Felix Guattari, sought to liberate desire from the centricity of the subject – particularly the subject described by psychoanalysis – thus dispersing the subject amongst a multitude of 'assemblages' and 'desiring machines'. The second approach is one that derives in part from psychoanalysis itself, and which seeks to resurrect the problematic of the Cartesian subject, although this time seeing it as anchored in unconscious doubt rather than rational certainty. Unlike the first strategy of dispersal, this Lacanian approach allows us to retain the category of the subject while, at the same time, removing it from both essentialist and structuralist understandings. Instead, the subject is seen in terms of a central void or 'constitutive lack' which remains open to different identifications and political struggles. Moreover, this understanding of the subject has informed the work of a number of thinkers who might be more accurately described as 'post-Althusserian', and whose different approaches to the question of political subjectification will also be discussed here. These include Žižek, Laclau, Badiou and Rancière – all of whom see the subject in terms of a sort of 'empty place', a place of militant identification that emerges from inconsistencies in the socio-political order.

My argument here will be that the former approach – that which emphasises the radical dispersal of the subject – while interesting and important, has certain limitations when it comes to thinking about radical politics today. The second approach – that which seeks to retain the central category of the subject, while seeing it at the same time as 'empty' – is a much more fruitful and productive one because it allows us to hang on to the idea of a universal political dimension without reintroducing the notion of the universal Subject. Indeed, what is characteristic of the latter approach is that rather than trying to disperse universality amongst a multitude of particularities – as in the logic of 'postmodern' identity politics – it shows the way that a universal political dimension emerges, in a contingent way, from a point of singularity or from an unexpected event. This universal political dimension is not thinkable from the former perspective. Therefore, in this chapter, I will attempt to rethink the category of the political subject, not through the metaphor of dispersal, but instead through that of *displacement*: as we shall see, what constitutes the political subject, what forms his ontological ground, is not some essentialist notion of pre-existing interests, or some dialectically unfolding human potential, but rather a certain process of 'dis-identification'.

The problem of self-domination

Classical political theories of emancipation – whether liberal or radical – were based on a certain Enlightenment conception of the subject: the subject was seen as having essential rational and moral capacities and certain inalienable rights, and, at the same time, as being oppressed by external forces, whether the obfuscations of religion, the dead weight of political authority or the fetters of economic exploitation. Thus the subject's rights and qualities were set in stark relief against the oppressive forms of power that darkened his world. Implied here, of course, was the idea of liberation – the subject would throw off these chains, upon which his full human potential could be realised. However, what these classical theories of emancipation did not take into account was the phenomenon of self-repression. In other words, why does the subject seem at times to be complicit in the power that dominates him, to willingly submit to excessive forms of authority, to even actively desire his own enslavement? This was the problem hinted at in the preceding chapter – one touched on, although inadequately, by Foucault – and it remains a central problem for radical politics. What hopes can be held for radical politics today when we seem ever more ready to support the conservative and authoritarian agendas of governments, when we turn once again to religion and 'family values', and when we clamour for harsher law-and-order measures and more police powers? Our obsession with 'security', our calls for governments to protect us from the spectre of terrorism at any cost – even at the cost of our freedom and privacy – suggests a kind of *infantilisation* of the body-politic: the prevailing subject-position in today's 'war on terror' seems increasingly that of a helpless infant, seeking from the state not only protection and security, but a more general level of regulation, control and surveillance. No wonder the so-called 'security-moms' in the United States featured so prominently as a symbol of George Bush's re-election in 2004. Is this willing abrogation of one's power and autonomy to the state simply the result of the way we have been positioned or constructed by the power – as Foucault believed – or does it also suggest a deeper psychological dependency on the part of the individual? In other words, what is it that ties us to the power that dominates us; why are we so enthralled to power and authority that we actively participate in our own repression? Self-repression forms the other side – or, to use Balibar's term (borrowed from Freud) the 'other scene'[4] – of power. Let us start, then, with this problem of *voluntary servitude*.

The problem of voluntary servitude, of self-subjection was, for the sixteenth-century thinker Etienne de La Boetie, the central enigma of politics. In his work, *De la servitude volontaire*, he raises this fundamental question of why it is that so many people can be ruled by so few:

> I should like merely to understand how it happens that so many men, so many villages, so many cities, so many nations, sometimes suffer under a single tyrant who has no other power than the power they give him; who is able to harm them only to the extent to which they have the willingness to bear with him; who could do them absolutely no injury unless they preferred to put up with him rather than contradict him.[5]

Here La Boetie recognises that power only operates through our acceptance and consent. Indeed, it is simply not possible for one man or one government to rule over us without our willing it. Tyranny cannot rely on force of arms alone – indeed, this is when it is at its most desperate and vulnerable. Rather, it relies on our daily acquiescence. This is surely a modern problem too: even though the functioning of power is far more complex and sophisticated than it was in La Boetie's time, governments still rely on our agreement and complicity – on our readiness to obey the law and to submit to their authority. Even when we realise that a government may be acting illegitimately – when it goes to war under false pretences, as it did in Iraq for instance – we still recognise its symbolic authority over us. We should not imagine, either, that democratic governments have any more claim to legitimacy here – La Boetie points to the way that tyranny can also come through democratic elections.[6] Moreover, according to La Boetie, resistance to illegitimate authority does not have to amount to a violent insurrection, but to a simple turning away – a refusal, in other words, to recognise this authority. There is a sort of master/slave dialectic going on here, in which the master only exists in so far as he recognised as such by the slave: once the slave no longer recognises his authority, the position of the master collapses.

This also suggests that the authority is simply a construction of the one who submits to it – that the paradox of authority lies in the way that it is retroactively constituted through one's recognition of it.

La Boetie's analysis of voluntary servitude provides us with a radical account of power and the hold that it has over us. Here La Boetie can be seen as the radical counterpart to Hobbes – the anti-Hobbes: while, for Hobbes, it is only natural that people in the state of nature transfer their power to a sovereign authority who, in return, guarantees their security, for La Boetie this is the fundamental mystery of politics. The real question for La Boetie is, therefore, not that of power, but rather that of the subject: why is it that the subject submits to tyranny? He does not find any satisfactory answer to this, falling back on the idea that man has been 'de-natured', that he has lost his 'animal' love for freedom and, therefore, through force of habit, willingly complies with those who rule over him.

Perhaps a more convincing and sophisticated understanding of self-domination is provided by Stirner, whose critique of Feuerbachian humanism and the Hegelian dialectic constituted one of the most radical interventions in nineteenth-century continental philosophy. In his work *The Ego and Its Own*, Stirner points to the new forms of subjection that have emerged with the discourse of humanism, the discourse which was supposed to liberate the individual from the alienation and oppression of religion. According to Stirner, all humanism has done is replace God with Man, thus reinventing the same religious idealism – and thus the same oppression and alienation – in a new secular and humanist guise.[7] Man has become the new abstract figure – the new ideological construct – to which the individual is now subordinated. The problem with humanism is that it assumes that there is a universal and unchanging human essence to be found at the basis of existence, behind every concrete individual, and this essence, according to Stirner, is simply a new form of religious idealism – it is just as abstract and oppressive as Christianity. This notion of essence has a subjectifying effect on the individual: it establishes a moral and rational norm and a universal *idea* of Man which supposedly exists within the individual, and which the individual is required to venerate and live up to. However, this only creates a new form of alienation, more intense than that of Christianity: when the individual finds that he cannot live up to this impossible humanist ideal, he becomes alienated from himself, from his own essence.[8]

According to Stirner, this humanist subjection – in which the individual is tied to an impossible idealised version of himself – also has political effects. The moral and rational norms imposed upon the individual are used to police his behaviour: they become part of a liberal political rationality whose underside is discipline and normalisation. In other words, while liberalism ostensibly is a discourse of individual rights and freedoms, it also at the same time 'constructs', through disciplinary and normalising procedures, a certain liberal mode of subjectivity: the liberal subject as rational, autonomous, an effective agent in the marketplace etc. Here Stirner is making an argument surprisingly similar to Foucault's: liberalism is a mode of government that promotes a particular form of life as free; it can be seen as a kind of discursive threshold where individual freedom meets the regulative power of the state. In other words, the humanist subjection of the individual has the effect of tying the individual to the state.

Moreover, like La Boetie, Stirner believes that the state cannot operate through simple coercion or repression. Rather, the state relies on our willing submission, on the abdication of our own will:

> The state is not thinkable without lordship (*Herrschaft*) and servitude (*Knechtschaft*) (subjection) ... He who, to hold his own, must count on the absence of will in others is a thing made by these others, as a master is a thing made by the servant. If submissiveness ceased, it would be all over with lordship.[9]

Stirner is not suggesting that the state is an abstraction or a simple figment of our imagination that we have created and can simply will away – as Marx and Engels accused him of doing in *The German Ideology*. Rather, the state, as a political institution, is supplemented by and relies upon an ideological dimension which interpellates us, which constructs us as its willing subjects. In other words, it is the *idea* of the state which dominates us, more than perhaps the actual institution itself. The state's power is really based on *our* power. It is only because the individual has not recognised this power, because he humbles himself before authority, that the state continues to exist. The mechanism by which we are subjected in this way is one that operates at the level of our desire. Stirner recognised that that state does not repress desire, but rather 'channels' it to itself, so that we actively desire our own domination: 'The state exerts itself to tame the desirous man; in other words, it seeks to direct his desire to it alone, and to *content* that desire with what it offers.'[10] So, for Stirner, our subjection by humanist ideology has led to a contortion of our desire, so that, at some level, we come to desire our own repression. Like La Boetie, Stirner is not so much interested in power itself, but in the reasons why we allow ourselves to be dominated by power; power is not only concerned with economic or political questions – it is also rooted in psychological needs. Stirner therefore continues this line of libertarian thinking established with La Boetie, exploring the ways in which we as subjects actively participate in our domination. In doing so, he touched on a problem which classical political theory could not grasp.

Deleuze and Guattari also consider the problem of self-domination, pointing to the way that desire can desire its own repression: 'To the question "How can desire desire its own repression, how can it desire its slavery?" we reply that the powers which crush desire, or which subjugate it, themselves already form part of the assemblages of desire.'[11] In other words, it is desire – rather than power, as Foucault believed – which is constitutive, constructing even those forces which act to repress it. Deleuze and Guattari explore a kind of ontology of desire, in which the socio-political field is itself composed of 'assemblages' of desire. While I will examine this ontology of desire in greater detail later, the value of Deleuze and Guattari's analysis is to again highlight the way that the subject can be complicit in his own domination, and therefore that any sort of radical politics must take place at the level of desire itself. We must free ourselves from our desire for repression, our desire for the state, otherwise we will never be released from its grasp. Indeed, similarly to Stirner, Deleuze and Guattari point to a mechanism of subjection by which the subject is constituted as a site of his own domination. Through our acceptance of existing signifying regimes and orders of meaning – statements which only reaffirm existing struc-tures of political power – we only tie ourselves to a subjectivity which has already been created for us by power: 'the more you obey the statements of dominant reality, the more you command as speaking subject within mental reality, for finally you only obey yourself ... A new form of slavery has been invented, that of being a slave to oneself'.[12] For Deleuze and Guattari, then, as for Foucault, it is the coherence and unity of the subject itself that must be ques-tioned: it is not simply that subjects engage in self-repression, but that the very form of subjectivity itself is what contorts desire, turning it against itself.

Postmodern subjectivities: Foucault and Deleuze

Here I have examined three approaches to the problem of self-domination – that of La Boetie, Stirner and Deleuze/Guattari – and have explored a certain line of libertarian thinking: one that does not simply oppose the individual to external forms of political power such as the state, but, in a much more sophis-ticated sense, shows the ways that individuals might be complicit in their own oppression through an *internalisation* of this power. This ambiguity of the subject within power is also highlighted by Foucault: not only is power exercised upon the individual in a myriad of ways – regulating his movements and activ-ities – but this operation of power also has a 'subjectifying' effect, actually constructing the individual as a subject upon whom this power can be exercised. It is through the subject's daily activities, and through his adherence to 'regimes of truth' which require him to speak about his sexuality, for instance, that he becomes a subject of power: these practices only tie the individual to a discur-sive identity which has been fabricated for him by power, and this in turn allows power to function more efficiently and smoothly. In other words, power is 'indi-vidualising' – it incarcerates the subject within an individual identity, an identity which the subject also conforms to and reproduces at the level of his daily practices. It is thus in this double sense that we are 'subjects': 'There are two meanings of the word "subject": subject to someone else by control or dependence, and tied to his own identity by a conscience or self-knowledge. Both meanings suggest a form of power that subjugates and makes subject to.'[13]

However, as Butler points out, there is a strange circularity in Foucault's argument: the subject upon whom power acts is always already a subject constructed by this power, so that the two different understandings of the 'subject' that Foucault posits actually presuppose one another. The paradox of subjection is precisely the impossible question of what comes first: power or the subject? Because power is the very condition of the subject – because, in other words, the subject is constructed by power – then in what sense can we speak of a subject who both exercises power and upon whom power is exercised? Conversely, in what way does the subject enter the world of power: in other words, if the subject is at the same time the precondition for the exercise of power, then how does the subject come to be at the same time subjected by it? There is a sort of impossible vanishing point in Foucault's analysis: power and the subject presuppose one another, and the subject enters the world of power as already constituted by it. As Butler argues, this ambivalence raises certain problems for the question of resistance and emancipation from power:

> How can it be that the subject, taken to be the condition for and instrument of agency, is at the same time the effect of subordination, understood as the deprivation of agency? If subordination is the condition of possibility for agency, how might agency be thought in opposition to the forces of subordination?[14]

Therefore, if the subject is the *other side* of power, as Foucault believes, then what is needed is some sort of understanding about the actual mechanism by which the subject comes to be subjected by power. In other words, how do we explain *why* the subject allows himself to be subjected: why does he attach himself to certain forms of power; why does he tie himself to a discursive identity which power has constructed for him and which thus allows him to be further dominated? For instance, why is it that the homosexual comes to identify with his constructed identity of 'homosexuality'? Conversely, how do we explain the fact that this process of subjection sometimes fails, that sometimes the subject actually *resists* his subjection and invents new forms of identity which, temporarily at least, are beyond the grasp of power? This is something that Foucault never adequately explains. It is not enough to point to the subjectifying effect of power without exploring, at the same time, the psychological mechanisms or 'passionate attachments' through which power is internalised. Here Agamben refers to the experience of *shame* as a kind of identification with one's own subordination: shame comes not only when one is passive, but when one is *moved by one's own passivity*, as in the sadomasochistic relationship where the masochist derives pleasure from his extreme subordination to another's power.[15] In other words, we would have to explain why the subject, in certain situations of power, becomes passionately attached to his own subordination. What is missing from Foucault's account is therefore some sort of understanding of the unconscious processes and 'irrational' drives which both bind us to power and cause us to try to free ourselves from it. In other words, what is needed is some notion of the psyche – understood as different to the subject and as forming the unpredictable underside of subjectifying power. As Butler argues:

> the psyche, which includes the unconscious, is very different from the subject: the psyche is precisely what exceeds the imprisoning effects of the discursive demand to inhabit a coherent identity, to become a coherent subject. The psyche is what resists the regularization that Foucault ascribes to normalizing discourses.[16]

Such an understanding of the psyche can only be provided, by psychoanalysis – something which Foucault remained hostile towards. I would suggest, then, that Foucault's account of subjection – 'the different modes ... by which human beings are made subject'[17] – is incomplete without this notion of the psyche, and this is why, as I shall argue later, Foucault can be supplemented by Lacan.

In any case, it is clear that there is a central ambiguity in Foucault's thinking about subjection, a deadlock that he tried to resolve, in a somewhat inadequate and fragmentary way, in his later histories of Greek and Roman attitudes towards sexuality and the 'care of the self'. The 'care of the self' refers to a series of stringent ethical exercises, regulations and even dietary restrictions that one imposed upon oneself in order to achieve self-mastery and, through this, a greater sense of autonomy.[18] Foucault suggested that in these practices there could be found a possible way out of subjection – a way for the modern individual, perhaps, to construct his own subjectivity, and to invent for himself his own modes of freedom which would go beyond the confines of power. According to Foucault, what was important about these ethical strictures and practices of the ancients was that they were applied by the individual to himself and therefore were not sanctioned by any sort of universal 'categorical imperative'. In other words, the subject followed a certain ascetic code or way of life, and this could be seen, according to Foucault, as a practice of freedom and ethics that had as its object the consideration and problematisation of the self.

This strategy of 'care of the self' might be understood as a kind of postmodern formula by which the subject invents his own identity and his own code of ethics, outside the moral norms sanctioned by society. Do we not see, in contemporary societies, all sorts of strategies that people follow for health, and mental and spiritual 'well-being' – everything from (increasingly bizarre) diets and rigorous exercise routines, to meditation and Eastern philosophy – in the belief that this will bring them some greater degree of autonomy and control over their lives? Witness the way that a couple of years ago, the philosophy of the Stoics – whom Foucault saw as key exponents of the 'care of the self' – came back into vogue: books of the Stoic emperor Marcus Aurelius' meditations became best-sellers. And what about the recent fetish for 'mentoring relation-ships', where, just like ancient Greeks, people once again turn to mentors who give them advice on certain aspects of the lives – usually on questions of career, but also on relationships? The idea of 'self-empowerment' or improving one's life through a kind of discipline that one imposes upon oneself is actively promoted today. Yet, it is difficult to see where the freedom lies in all this. There is instead, as Žižek would say, a vicious super-egoic (and indeed, biopolitical) injunction for the subject to engage in a continual quest for self-improvement – to be healthy, get fit, raise one's self-esteem, to 'get more' out of relationships, look after one's investments etc. Thus we see the way that, through the idea of 'self-discipline' or 'self-mastery', biopolitical norms are internalised in a much more oppressive way than if they had been authorised directly by external insti-tutions. Such postmodern strategies of 'care of the self' – strategies which Foucault believed might produce new forms of freedom and autonomy – lead instead to a new kind of tyranny, a tyranny made all the more pervasive and effective because it is one that the subject imposes upon himself.

However, perhaps the biggest problem with the strategy of care is that it signifies the more or less complete erosion of the political dimension: the subject retreats from politics into a private life of either quiet self-reflection or frenetic self-improvement. This withdrawal into the self as a way of fashioning one's own subjectivity – something which Foucault saw as a possible strategy for resisting power – produces instead a completely de-politicised subject, all the more at the mercy of power. It is interesting to note here the way that many feminists now speak about 'self-empowerment' rather than emancipation, suggesting a retreat from an active engagement in political struggles and, instead, a conservative strategy of playing the established power game. 'Self-empowerment' has replaced politics. So the problem with Foucault's later theorisation of the subject along the lines of the 'care of the self' is that it leads to a conservative withdrawal of the individual from politics into a life of ethical quietism. Today the 'care of the self' amounts to little more than carving out a niche for oneself in the capitalist universe, and 'liberating' oneself through experimenting with different 'lifestyles': even banks and investment strategies now cater for different 'lifestyle choices'. Moreover, for all this self-reflection that such strategies of 'care' require, the ethical subject that Foucault conjures up for us is remarkably one-dimensional, a kind of shadow-theatre where differ-ent modes of existence and ethical practices are performed, where different pleasures are tasted or denied, but where there is little of the subject 'himself'. The life devoted to the 'cultivation of one's soul' leads to a barren, a-political conception of the subject, and offers no real way out of subjectifying power.

As an alternative strategy for escaping power's subjectifying effects, Deleuze and Guattari propose – in their collaborative work in *Anti-Oedipus* and *A*

Thousand Plateaus – the abandonment, or at least the radical revision, of the very category of the subject. Indeed, they question the perceived unity and coherence of the subject, arguing that it is a kind of representative abstraction which imprisons and deforms desire. Their approach is based on a Nietzschean ontology of difference, which sees heterogeneous force relationships and, in particular, the struggle between 'active' and 'reactive' forces, as primary. In a similar manner to Foucault, who also takes Nietzschean genealogy as his point of departure, Deleuze and Guattari see this struggle of forces and differential power relations, driven by the *will to power*, as constitutive of all social relations and identities, even of physical bodies.[19] Indeed, individual bodies are simply a haphazard collection of different and heterogeneous forces, deriving their power from their affective relations with other forces. From this perspective, then, it is impossible to speak of a coherent subject or agent who exercises power in a conscious or goal-oriented manner: rather, as Nietzsche believed, there is no 'doer behind the deed', simply a relationship of forces that are transformed or reconstituted in different actions.

Developing this Nietzschean analysis, Deleuze and Guattari see the subject as situated in an immanent field of desire. Desire is not an internal property of the subject: rather, subjectivity itself is actually an *effect* of desire. Desire is seen here in terms of an immanent positivity, a field of heterogeneous forces which is coextensive with, and constitutive of, the socio-political field. The socio-political field is composed of what they call *assemblages of desire*. Desire is fundamentally productive, always seeking connections, and producing intensities and affective states. Desire can be seen as a system of 'a-signifying signs with which fluxes of the unconscious are produced in a social field'.[20] Here Deleuze and Guattari claim that their productive notion of desire is fundamentally different from that proposed by psychoanalysis: psychoanalysis sees desire in terms of *lack* – in other words as emerging from absence of the object of desire – whereas, for Delezue and Guattari, desire is actually positive, productive and, in Nietzsche's terms, 'life-affirming'. According to Deleuze and Guattari, psychoanalysis has succeeding in imposing images of negativity and castration on desire through the representative fiction of Oedipus. It is not so much that Oedipal desires are repressed, as Freud believed, but that the discursive figure of Oedipus is a trap that misrepresents desire to itself *as* repressed: 'Oedipal desires are the bait, the disfigured image by means of which repression catches desire in the trap.'[21] Desires are interpreted in psychoanalysis as signifiers of the Oedipal unconscious, and it is through this process that desire is pulled into line and made safe. In psychoanalysis, then, according to Deleuze: 'All real desire has already disappeared: a code is put in its place, a symbolic overcoding of utterances, a fictitious subject of enunciation who doesn't give the patients a chance.'[22] Moreover, the subject as defined through Oedipal representation is a kind discursive fiction which fixes and captures desire, attaching it to repressive forms. Indeed, Oedipal representation has the precise function of repressing desire and channelling it to the state, because untrammelled, unfettered desire is a threat to the existing state-capitalist social order. In Deleuze and Guattari's analysis, then, the subject – and in particular the Oedipal subject as posited by psychoanalysis – plays a fundamentally reactionary role, acting to deform and repress desire, tying it to notions of lack and castration, and thus perpetuating existing social relations.

We can see a parallel here with Foucault, for whom the subject is also a kind of discursive 'fiction' and a threshold through which power functions. The aim for Foucault, and Deleuze and Guattari, is to try to escape from subjection. Therefore, Foucault speaks of liberating ourselves not only from the state, but 'from the type of individualization linked to the state',[23] while Deleuze and Guattari talk about creating 'lines of flight' (*lignes de fuite*) from the figure of the subject and other forms of representation which crush desire and tie us to the state. We are crossed and re-crossed by different lines: lines are intensities through which we are connected to other social assemblages and multiplicities, and it is through such lines that we are connected to the state. Therefore, the aim of radical politics, for Deleuze and Guattari, is to invent new lines that escape subjection, lines which open up new ways of thinking about identity and therefore new possibilities for political action. Politics is an active experimentation with different and non-representative modes of thought. Here Deleuze and Guattari invoke the figure of the *rhizome* as an alternative to representative or 'arborescent' models of thought (based on the metaphor of tree and root). Arborescent thought presupposes the primacy and centricity of the thinking subject, and is based on stable identities, absolute notions of truth and consistent patterns of representation. It thus has the effect of imprisoning desire and thought within centralised structures and binary divisions. Rhizomatic thought, by contrast, emphasises connection, heterogeneity, multiplicity and rupture, thus undermining these stable identities and concepts. From the perspective of rhizomatic thought, then, the category of the subject is dispersed amongst a heterogeneous series of fluxes and *becomings*: the binary of man and woman, for instance, is destabilised by a series of connections that form between these two poles, and also between collective identities.[24] Similarly, the figure of the 'Body without Organs' is a kind of pure field of intensity, a smooth surface in which unities and representative structures are broken down into flows and becomings. Here there is a constant shifting and fragmentation of identities, and a multitude of connections forming between different assemblages. For Deleuze and Guattari, it is through these new figures of thought – models which emphasise dispersal, flux and multiple connections rather than stable and unified identities – that we can escape from what they see as the authoritarianism of Oedipal subjectivity and the forms of power that are linked with it. Seeking new lines of flight in this way is an inherently risky enterprise, because there is no telling where a particular line might lead. However, such experiments are an essential part of any politics of resistance. Radical politics today, according to Deleuze and Guattari, is the attempt to liberate desire from subjection through the development of new collective assemblages. It is the attempt to escape from existing modes of subjectivity through a 'long labour which is aimed not merely against the state and the powers that be, but directly at ourselves'.[25]

Deleuze and Guattari's analysis makes an important point about our complicity with power, and the need to free ourselves from authoritarian ways of thinking before we can liberate ourselves from authoritarian institutions themselves. The state exists as much in our heads and hearts as it does in reality, and there is a need, then, to develop new ways of thinking and new forms of politics which go beyond the figure of the state – to promote, as Foucault said in his Preface to *Anti-Oedipus*, a 'non-fascist' life. However, where I would disagree with them is in their contention that the subject is necessarily an authoritarian and conservative figure. Deleuze and Guattari, as we have seen, regard the subject as a kind of abstraction of thought which acts to imprison desire and block its flows, directing it to the state. Here they go further even than Foucault in their deconstruction of the subject. While Foucault later recognised the potential importance of the category of the subject, trying to retrieve it through the ethics of 'care of the self', Deleuze and Guattari seek to completely undermine the sovereignty of the subject. In their analyses there is simply no place for the subject as such, except as a discursive fiction and an authoritarian image through which desire turns against itself. Through their 'machinic' metaphor for desire, the subject is fragmented, dispersed into a million shards: subjectivity becomes a heterogeneous multitude of intensities and becomings, an infinite series of connections with different social assemblages, in such a way that a stable identity can never established. There is no coherent or unified place for the subject here. Thus we have a completely 'postmodern' experience, where, instead of a central subject, there is a giddying series of flows, fluxes and becomings.

However, as I have suggested before, we should not necessarily see this fragmented, polymorphous subject as liberating or subversive: in many ways, it is the ideal figure of contemporary capitalism, an economic logic which is, at its heart, 'deterritorialising', as Deleuze and Guattari themselves recognised. That is, capitalism acts to destabilise identities and structures: its ideal subject is not necessarily one with a coherent identity and stable desires and tastes, but rather a kind of hybrid subject in a continual process of becoming and flux, who experiments with different identities and patterns of consumption. Capitalism, in other words, thrives on the transgression of fixed and stable identities – it revels in the motifs of difference, flux and instability. As Eagleton points out: 'Capitalism wants men and women to be infinitely pliable and adaptable. As a system, it has a Faustian horror of fixed boundaries, of anything which offers an obstacle to the infinite accumulation of capital.'[26] In other words, we should recognise that the structure of contemporary capitalism is already *postmodernised*, and therefore the postmodern figure of the hybrid subject – the subject in a permanent state of flux and becoming, connected to different 'assemblages' and dispersed along paths of infinite desire and transgression – no longer represents any real threat to capitalism: on the contrary, it seems to reflect its very truth. We should perhaps also be cautious of this 'machinic' metaphor for subjectivity, celebrated not only by Deleuze and Guattari but also by other postmodern thinkers like Donna Haraway, whose figure of the 'cyborg' replaces that of the human: the idea of the individual with prosthetic parts, 'plugged in' to different machines and computer programs, and whose reality is a 'virtual reality', is becoming the emblematic figure of our technology-saturated age. Do we not see already the blurring of the division between man and machine: earpieces for mobile phones being now worn permanently by people, or even scan-able computer chips being implanted under the skin? Is not Deleuze and Guattari's figure of the 'assemblage' – in which we form a kind of synthesis with the different machines that we use – simply a fetishisation of what is already proving to be both the ultimate fantasy of capitalism and the ultimate nightmare of technology? The 'desiring-machine' becomes simply the ultimate 'consuming-machine' in an orgiastic immersion of the subject in technology.

Furthermore, this experience of fragmentation and infinite flux which Deleuze and Guattari celebrate, deliberately evokes the experience of schizophrenia: schizophrenia, with its disorders of speech, is seen as a producing a liberating discourse which has the potential to 'deterritorialise' and explode existing social and political formations. 'Schizoanalysis' is opposed here to psychoanalysis, which Deleuze and Guattari see as a reactionary signifying regime which sustains state-capitalism. Here, though, one could say that 'schizoanalysis' with its emphasis on fragmentation, flux and becoming, seems to be at the same time enthralled by psychoanalysis – its Dionysian reaction against it somehow mirroring and reaffirming it. Is not the body-without-organs – a metaphor borrowed from Artaud – the exact reverse of the 'body in pieces' (organs-without-a body), the image used by Lacan to characterise the pre-Oedipal 'mirror stage'? Does 'schizoanalysis' not simply amount to a kind of infantile parody of psychoanalysis?

More importantly, in their attack on the psychoanalytic notion of the subject – something I shall explore later – Deleuze and Guattari neglect the central importance of the subject in any political analysis. For instance, as they correctly point out, fascism, as a political formation, is not only about domination and control but also about *desire*: fascism emerges from a collective desire, a desire even for self-repression. They also mention the danger that the collective assemblages and 'becoming-minorities' – which they see as new political figures of resistance and deterritorialisation – can themselves turn fascist: the problem of 'micro-fascisms'.[27] However, it is difficult to understand this deformation of desire into fascism and the emergence of 'micro-fascisms' without some under-standing of the psyche and the field of drives and 'passionate attachments'. As Freud recognised, the emergence of the group as a distinct political formation – whether it be the mob or institutional groups like the Church and the army – involves a specific combination of unconscious forces and a complex relation-ship of love and identification between members of the group and their leader: the Leader is a libidinally invested figure, the object that takes the place of the ego-ideal for the members of the group, thus functioning as a kind of cipher through which members of the group can love and identify with one another.[28] Here the collective identity of the group is held together through a series of libidinous ties and unconscious drives. Deleuze and Guattari condemn psycho-analysis for being individualising – for focusing on the individual psyche and thus closing itself off to social forces and relationships. However, as Freud's analysis shows, psychoanalysis is concerned with the individual's relations with those around him, not only with family members but with society more broadly. As Freud demonstrates, psychoanalysis is eminently concerned with 'social phenomena', including the formation of groups, and is thus equipped for socio-political analysis.[29] The psychoanalytic unconscious is not individualising and therefore reactionary, as Deleuze and Guattari alleged: on the contrary, it is *intersubjective* and can therefore be applied not only to an analysis and critique of existing socio-political relationships, but also to an understanding of radical political identities. I shall return to this point later.

Postmodernity and the end of Man

I have suggested above that Foucault's and Deleuze and Guattari's approaches to the question of subjectivity are ultimately inadequate and offer no real radical alternative to the problem of subjection: Foucault's desire to re-invent the subject through the ethical strategies of 'care of the self' presents us with a one-dimensional figure of the subject which only reflects the 'cult of the self' in contemporary society; Deleuze and Guattari's wholesale abandonment of the subject not only mirrors the fully postmodern experience of hybridity and frag-mentation central to capitalism today, but also seems to deprive us of an adequate figure of resistance. For radical politics to be considered and re-invig-orated today, we need some notion of subjectivity – some understanding of agency or a central discursive category through which radical political identifi-cations occur – and yet this is precisely what is denied to us in the two approaches described above.

Postmodernism therefore presents us with a problem when it comes to considering subjectivity. As Foucault believed, our time is characterised by the immanent end of Man – the disappearance of this discursive figure through whom we identify ourselves as subjects. However, the question that confronts us here is how to interpret this 'disappearance of Man'. Can we accept the disappearance of Man while retaining some idea of the subject, or does the disappearance of Man mean also the disappearance of the very category of subjectivity itself? Derrida has suggested that this 'disappearance of Man' – so central to the experience of postmodernity – is fundamentally ambiguous, and that we may have even been too hasty in sounding his death-knell. He shows that the figure of Man is still with us, and that Heidegger's destruction of metaphysical humanism has not succeeded in displacing Man – as many postmodern thinkers imagine – but has simply re-inscribed Man in the notion of Being. This intransigence of Man confronts us with two opposed strategies – what Derrida describes as 'false exits' from the system of meaning still caught within metaphysical humanism. The first strategy is to 'attempt an exit and a deconstruction without changing terrain' – in other words to try to transcend this system of meaning by using its language and founding concepts; whereas the second strategy is to seek a violent exit from this system, '[T]o decide to change terrain, in a discontinuous and irruptive fashion, by brutally placing oneself outside, and by reaffirming an absolute break and difference.'[30] This latter strategy might be seen as the one adopted by Foucault, and more so by Deleuze and Guattari in the radical attempt to go beyond the category of Man by abandoning the category of the subject altogether. This desire to violently 'change terrain' is even expressed in the attempt to formulate an entirely new language: that of 'desiring-machines', 'war-machines' and 'assemblages'. Indeed, as Derrida says, this latter strategy of deconstruction is the dominant one in France at the time (*Marges de la philosophie* was first published in 1972, in the same year when *Anti-Oedipus* appeared). The point is that, as Derrida argues, *both* strategies are inadequate: they fail to fundamentally 'change the terrain', the first because it uses the tools and concepts of the existing terrain; and the second because, in the excessive violence and haste with which this terrain is transgressed, it inhabits 'more naively and more strictly than ever the inside one declares one has deserted'.[31]

However, according to Derrida, there still needs to be a 'change of terrain' and, therefore, as a way out of this quandary, he suggests that the two strategies be combined or 'woven' together in a new form of 'writing'. We must remember that deconstruction is not a single strategy but a combination of strategies or 'moves' operating on different levels. In a similar way, I would argue here for a different approach to the question of subjectivity: one that combines both the desire to retain the subject and the desire to abandon him. How can this 'double writing' – to use Derrida's term – be achieved? Here I would suggest a radical re-thinking of the subject – one that allows the central category of subjectivity to be retained, but at the same time rejects the essentialist and rationalist foundations upon which the subject has traditionally been based. In other words, the

Enlightenment problematic of the subject must not be abandoned but, rather, *revised* – and revised in such a way that its radical potential can be realised. In order to explore this radical dimension of subjectivity, I shall now turn to Lacanian psychoanalytic theory.

The Lacanian subject

I have already touched upon the importance of the Freudian notion of the unconscious in socio-political analysis. Freud demonstrated the central place of the unconscious in the subject, and showed the way that this enigmatic and opaque field of drives, impulses and 'passions' determined our behaviour in all sorts of ways, ways that we were no longer even aware of. Any analysis of political behaviour could no longer be modelled entirely on the autonomous and 'utility-maximising' individual who was aware of his motives and who pursued his interests in an entirely rational way: politics now had to take into account the 'irrational' and passionate dimension of the subject. Freud's so-called 'Copernican' revolution – in which the conscious ego was found to be no longer at the centre of our experience, now having to contend with the 'other scene' of the unconscious – thus mounted a fundamental challenge to the subject of the Cogito, the subject whom Descartes based on the primacy and certainty of conscious reflection. After Freud, we can no longer think of the subject as autonomous and transparent to himself. The subject was, henceforth, irretrievably 'split', not simply between his conscious and unconscious 'selves', but between two different places of enunciation: the position from where one speaks is no longer consistent. However, it is important to realise that this critique of the Cogito did not mean an abandonment of the subject itself: Freud saw his exploration of the unconscious as a continuation of the Cartesian problematic; the subject was not being undermined by psychoanalysis – on the contrary, a new dimension of the subject had been discovered, one that allowed the subject to be understood in radically different ways. The paradox of the Freudian revolution is that while it reveals this unconscious dimension which entirely unsettles traditional Cartesian notions of the subject and models of rational thought, it still takes place within the Enlightenment and Cartesian paradigm of rational and 'scientific' enquiry.

This Cartesian mode of inquiry is continued with Lacan:

> in the term *subject* . . . I am not designating the living substratum needed by this phenomenon of the subject, nor any sort of substance, nor any possession of knowledge in his *pathos*, his suffering, whether primal or secondary, nor even some incarnated logos, but the Cartesian subject, who appears at the moment when doubt is recognised as certainty – except that, through my approach, the bases of this subject prove to be wider, but at the same time much more amenable to the certainty that eludes it. This is what the unconscious is.[32]

There are a couple of important points to be made here. Firstly, Lacan rejects any idea of an essence or an essential foundation of the subject: by the 'subject' he does not refer to a *living substratum* or *any sort of substance*. The truth of the subject lies elsewhere, neither in a biological dimension nor in an essential substance. Moreover, the subject cannot be seen in terms of some sort of transcendental rationality or *logos*. Secondly, the subject for Lacan (as for Freud) is the Cartesian subject; however, this is a Cartesian subject which is no longer based on the certainty of its conscious thought, but on the *certainty that eludes it*. In other words, what the Lacanian subject is certain of is that there is some aspect of himself that he is *not* certain of – some sort of knowledge within himself that remains hidden to him – and this is, of course, the unconscious.

What we find here is a radically new way of thinking about the subject: the subject is not founded on some sort of essence or an immanent rationality – as in classical humanism – but rather on a kind of doubt or uncertainty: the unconscious is that which, at the same time, founds and displaces the subject. The subject is not abandoned or fragmented here – the subject is still the central category – but it is at the same time de-centred, thrown off its course of certainty and rational self-understanding. For Lacan, the subject is constitutively split and based on lack, on the absence of complete self-knowledge. In other words, the self is somehow not consistent with itself: it is *outside* itself, because the unconscious is something that is both within the self and yet beyond its understanding. Moreover, the unconscious must be understood as radically *intersubjective* because it is, as Lacan says, *'structured like a language'*.[33] That is to say, unconscious is structured fundamentally through the external order of language, through signifiers: indeed it is only when the subject enters the world of language, when he becomes a speaking being, that the unconscious is formed. So there is a sort of double alienation or displacement here: the subject is not only alienated from the knowledge of the unconscious – the unconscious which is at the same time internal and external to him – but also within the external order of language itself, where he is 'misrepresented' or mistaken for another signifier. Put simply, the subject can only construct a meaning for himself and develop a coherent identity through language, through the signifiers that 'name' him as a subject. The 'I' only has meaning and a sense of its 'self' in relation to the signifier that stands in to represent it.[34] However, because signifiers only refer to each other within a chain of signifiers, then the subject cannot wholly identify with, or find a place for himself within, this symbolic order. This means that the subject cannot develop a coherent sense of identity: there is always a sense in which language fails to fully account for or represent the subject. Therefore, there is an irreconcilable lack between meaning and being, and, because of this, identity itself is always lacking, incomplete and only partially constituted.

So the subject in Lacanian psychoanalysis refers not to a coherent individual but rather to a kind of structural lack or gap – a gap not only between the unconscious and the speaking being, but also between the speaking being and language itself. Subjectivity is therefore based on a *failed* identification, and thus identity itself is to some degree incoherent and unstable. That is why Lacan writes the subject as *s(Ø)* – *s* barred: this recognises the failure of the signifier to represent the subject. Furthermore, the reason why the subject cannot be wholly represented within the external order of signifiers is because this order is itself incomplete – there is something missing from its structures of meaning, an internal structural void or gap. This is what Lacan calls the 'real': the real, as I showed in Chapter 1, is a kind of 'impossible' domain that is outside language, something which *cannot be symbolised*, and which simultaneously destabilises the order of meaning and constitutes it by acting as its limit. So it is this real which disrupts the subject's identity: 'This cut in the signifying chain alone verifies the structure of the subject as discontinuity in the real.'[35] The real, in Lacan's formulation, has nothing to do with *reality* as such; rather, it is what displaces what is commonly understood by 'reality'. In other words, our reality – the reality of our identities and our way of seeing the world – is fundamentally conditioned by symbolic and fantasy structures; and it is the real – that which cannot be integrated into these structures – which jeopardises this reality, making our identities precarious and at times incoherent. The real is therefore the point at which these symbolic structures break down and the contingency of their operation is revealed. It may be seen as an irreducible void around which identity is both partially constituted and dislocated. It is here that we could point to the 'poststructuralist' logic of Lacan's argument, although I accept that this label is not unproblematic when applied to Lacan.[36] However, unlike Žižek, who goes to great lengths to insist on the distinction between poststructuralism/deconstruction and Lacanian psychoanalysis, I would suggest that Lacan's notion of the real as that element which destabilises the structure of meaning by forming its internal limit, can be understood in terms of a poststructuralist approach to identity, albeit one that is very different from Foucault's and Deleuze/Guattari's. The former retains the structure of meaning and subjectivity, seeing it, however, as unstable and undecidable; while the latter approach, as we have seen, seeks to disperse both structures into multiple relations of power, flux and intensity.

The advantage of Lacan's approach is that the central category of the subject is retained yet, at the same time, destabilised through a structural element that is beyond its limits of representation: the real, in this sense, refers to the place of the impossible enjoyment (*jouissance*) that is forever lost to the subject. This is the lost object of desire through which the subject is defined as the subject of lack. However, rather than this notion of lack leading to an enclosure of desire within the subject and thus to reactionary and repressive social structures and forms of politics, as Deleuze and Guattari claim, I would argue that lack not only opens the structure of subjectivity to what lies beyond it, but also allows radical political identifications to emerge. Firstly, it suggests a way out of subjection – or at least the possibility of a radical critique of it. If we compare Lacan to Foucault on this point, a crucial difference becomes apparent: both thinkers accept that the subject is constituted through external structures – power/knowledge for Foucault and language for Lacan; however, the difference is that, for Foucault, the subject is *wholly* constituted by these structures (there is no aspect of the subject that is not colonised by power/knowledge) whereas for Lacan, they only *partially* constitute the subject. In other words, from the perspective of Lacanian theory, subjection is *not* completely successful: the subject's integration into language, the process which bestows meaning upon the subject and fixes his identity, is only partial and incomplete. There is always a kind of remainder or 'leftover' from this process of subjection – the site of the unconscious which could serve as a point of resistance to subjection itself. Therefore, the subject refers not to any fixed identity but rather to the structural gap between being and identity. What emerges here, at the limits of subjection, is the possibility of a radical *de-subjection*. I shall return to this point later.

Secondly, because the subject lacks the object that he imagines will make him whole – and because he lacks full recognition of himself with the symbolic order – he engages in a continual process of identification, searching for a signifier through which he believes he will gain access to this lost enjoyment. As Yannis Stavrakakis shows, this is how advertising functions. It sells us a certain product and, through this, a certain 'lifestyle' or identity which promises to gives us access to the lost object of desire, to full satisfaction – something which, of course, it never delivers, thus perpetuating the desire to consume.[37] However, this notion of partial identification can also be applied to an understanding of the political field: the process of political identification – our identification with certain parties, movements or political ideologies for instance – can be seen as the attempt to fill in the lack in social objectivity, or to make sense of the world and act within it politically. Without this lack – both within the subject and the social order itself – there can be no politics. For Stavrakakis: 'This state of happiness, embodying the lost/impossible *jouissance*, has to be posited as lost if our life in the socio-symbolic world is to have any meaning; without it no desire for social and political identification would arise.'[38] Of course, the absence of the object of desire and the constitutive lack it creates within the subject can lead to all sorts of political identifications, not just radical ones but reactionary ones as well. However, as thinkers like Lefort and Laclau argue, this notion of constitutive lack, because it resists the idea of the fullness of identity, tends to be associated with a certain understanding of democracy. I shall explore this in later chapters.

The politics of subjectification

It is possible now, following the insights outlined above, to give a preliminary definition of the subject: the subject is an empty place, a structural gap within the order of language, which comes to be occupied – temporarily and contingently – by the individual. In other words, the subject has to be distinguished from the individual: the subject is the *place* with which individuals come to identify. Thus political struggles involve a process of *subjectification* (as opposed to subjection) in which the individual transcends his ordinary, everyday existence to take up a position of a full political subject. It is in this sense that subjectification should be distinguished from subjection: subjection refers to a process by which power constructs an identity and imposes it on the individual in the Foucauldian sense; whereas subjectification involves a rejection of, and indeed, an *insurrection against* this established discursive identity. To give an example: the woman who rejects her established role within society, who comes to see this position precisely as one of subordination and oppression, and who challenges it through social and political struggles, becomes a feminist subject.

However, this notion of subjectification means more than simply a postmodern experimentation with different identities: it is not through a simple abandonment of her identity as woman, but rather through a problematisation of what it means to be a woman, that she becomes a political subject. In other words, it is on the basis of her identity *as* a woman demanding full political, social and economic equality, that she at the same time rejects what society tells her a 'woman' is or should be. By contrast, the simplistic postmodern 'play' of identities amounts to nothing more than an experimentation with established social roles and practices, which, in our contemporary society, can be very varied indeed and even marginal: thus one can be a lesbian mother, an S/M practitioner, a gay preacher. But these are 'subject positions' which remain unpoliticised, and thus cannot be seen acts of subjectification in the sense that I am describing. We see, then, that subjectification is also at the same time a *de-subjection or 'dis-identification'*: it involves a separation or a disengagement from one's established social identity or role, a kind of rupture of, or as Badiou would say, a 'subtraction' from one's normal existence. Politics, in this sense, does not emerge on the basis of one's essential or pre-existing identity, but through a rupturing and radical break with such identities. I realise that this might seem a very paradoxical and idiosyncratic understanding of subjectivity: the subject is one who becomes what one *is not*, not what one is – in other words, the subject is one who removes himself from himself, who radically detaches himself from his normal social identity. But here we are trying to describe a very specific experience of political identification, one that is crucial to the theorisation of radical politics.

There are a number of contemporary continental thinkers who employ a similar notion of subjectification in their radical political analyses. Furthermore, as I shall show, their understanding of political subjectification points to a universal political dimension that goes beyond a simple politics of difference, while at the same time avoiding essentialist claims about the human subject.

For instance, according to Jacques Rancière, politics emerges from a fundamental dispute or 'disagreement' (*mesentente*) between a particular group which is excluded and the existing social order: this excluded social group not only demands that its voice be heard, that it be included in the social order, but, more precisely, it claims in doing so to represent the whole of society. What is central to politics, then, according to Rancière, is that an excluded part not only demands to be *counted* as part of the social whole, but that this part claims to actually embody this whole. Rancière shows the way that in ancient Greece the demos – or 'the people', the poor – which had no fixed place in the social order, demanded to be included, demanded that its voice be heard by the aristocratic order and, in doing so, claimed to represent the universal interests of the whole of society. In other words, there is a kind of metonymical substitution of the *part for the whole* – the part represents its struggle in terms of a universality: its particular interests are represented as being identical to those of the community as a whole. In this way, the 'simple' demand to be included causes a rupture or dislocation in the existing social order: this part could not be included without rupturing the very logic of a social order based on this exclusion. To give a contemporary example: the struggles of 'illegal' immigrants – perhaps the most excluded group today – to be given a place within society, to have their status legitimised, would create a kind of contradiction in the social order which refuses to include or even recognise them, which promises equal and democratic rights to everyone, and yet denies them to this particular group. In this way, the demand of the 'illegals' to be counted as 'citizens' highlights the inconsistency of the situation in which universal democratic rights are promised to all, but in practice are granted to only some; it shows that any fulfilment of the democratic promise of universal rights is at the very least conditional on *their* recognition also as citizens with equal rights. The discursive 'stage' upon which politics takes place is therefore an inconsistency within the structure of universality, between its promise and its actualisation. To give a further example: the protests that took place in France in 2004 over the ban on Islamic headscarves in schools, pointed to the inconsistency of a situation in which, on the one hand, everyone is formally recognised as having equal rights as citizens of the French Republic, while on the other, laws are introduced, *in the very name of this Republican ideal of equality*, which obviously discriminate against and target certain minorities – particularly Muslims. Indeed, the explosion of violence in Paris in November 2005 was a direct expression of the frustration felt by people from North African and Islamic backgrounds at the racism and exclusion that they suffer on a daily

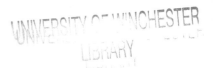

basis. It is thus a mistake to claim, as both conservative and socialist MPs did, that these protests and acts of resistance were anti-Republican: on the contrary, the Muslim women protesting against the headscarf ban waved the tricolor and held placards emblazoned with the words *Liberte, Egalite, Fraternite*. By identifying with the ideals of the Republic, they highlighted, in a very effective way, the fact that they were excluded from these ideals. Their message was that they believe in the Republic *but the Republic does not believe in them*. Here we see the excluded part claiming to represent the universality of the egalitarian ideal through the simple demand to be counted. So for Rancière: 'politics exists whenever the count of parts and parties of society is disturbed by the inscription of a part of those who have no part'.[39]

Central here is a tension between two different logics: *politics* and *police*. Police refers to the rationality of 'counting' that founds the existing social order – a logic that regulates the different identities in society, assigning each to its place within the social hierarchy. In this sense, police would include the usual coercive and repressive policing functions, but it also refers to a much broader organisation and regulation of society – the distribution of places and roles. Politics, on the other hand, refers to the logic I have just described: the claim of the part to be the whole, the claim which fundamentally disturbs the social order. In this sense, political subjectification, for Rancière, involves a rupture of existing social identities, a kind of de-subjection or 'dis-identification' in which one detaches oneself from one's normal social role and fundamentally questions one's 'normal' position of subordination:

> political subjectification forces them out of such obviousness by questioning the relationship between the *who* and the *what* in the apparent redundancy of the positing of an existence ... 'Worker' or better still 'proletarian' is similarly the subject that measures the gap between the part of work as social function and the having no part of those who carry it out within the definition of the common of the community.[40]

In other words, subjectification involves a questioning and violent separation from one's established, even 'natural', position of subordination and exclusion. There is a 'measuring of the gap' between, for instance, the role of the worker in the productive process, and the actual exclusion or subordination of the worker in the capitalist social order – thus revealing an actual contradiction within this social order. So, as Rancière argues, 'any subjectification is a disidentification, removal from the naturalness of place'.[41] Here we see a *non-essentialist* approach to subjectification: becoming a political subject is not based on some sort of given essence or intrinsic set of interests, or even on an immanent social rationality – these are, in Rancière's analysis, on the side of the 'natural' social order. Rather, the political subject comes about through a rupture of this natural order.

We can also see here a clear reference to a universal political dimension – in the claim of the excluded part to represent the universality of interests. However, this universal dimension is again not based on any pre-given, essentialist identity or set of interests: rather, it only emerges in a contingent way when a particular group claims to embody this universality. In other words, instead of a universal political dimension being posited as pre-given, as something that emerges in a dialectical unfolding of an immanent social logic, it only appears, in a temporary and irruptive fashion, *through a point of particularity*, a particularity which 'stands-in' for this universality, claiming to embody it. However, universality, for Rancière, is not simply an empty space – as Laclau might argue – but is actually constructed around the idea of *equality*. The radical premise upon which Rancière's argument is based is that equality is primary and forms the ontological ground of politics itself. This equality is presupposed by the fact that we are all speaking beings, and therefore all have access to thought and discourse. However, this fundamental equality is at the same time not recognised by the social or police order, which is based on a hierarchical regulation of statements and positions in which only some are authorised to speak. However, we can see how Rancière's approach differs from the 'postmodern' celebration of difference: rather than emphasising, as Lyotard does, the incommensurability of statements and speaking positions, Rancière emphasises their radical sameness and equality. He is not interested so much in difference and heterogeneity, but rather in a radical disagreement that emerges around a fundamental equivalence: 'An extreme form of disagreement is where X cannot see the common object Y is presenting because X cannot comprehend that the sounds uttered by Y form words and chains of words similar to X's own.'[42] There is thus a fundamental equality between speaking positions, an equality which at the same time is not recognised and, indeed, is repressed or disavowed by the social order upon which it is based. Politics, for Rancière, is therefore the revelation and irruption of this moment of equality, an act of recognition which disturbs the police order and unmasks the contingency and fundamental injustice of its hierarchies and social arrangements. The idea that we all belong to the same 'community' of those who speak and think, and, yet, that certain subjects are at the same time excluded from this community and so challenge their exclusion on the basis of the universality of this community, is, for Rancière, the very definition of politics. The universal horizon of equality thus looms up as an ever-present possibility behind any struggle for liberty:

> It [politics] begins when the equality of everyone and anyone is inscribed in the liberty of the people. This liberty of the people is an empty property, an improper property through which those who are nothing purport that their group is identical to the whole of the community.[43]

Badiou is another thinker for whom a universal dimension is central to any theorisation of politics and to any proper consideration of the subject. Indeed,

he argues that the so-called 'politics of difference' – the struggles of incommensurable particularisms for recognition so closely associated with the
'postmodern condition' – cannot be seen as worthy of the designation 'politics':
the insistence upon the difference or particularity of any identity or community
– whether it be ethnic, sexual, religious – amounts to the abandonment of a
universal political terrain, and thus can be easily accommodated within the
contemporary capitalist system, a system which constantly seeks new markets
amongst niches. For Badiou, the only real threat to the universality of this capitalist order is another universalism.[44] Badiou's hostility to the postmodern
politics of difference and his insistence on a universal form of politics makes
him, seemingly, a curious figure to be included in any discussion of poststructuralist, or even post-Althusserian, theory (he would almost certainly reject the
former label). However, I would argue that Badiou, like Rancière, develops a
notion of universality and a theory of the subjective processes through which it
emerges, which eschews essentialist foundations, dialectical unfoldings and
structuralist determinations, emphasising instead a singular and unpredictable
moment of rupture – what Badiou calls the *event*.

So, what is this event through which the universal dimension appears, and
how does it relate to the question of subjectivity? The event is a moment – one
that is wholly unpredictable and contingent and that cannot be seen as determined by preceding conditions – in which the subject becomes the bearer of a
universal truth. Not only is this universal truth revealed to the subject, but the
subject himself becomes its point of articulation – he declares it and remains
faithful to it. Moreover, it is through this declaration and fidelity that one's
subjectivity is constituted: one becomes a subject in relation to this truth and
through its articulation. What we see here is the moment of *subjectification*.
Paradigmatic here, for Badiou, is the figure of St Paul, whose conversion on the
road to Damascus to the universal 'truth' of Christ's resurrection symbolises
this moment of subjectification: he is 'caught up' by the revelation of this truth,
and henceforth remains faithful to this event by not only declaring it, but by
founding a new militant political movement around it. The important point
here is that this event, and the moment of subjectification created by it, are
completely contingent and singular – the event comes to the subject from the
'outside':

> First, since truth is eventual, or of the order of what occurs, it is singular. It is
> neither structural, nor axiomatic, nor legal. No available generality can
> account for it, nor structure the subject who claims to follow in its wake ...
> Second, truth being inscribed on the basis of a declaration that is in essence
> subjective, no preconstituted subset can support it; nothing communitarian
> or historically established can lend its substance to the process of truth. Truth
> is diagonal relative to every communitarian subset; it neither claims authority
> from, nor constitutes any identity. It is offered to all, or addressed to all,

without a condition of belonging being able to limit this offer, or this address.[45]

There are a number of important points to be made here. We see the way that, firstly, universal truth is singular – that is, it emerges from an event which is wholly unpredictable and contingent. This is very different from a simplistic 'postmodern' assertion of difference: instead of a universal order of differences and singularities – which, as Badiou has argued, fits hand in glove with the universal market – we have a *singular universal*, a universal truth which emerges through a point of singularity. This singular universal, what is more, consists of a radical sameness and – like Rancière's formulation of politics – invokes a radical equality. It is not so much intolerant of differences but simply *oblivious* to them, refusing to see them as important: St Paul declares that 'there is neither Jew nor Greek, there is neither slave nor free, there is neither male nor female'.[46] I would argue that the radical equivalence that is proposed in this statement is far more subversive than the politics of difference, which insists on the recognition of difference; how often is 'difference' simply a polite word for inequality? Furthermore, as I have already suggested, the politics of difference risks falling into another form of essentialism – one that sees difference itself as a stable identity whose particularity is asserted as absolute. By contrast, Badiou's approach shows that not only is a pre-existing identity unimportant in the face of this universal truth, but that it is never stable or fixed in any case: pre-existing identities are always ruptured and destabilised by the event, and are thus opened to something beyond their immediate experience. This brings me to my second point: central to Badiou's notion of universal truth is a radical understanding of subjectification. Becoming a subject of universal truth involves – in a similar manner to Rancière's 'dis-identification' – a separation or detachment from one's established identity or mode of living. Paul's followers were introduced to a new form of living, a new mode of subjectivity, in which one's background or ethnicity or social status were absolutely unimportant, in which one separated from one's normal identity and social role, embracing instead the principle of complete equality and affirming one's fidelity to the event. So here with Badiou, as with Rancière, we see subjectification as simultaneously involving a 'de-subjection'. The subject's emergence through the truth event is what, at the same time, punctures and suspends his normal existence:

> I am altogether present there, linking my component elements via that excess beyond myself induced by the passing through me of a truth. But as a result, I am also suspended, broken, annulled; dis-interested. For I cannot, within the fidelity to fidelity that defines ethical consistency, take an interest in myself, and thus pursue my own interests.[47]

Thus, for Badiou, politics involves an 'un-binding', an undoing of the social bond and a detachment from normal social roles and identities.[48] Politics is therefore one of the privileged sites of de-subjection, one that is shared with art, science and love.

A similar understanding of subjectification is employed by Žižek, who calls for a return to the problematic of the Cartesian subject through the psychoanalytic notion of the unconscious.[49] Therefore, his account of the subject largely follows Lacan's: the subject is the name of the void or the gap between being and the symbolic order. However, Žižek emphasises the idea of the Act as fundamental to the experience of the subject: subjectification refers to an act or decision through which the subject is retroactively constituted. There is a paradox here, one that emphasises this theme of *coming to subjectivity* that I have been pursuing: it is not a pre-existent subject who makes a decision; rather it is the decision or act which constitutes the subject. Subjectification involves a sort of 'leap across the void' – it comes about, not on the basis of already existing interests, motivations or social positions but, rather, *ex nihilo* (out of nothing). Furthermore, for Žižek, subjectification through the act involves a universal political dimension, one that is often disavowed in the postmodern universe of differences: the act is something that has the potential to fundamentally alter existing politico-ideological coordinates, creating a new political space, in the same way that, for Lacan, the Master Signifier re-grounds the Symbolic Order. As such, it has, for Žižek, a real emancipative potential: in this sense, the act is similar to Badiou's event. As an example of the act, however, Žižek valorises a Leninist politics (indeed the figure of Lenin is also invoked by Badiou): this is a universal revolutionary politics which, unlike what Žižek dismisses as 'liberal Leftism', is fully prepared to assume the consequences of its act – the Bolshevik revolution – by ruthlessly exercising the power it has seized and by crushing opposition to it: 'a Leninist, like a Conservative, is *authentic* in the sense of *fully assuming the consequences of his choice,* of being fully aware of what it means to take power and exert it'.[50]

The willingness to assume the consequences of one's act – the preparedness to exercise power ruthlessly if need be – is Žižek's version of Badiou's *fidelity to the truth-event*: both approaches invoke the idea affirming an event, of following its consequences to the end and, thus, allowing oneself to become subjectified by it. However, Badiou also cautions us about the dangers of the *passage a l'acte*, of pursuing the Good without moderation and thus subordinating every truth to its authoritarian and terroristic injunctions: this is one of the illegitimate and excessive functions of the Good which leads only to *disaster*. Stalinist terrorism and totalitarianism could be seen as one of the consequences of this excessive pursuit of the Truth of the Bolshevik revolution.[51] Thus, while Badiou calls for 'moderation' in philosophy – its 'critical virtue' – Žižek's notion of the act recognises no such limit: in Žižek's more recent work, there is a celebration of revolutionary violence and authoritarianism. In his desire to affirm the heroism of the act, Žižek is drawn to a terrorist politics of the absolute and the blind will to destruction which recalls the lures of the *death-drive*. This is a point that I shall take up with him in the following chapter on Ethics.

Lastly, we come to Laclau, whose notion of hegemonic politics also involves radical rethinking of the subject and universality. While Laclau accepts the consequences of the postmodern condition – the breakdown of 'metanarratives' and the displacement of the proletariat as the universal revolutionary identity – he nevertheless remains suspicious of the 'politics of difference' associated with postmodernism. The idea of a purely particular or differential 'subject position' is problematic because it implies a fixed position or location within a totality – and, as Laclau argues: 'What could this totality be but the object of experience of an absolute subject?'[52] In other words, what is implied, yet disavowed, in the 'politics of difference' is precisely a place of enunciation which forms a background upon which these differential 'subject positions' and identities are constituted. However, rather than re-invoking the idea of the universal Subject – the idea central to classical theories of emancipation – Laclau shows the way that there is a mutual contamination between these different subject positions and the universal background in which they are constituted. In the political field abandoned by the notion of the universal Subject, there is only an 'empty' horizon of universality which can be embodied by different particular identities. The universal is an 'empty signifier' that cannot be filled and, yet, because of this generates the desire (in the Lacanian sense described above) in different political identities to fill or embody it. 'Society', for instance, may be seen as an example of an empty universality: society is ultimately a meaningless and inconsistent identity and thus has no objective content as such, but rather embodies an 'absent fullness' which awaits embodiment. However, at the same time it is structurally impossible to completely embody this identity. It is this political operation of attempting to fill the 'unfillable' place of politics that Laclau refers to as the logic of 'hegemony': '*The universal is an empty place, a void which can be filled only by the particular, but which, through its very emptiness, produces a series of crucial effects in the structuration/destructuration of social relations.*'[53]

Hegemony involves, then, a relationship of mutual contamination between the universal and particular. Because the universal is formally empty, it can only articulate itself if it is represented by a particular political identity. However, at the same time, this particular identity is never self-enclosed in its difference and, if it is to engage in political struggles and pursue a series of demands, it must increasingly form alliances or what Laclau calls 'chains of equivalence' with other groups and identities united in opposition to a common enemy – the identity who denies them their demands. So the subject, for Laclau, refers to this place of hegemonic operation: the identification of a particular element with this empty space of universality is the moment of subjectification. However, we see that this moment of subjectification also involves a de-subjection: the groups involved in political struggles are increasingly split between their own demands and identity, and the necessity for them to appeal to a broader coalition of forces in their attempt to represent the universal dimension they are seeking to occupy. In other words, their involvement in hegemonic political struggles increasingly takes them 'out' of their established identity and forces them to construct alliances with other groups.

There are significant differences between the four thinkers discussed here. However, I have attempted to tease out two major themes upon which they all converge. Firstly, there is the theme of subjectification – which involves the coming into the place of subjectivity, not on the basis of any kind of essence or pre-existing identity or series of interests but, on the contrary, through a kind of *rupture of and separation from these categories*. Subjectification – the process of becoming a subject – involves at the same time a *de-subjection*: a removal from one's given social role and position. Secondly, I have shown the way that, for these thinkers, universality – particularly in politics – emerges not on the basis of some pre-given rationality or structure, but rather through a *contingent moment of singularity*: for Rancière, the part that claims to the whole; for Badiou, the unpredictable event; for Žižek, the absolute act; and for Laclau, the hegemonic contamination of the universal and particular.

I started with the problem of self-repression in the process of subjection, and have ended with a notion of *subjectification*: a positive notion of subjectivity, which not only suggests a working of oneself out of the immediate grasp of power, but also the invention of new, radical modes of political identification. In charting this course for the subject, I have also touched on different understandings of ethics: for instance, the individual ethics of 'care for the self' in Foucault, and the singular/universal ethics of the act for Žižek. The question posed here is what is the relationship between ethics, subjectivity and politics, and to what extent is radical politics dependent on the notion of ethical action? This will be the central question addressed in the next chapter.

Notes

1 M. Foucault, 'What is Enlightenment?', in P. Rabinow (ed.) *The Foucault Reader* (New York: Pantheon, 1984) pp. 32–50, p. 41.
2 Žižek, *The Ticklish Subject*, p. 220.
3 M. Foucault, *The Order of Things: an Archaeology of the Human Sciences* (London: Routledge, 2003), p. 422.
4 See Balibar, *Politics and the Other Scene*.
5 E. de La Boetie, *The Politics of Obedience: The Discourse of Voluntary Servitude*, trans. H. Kurz (New York: Free Life Editions, 1975), p. 46.
6 La Boetie, *The Politics of Obedience*, p. 58.
7 Although here we might say that the continued existence of God in the shape of Man has, in contemporary postmodern societies, led to the paradoxical return of more virulent forms of religious fundamentalism: a fundamentalism which is not simply a reaction to secular humanism, but rather a kind of 'return of the repressed', where

God, who never really went away, now reasserts himself *without* the secular humanist disguise.

8 Stirner, *The Ego and Its Own*, p. 38.

9 Stirner, *The Ego and Its Own*, pp. 174–175.

10 Stirner, *The Ego and Its Own*, p. 276.

11 G. Deleuze and C. Parnet, *Dialogues*, trans. H. Tomlinson and B. Habberjam (New York: Columbia University Press, 1987), p. 133.

12 Deleuze and Guattari, *A Thousand Plateaus: Capitalism & Schizophrenia*, p. 162.

13 Foucault, 'The subject and power', *Essential Works*, p. 331.

14 J. Butler, *The Psychic Life of Power: Theories in Subjection* (Stanford, CA: Stanford University Press, 1997), p. 10.

15 See G. Agamben, *Remnants of Auschwitz: The Witness and the Archive*, trans. D. Heller-Roazen (New York: Zone Books, 2002).

16 Butler, *The Psychic Life of Power*, p. 86.

17 Foucault, 'The subject and power', *Essential Works*, p. 326.

18 M. Foucault, *The Use of Pleasure, Vol. 2 of The History of Sexuality*, trans. R. Hurley (New York: Pantheon Books, 1985), pp. 29–30.

19 See G. Deleuze, *Nietzsche and Philosophy*, trans. H. Tomlinson (London: Athlone Press, 1983), p. 40.

20 See Deleuze and Parnet, *Dialogues*, p. 78

21 G. Deleuze and F. Guattari, *Anti-Oedipus: Capitalism and Schizophrenia* (New York: Viking Press, 1972), p. 116.

22 Deleuze and Parnet, *Dialogues*, p. 80.

23 Foucault, 'The subject and power', *Essential Works*, p. 336.

24 Deleuze and Parnet, *Dialogues*, p. 131.

25 Deleuze and Parnet, *Dialogues*, p. 138.

26 Eagleton, *After Theory*, p. 118.

27 See Deleuze and Parnet, *Dialogues*, p. 144.

28 See S. Freud, 'Group psychology and the analysis of the Ego' (1921), in *The Standard Edition of the Complete Psychological Works of Sigmund Freud*, trans. James Strachey (London: Hogarth Press, 1953–1975), pp. 69–143.

29 Freud, 'Group psychology and the analysis of the Ego', p. 69.

30 J. Derrida, *Margins of Philosophy*, trans. A. Bass (Chicago: University of Chicago Press, 1982), p. 135.

31 Derrida, *Margins of Philosophy*, p. 135.

32 J. Lacan, *The Four Fundamental Concepts of Psychoanalysis: The Seminar of Jacques Lacan, Book XI*, ed. J.-A. Miller and trans. A. Sheridan (London: W.W. Norton & Co, 1998), p. 126.

33 Lacan, *The Four Fundamental Concepts of Psychoanalysis*, p. 20.

34 J. Lacan, *Ecrits: A Selection*, trans. A. Sheridan (London: Tavistok, 1977), p. 3.

35 Lacan, *Ecrits*, p. 299.

36 See Yannis Stavrakakis' entry on Lacan in J. Simons (ed.) *Contemporary Critical Theorists: From Lacan to Said* (Edinburgh: Edinburgh University Press, 2005), pp. 18–33.

37 Stavrakakis in Simons, *Contemporary Critical Theorists*, pp. 28–29.

38 Stavrakakis, *Lacan and the Political*, p. 52.

39 J. Rancière, *Disagreement: Politics and Philosophy*, trans. J. Rose (Minneapolis: University of Minnesota Press, 1999), p. 123.

40 Rancière, *Disagreement*, p. 36.

41 Rancière, *Disagreement*, p. 36.

42 Rancière, *Disagreement*, xii.
43 Rancière, *Disagreement*, p. 123.
44 See A. Badiou, *Saint Paul: The Foundation of Universalism*, trans. R. Brassier (Stanford, CA: Stanford University Press, 2003), pp. 6–7.
45 Badiou, *St Paul*, p. 14.
46 See Badiou, *St Paul*, p. 9
47 A. Badiou, *Ethics: An Essay on the Understanding of Evil*, trans. P. Hallward (London: Verso, 2001), pp. 49–50.
48 Badiou, *Metapolitics*, p. 77.
49 See Žižek, *The Ticklish Subject*.
50 Žižek, *The Ticklish Subject*, p. 236.
51 See Badiou, *Manifesto for Philosophy*, pp. 130–132.
52 Ernesto Laclau, *Emancipation(s)* (London: Verso, 1996), p. 21.
53 Laclau, Butler and Žižek, *Contingency, Hegemony, Universality*, p. 58 (original emphasis).

4

Ethics

THE PREVIOUS chapter explored the question of subjectivity in radical politics, and it tried to formulate a new mode of political subjectification – understood in terms not of simple identification but, rather, a *dis-identification* from prevailing subject positions and social identities. We found also that this raised certain ethical questions, namely the extent to which this attempt to escape subjectifying power and explore new forms of subjectivity suggests at the same time a new conception of ethical action. Foucault, for instance, saw the possibility of a new form of subjectivity – or a new way of relating to the self – in the 'ethics of care' of the ancients. Deleuze and Guattari's *Anti-Oedipus*, in which they attempt to forge 'lines of flight' from Oedipal subjectivity, was described by Foucault as nothing less than a book of ethics.[1] Žižek talks about the 'ethics of the act', in relation to which the subject is retroactively constituted. It would seem that in dealing with the subject – particularly the radical political subject – we cannot really avoid the question of ethics.

Indeed, it is said that continental philosophy itself has, in recent times, been marked by a general return to the question of ethics. Thinkers such as Derrida and Lyotard, for instance, turned later in their work to more explicit ethical concerns, the former through Levinas, and the latter through Aristotle and Kant. The seeming paradox here is that the postmodern condition, with which such thinkers have been generally associated, is seen to imply a breakdown of moral metanarratives and a decline of the idea of a universal moral position. Instead of Kant's categorical imperative – in which ethics is seen as absolute obedience to a universal moral law – our contemporary world would appear to be characterised by a plurality of different and often conflicting beliefs, attitudes and perspectives from which it is impossible to derive any kind of universal moral standpoint. As Lyotard argues, the metanarrative has given way to kind of 'paganism' of different and incommensurable language games or 'phrase regimens' between which it is impossible to establish any consensus. However, as

Lyotard shows, paganism also implies the possibility and, indeed, the necessity, of judging, of making judgements – including ethical and political judgements – *without criteria*. In other words, in this postmodern experience marked by the collapse of the metanarrative and therefore the absence of firm moral and rational foundations which once guided our judgements, we must nevertheless make judgements, and, indeed, we do so every day: 'And one judges not only in matters of truth, but also in matters of beauty (or aesthetic efficacy) and in matters of justice, that is, of politics and ethics, and all without criteria. That's what I mean by paganism.'[2] Here Lyotard invokes an Aristotelian notion of ethical judgement, in which one judges not according to absolute criteria or pre-given models, but rather on a case by case basis, employing one's 'prudence'.[3] Indeed, for Aristotle, as Lyotard suggests, we have a good or virtuous ethos because we make good judgements, rather than our ability to make good judgements emanating from some prior essence of the good within us.

It is therefore not the case that postmodernism amounts simply to ethical nihilism – to an abandonment of the responsibility to make judgements; on the contrary, precisely because we lack firm foundations and universal criteria to guide us, we are all the more responsible for the judgements we make. In other words, ethics can no longer be seen as the mere application of a rule or moral law, but rather as a *phronetic* process in which we rely on our skills and expertise to make judgements in particular situations. Lyotard is concerned with arriving at an understanding of justice in a groundless world, in a world in which the social bond has irretrievably broken down. Therefore, justice cannot be determined on the basis of some sort of social totality or whole, but rather from the perspective of the multiplicity, diversity and heterogeneity of different positions and language games that are found in society. Justice as ethics, for Lyotard, therefore comes down to the ability not only to make judgements in this groundless world, but more so to remain faithful to its heterogeneity – to respect and preserve, in other words, the plurality and incommensurability of language games and to not try to subsume them under some sort of totality or consensus.

While I accept Lyotard's premise about the need to make ethical and political judgements in a world without absolute foundations, I find his notion of ethics somewhat unsatisfactory. Because ethics ultimately has to coincide with – or at least not intrude upon – the incommensurability between different positions and language games, it implies a highly individualistic and particularised experience of judgement-making, one that would seem to preclude any notion of collective activity. In other words, what is rejected in Lyotard's account of ethics is any sort of universal politico-ethical dimension, and any sort of possibility of collective ethical action – and it is therefore difficult to derive from this a notion of ethics that would be relevant to radical politics. Radical politics relies on some sort of universal dimension, and some possibility of a collective ground being constituted – even in a highly contingent manner – between different perspectives and identities, and this is what seems to be occluded in Lyotard's notion of ethics.

It is perhaps for this reason that Habermas tries to develop a post-foundational understanding of ethics based on a rational consensus achieved between interlocutors. Habermas accepts the idea of a world without absolute moral foundations: there is no universal moral law governing our actions; there is no rationally perceivable categorical imperative that exists in a de-ontological sense outside empirical contexts. In its place, though, Habermas tries to develop a notion of 'discourse ethics' which is based on a consensus that is arrived at through rational deliberation, where the participants agree on the rules and norms of rational discussion. Here we see the possibility of a context-dependent understanding of ethical speech and action emerging through a rational consensus, rather than on the basis of a non-negotiable universal moral law. So, whereas Lyotard's notion of justice and ethics rejected any notion of consensus, Habermas sees consensus as the *only* way of arriving at ethical decisions. There are, however, a number of problems with Habermas' understanding of discourse ethics – problems which have already been touched upon in the first chapter. Habermas, I would suggest, has merely substituted one form of foundationalism for another – universal rational consensus instead of universal moral law. Both are equally implausible and unsustainable. Furthermore, we should recognise that this idea of rationality serving as the basis for a universal consensus conceals the potential exclusion of perspectives and language games that would be deemed to be 'irrational' and therefore beyond the limits of rational deliberation. At least Lyotard's notion of justice remains open to the *differend*, whereas Habermasian discourse ethics is totalising, subsuming the differend under the universal law of the rational. Moreover, and perhaps more importantly, should ethics be determined by consensus? We can easily imagine all sorts of things being agreed to, under the conditions of rational deliberation, that are entirely unethical and unjust. Rationality is by no means a guarantee of ethical action, and indeed, as thinkers like Adorno and Horkheimer have pointed out, modern ethical tragedies such as the Holocaust came about not because of the breakdown of rationality, but rather as a result of the technical and instrumentalist mentality produced by the rational categories of the Enlightenment – the very categories that Habermas wants to preserve. While there is no harm, of course, at arriving at ethical decisions through rational deliberation, we need to recognise that ethics cannot be seen as being wholly determined by this. Ethics goes beyond the limits of rational agreement: indeed, it is what, at times, goes against and *disrupts* consensus.

To develop a notion of ethics which conforms to the general conditions of postmodernity – namely the absence of foundations – and yet at the same time allows a collective, universal political dimension to emerge, will involve finding a 'middle road' between Habermas and Lyotard. The challenge of this chapter will therefore be to investigate the conditions for a radical political ethics within the poststructuralist theoretical 'framework'. Here I will explore the relevance of ethics to radical politics today – something that is not at all obvious – and then examine a number of different approaches to the question of ethics, pointing out their applications and limitations when it comes to theorising contemporary radical politics. This will include: the ethics of postmodern irony – Richard Rorty; the ethics of psychoanalysis – Lacan and Žižek; and the ethics of the Other – Levinas and Derrida.

Ethics and radical politics

The conditions of postmodernity are marked, as I have argued, not only by the death of God, but also the breakdown of the Enlightenment moral metanarratives that were developed to fill His place. Kant formulated ethics as duty to a universaliseable moral law which was suprasensible, and beyond empirical observation and pathological considerations. Thus we had the notorious categorical imperative – formalised as acting *'only on that maxim whereby thou canst at the same time will that it should become a universal law'*.[4] However, even this guide to ethical action has broken down, and we 'postmoderns' are left perhaps like Nietzsche's madman, faced with an unbearable and, at the same time, exhilarating sense of uncertainty – of having lost our footing, our moral compass. What kind of effect has this loss of an absolute moral ground had on radical politics? Undoubtedly, it has liberated it from the crippling morality of Kant and has alerted it to a sense of historical contingency. However, can radical politics do wholly without any notion of ethics – without any notion of a 'right course of action', or of justifying one's measures and goals according to some sort of ethical standard? Surely, if it is to be distinguished from nihilism, radical politics must involve some sort of ethical dimension; political action must be conditioned by some kind of ethical standard or limit.

However, when considering the question of ethics, radical political theory today is confronted with a highly ambiguous and contradictory situation. As I have suggested, postmodernity, while it implies the shattering of universal foundations and metanarratives, is also characterised, paradoxically, by a paranoid desire to restore traditional moral foundations and values as a kind of reaction to this moment of dislocation. Thus we see the proliferation today of conservative moral discourses and religious fundamentalisms, all animated by a desire to restore some imagined moral foundation to society. We hear politicians from across the political spectrum calling for a return to traditional community and family values; we see the evangelical Right, with its morally conservative agenda, flourishing in the United States; we see the open questioning of modern principles of secularism in the name of a more fundamental and non-negotiable doctrine; we see the religious fervour of the suicide bomber, willing to sacrifice his life for some obscure higher cause. How does a radical political ethos situate itself in relation to this? Clearly it must stand opposed to it, and point out its hypocrisy and inconsistency – the way that it is an artificial, false reaction to the destabilisation created by postmodernity and global capitalism: here we should remember that most religious conservatives are at the same time ideological proponents of the very 'free market' which is rending apart and destabilising the organic communities and traditional values they claim to uphold. However, the problem is that at a time characterised by a stifling and hysterical moralism, the question of ethics becomes more ambiguous – to what extent, in other words, does the recourse to an ethics of any kind buy into and perpetuate this return to 'moral values'?

On the other hand, we could also say that our world is desperately *in need* of ethics, even of the rigorous Kantian kind. Look at the way that the ethical norms, which in theory at least governed the international system, have now been transgressed and openly disavowed by the global superpower and its obsequious satellite states: we have seen the United States pulling out of the Kyoto Protocol, defying the United Nations and world public opinion by invading Iraq, exempting itself from the jurisdiction of the International War Crimes court (while at the same time urging it to pursue Bosnian-Serb war criminals) and defying numerous international conventions and norms on human rights and the treatment of prisoners by running off-shore extra-legal detention camps and denying detainees even basic rights. Indeed, we might say that the appalling moralism shown in the pronouncements of George W. Bush and Tony Blair in the international domain – with their continual references to God, 'democratic values' and the 'evil' of terrorism etc – finds its ultimate answer in the complete evacuation of moral standards and limits from this domain. It would seem that what is needed, in the international arena at least, is a more rigorous and unconditional application of ethical and moral laws, an insistence that such laws and rules are non-negotiable and cannot be transgressed, even for matters of 'national security'. The ongoing debate on the torture of terrorist suspects – especially after revelations of torture and prisoner abuse at Abu Ghraib, Guantanamo Bay and in the secret CIA prisons in Europe – shows how far our 'civilised' Western societies have already gone on the road to moral destitution. Here we have seen the worst kinds of moral contortions and prevarications taking place – when, for instance, Condoleeza Rice insists that the United States does not practise torture and piously states that it is contrary to American values while, at the same time, it is common knowledge that the US 'out-sources' its torture to other countries.[5] We also see people with impeccable liberal credentials, such as civil liberties lawyer Alan Dershowitz, making allowances for torture against terrorist suspects, provided that it is harmonised with the 'rule of law'. According to Dershowitz, torture goes on in any case in liberal regimes, so why not have it out in the open and under judicial control and oversight, rather than have it practised covertly and illegally? He proposes the creation of 'torture warrants' which would be sanctioned by the judiciary and given to government agents prior to the torturing of a terrorist suspect. However, as Dershowitz notes, when he raised this possibility in a series of public lectures in Israel during the 1980s, a time when it had been revealed that the Israeli internal security service routinely practised torture or 'tough interrogation' on Palestinian terrorist suspects:

> The Israeli government and judiciary rejected my proposal. The response, especially of the Israeli judges, was horror at the prospect that they – the robed embodiment of the rule of law – might have to dirty their hands by approving so barbaric a practice in advance and in specific cases.[6]

Dershowitz then goes on to point out the difficulties with such an objection – the way that it amounts to governments and the judiciary simply turning a blind eye to the covert use of torture, while at the same time officially denying it and thus keeping their hands clean.

At one level, Dershowitz is of course right to highlight this hypocrisy. However, the trouble with his proposal to bring torture out in the open is that it bestows on torture a kind of legitimacy and acceptability. Here I agree with Žižek that if torture is to take place, in some ways it is better that it remain covert and secretive: if torture remains a 'dirty little secret' – something that the law turns a blind eye to – then at least torture continues to be seen as illegitimate; if it comes out into the open and is sanctioned by law, then the moral taboo on torture falls away and it would gain eventual moral and social legitimacy. In other words, in certain cases it is important to 'keep up appearances' – to maintain the symbolic legitimacy of the law through official denials of the practice of torture, even though this position might in reality be false and hypocritical.[7] The obscenity of Dershowitz's suggestion lies its 'reasonableness' and in what it considers to be its virtue in removing this hypocrisy: can we imagine a situation in which torture becomes a normal, routine judicial matter, something that we not only know is about to take place but which is actually sanctioned by the judiciary; would courts start making determinations on how much pain is to be inflicted, or on what level of physical injury is permissible, or on what kinds of torture techniques are to be used, etc?[8] Even the fact that such debates on torture are now accepted – where previously they would be unthinkable – shows how much the moral ground has already shifted.

It is against such moral pettifogging – particularly on the question of torture – that a poststructuralist political ethos must insist on the most unconditional and stringent application of ethical limits, moral law and universal human rights. Here Derrida, for instance, insists on the ongoing and universal importance today of human rights, particularly in the face of their increasing transgression in the 'war on terror': 'We must [*il faut*] more than ever stand on the side of human rights. *We need* [*il faut*] *human rights.*'⁹ Or perhaps we might invoke Foucault when he calls for the unconditional mobilisation of rights and laws against the incursions of power: 'Against power one must always set inviolable laws and unrestricted rights.'¹⁰

The 'war on terror' exposes liberalism for what it is – particularly when we see liberal societies transforming themselves into police states in the name of the very liberal principles they purport to uphold, and when we see liberal thinkers openly discussing and debating the legal merits of judicial torture. While Dershowitz does not, of course, speak for all liberals, or even represent mainstream liberal opinion on this question, it is interesting to see that in his argument there is little difficulty in accommodating torture under a liberal regime. And it is even more striking to see a poststructuralist position – at least that which is represented here by Derrida and Foucault – defending the ethical principles of unconditional human rights much more vigorously than a liberal like Dershowitz. Ironically, it is poststructuralism, with its deconstructive interrogation of the categories of universality, natural rights and normative morality – a deconstruction for which it has been heavily criticised by liberals on the grounds that it leads to moral ambivalence – which ends up insisting in a much more unequivocal way on human rights and ethical injunctions, while it is the liberals themselves who get caught up in the miserable game of moral negotiation, of trading certain rights for 'security'. It would seem, in a strange kind of way, that it is the poststructuralists who are the true Kantians, the true defenders of the categorical imperative.

However, what is more the case is that for poststructuralist thinkers like Derrida and Foucault, the significance of ethics and human rights, while it is universal, arises in singular situations – particularly when these rights are pitted against institutional power. For instance, Foucault, in his analysis of the Iranian Revolution in 1979, saw the universality of human rights as emerging in a contingent, yet irreducible, way in a revolutionary situation, a situation where people rebel against power and are prepared to die to resist it. The fact that people who rebel are prepared to take this risk – something that we cannot, as casual observers, explain, only gaze upon with reverence, humility and awe – provides, according to Foucault, a much firmer and more immediate basis for rights than some abstract notion of 'natural rights'. Again, this does not mean that rights are historicised and thus negotiable: on the contrary, it means that the rights invoked by people against power are unconditional and universal because people are prepared to pay the highest price for them. It is here that Foucault talks about an ethics of revolt – what he calls an 'anti-strategic' ethics: 'to be respectful when something singular arises, intransigent as soon as power offends against the universal'.¹¹ What we have here, when Foucault is compared to Dershowitz, is a 'true' universality and a 'false' one. Dershowitz invokes a 'universal' liberal notion of rights, and yet we see that in singular, exceptional 'ticking bomb' situations these rights do not apply. Thus, the universal is transgressed and violated in singular situations – a 'false' universality. However, with Foucault we see a 'true' and unconditional universality of rights emerging from singular, concrete and 'exceptional' situations – the situation of revolt. With Dershowitz, the universal is made destitute in singular situations; whereas with Foucault, the universal becomes unconditional, exalted and thus *truly* universal in singular situations.

Furthermore, the way that in both Derrida and Foucault's accounts, human rights are pitted against power – the power of institutions and governments – suggests an ethics of anti-authoritarianism. Again we see, by contrast, how impoverished and ethically abject Dershowitz's notion of liberal rights is: for Dershowitz, torture is justified in exceptional situations as long it is carried out openly by liberal institutions, sanctioned by the judiciary and in accordance with liberal principles. By contrast, the *anti-authoritarian* – rather than simply liberal – politico-ethical stance of poststructuralism always aims at unmasking and opposing power in whatever form it takes, whether it appears in the form of the most authoritarian and arbitrary of despotisms or the most 'enlightened' or 'civilised' liberal societies – a distinction which, in any case, is starting to look more and more uncertain. As I will show later, the poststructuralist ethical critique of power suggests that ethics must have an anti-authoritarian dimension, or at least it must go beyond, and provide the grounds to criticise, existing political institutions and practices.

Ethical ideology

If ethics must contain an anti-institutional, anti-authoritarian dimension, this suggests that if ethics is actually applied by institutions or endorsed by governments, then it becomes somewhat suspect, resembling more of an ideology than a real ethics. However, what we have seen in recent times are ethical discourses and norms being propounded by a multitude of institutions, government departments and corporate organisations. Paradoxically, while ethics in the sense of moral injunctions against practices such as torture seems to be increasingly absent from the political and international domain, we see, at the same time, an overwhelming return to ethics – or at least to the *semblance* of ethics – at the level of government and institutional discourses. Perhaps we could say that as a symptom of the general repression of a real politico-ethics, we are increasingly surrounded by the *simulacra* of ethics: the absence of a real ethical dimension finds its ultimate form in a saturation of political discourse by its semblance. This takes the dangerous form of the bureaucratisation of ethics: thus we see the proliferation of the so-called 'ethics committees' in government departments, hospitals, universities and corporations – committees which make

judgments and pronouncements on all sorts of 'ethical' questions and supposedly provide a guide to good conduct within a particular institutional setting; we
see the permeation of the notion of ethics into all sorts of realms from which it
had previously been absent – thus we have business ethics, scientific ethics,
medical ethics or 'bioethics'. We even see corporations signing up to voluntary
'ethical codes of conduct'. There have been numerous popular books on good
behaviour, providing guides to ethical conduct and even setting out the rules of
dating etiquette. Governments rattle on about the need to curb what they call
'anti-social behaviour', and bring in all sorts of rules – ranging from the petty to
the draconian – which are designed supposedly to regulate our conduct with
others and encourage us to 'respect' our neighbours and communities.

How do we account for this 'ethical' over-saturation? Again, this can be seen
as symptomatic of postmodernity. Postmodernity, and indeed modernity itself,
is characterised by the breakdown of traditional forms of authority – the *decline
of the paternal function* as Lacan would say. However, this decline of traditional
modes of prohibition and authority – the symbolic authority of God, the King,
the Father etc – results not in a new-found freedom but, on the contrary, in a
proliferation of new forms of authority, new forms of *unfreedom*. From a
psychoanalytic perspective, this is because the external voice of prohibition,
once symbolised by the authoritarian paternal figure, now becomes internalised
as guilt – or, as Lacan would claim, an obscene superegoic injunction to enjoy,
something which contains its own secret prohibition, resulting in the denial of
pleasure.[12] One of the great mysteries of psychoanalysis is the way that the
neurotic, whose life of repression and the denial of pleasure might be blamed on
an external authoritarian figure such as his father, cannot then enjoy his
freedom once this external figure dies or is removed from the picture: this death
simply results in an internalisation of repression, so that the neurotic carries on
as if the father is still alive. This paradox is summarised in Lacan's famous reversal of Dostoyevsky's dictum in *The Brothers Karamazov* that 'God is dead; now
everything is permitted'; for Lacan, on the contrary, 'God is dead; now *nothing*
is permitted.'[13] This raises interesting ethical questions about the relationship
between transgression and moral law, questions that will be explored later in the
chapter. However, the point is that with modernity and postmodernity come
new forms of authority, new kinds of constraint – not only the superegoic
injunction to enjoy that Žižek talks about, but also the myriad rules and norms
governing society and regulating the behaviour of individuals. Perhaps we
might understand this new obsession with 'ethics' in this sense: it would seem
that because we now no longer recognise the traditional forms of authority and
prohibition, it is left to institutions and 'ethics committees' to tell us what to do
and how to live our lives, guiding us towards ethical behaviour and 'responsible'
conduct towards others. A new superego not only orders us to enjoy – within
certain limits, defined by the capitalist market – but also burdens us with an

incoherent array of petty, stupid and meaningless rules and regulations, and all sorts of conflicting advice – about how to be healthy, what diets to follow, how to relate to others, how to raise our children etc. It is as if the whole sphere of human activities must be ceaselessly regulated, normalised, supervised and *guided*. While continuing to bemoan the 'lack of individual responsibility' that supposedly abounds today, governments increasingly take over this role, bringing in rules and regulations that are apparently for our own good, our own 'protection'. We see the old Victorian moral panic now dressed up in the new guises of political correctness and strictures on sexual harassment. Perhaps this ceaseless proliferation of rules about ethical and responsible behaviour – this minute regulation of social and personal life – is to prevent us from realising that there is no longer any absolute epistemological and moral authority in society, no more God, no more Father, no more Big Other as Lacan would say.

Again there is something strikingly artificial about the way that ethical behaviour is now promoted by institutions, something which should make us immediately suspicious. One could first point to its basic hypocrisy: business ethics, for instance, and the notion of corporate 'ethical responsibility' simply operates as a way of whitewashing corporations, who largely continue to carry on in the way they have always done. Here ethics operates as an ideological fetish for global capitalism. University 'research ethics' committees are the bane of any researcher, who has to deal with endless bureaucratic procedures simply in order to get his or her project approved, even in the humanities; and yet these ethics committees tend to be a symptom of the increasing corporatisation and commercialisation of universities, without anyone questioning the ethics of *this*.

Furthermore, one of the newest horizons in this brave new world of ethics is bioethics, and here one finds endless discussions and debates about medical practices, euthanasia, palliative care, abortion and so on. While there should certainly be ethical limitations imposed on the practice of medicine, the use of medical technology and the treatment of patients, bioethics is also problematic: like business ethics, it operates as the ideological supplement to the medical-pharmaceutical industry, providing the 'ethical' coordinates for the invasion of our lives and bodies by new medical technologies. Moreover, bioethics has to be seen as the *other side* of biopower, which I discussed in Chapter 2. The increasingly minute regulation and control of life – through new medical technologies, DNA research and the mapping of the human genome, and through more intrusive forms of biological surveillance etc – itself functions through the discourse of bioethics. In other words, by regulating medical practices and research, bioethics at the same time provides the discursive and normative framework through which they function and are extended. Furthermore, as Benjamin Noys points out, bioethics acts to conceal the political context of death.[14] As Agamben showed, 'bare life' – or life reduced to its biological substratum – is the political condition which is defined by the field of sovereign power: in other words, sovereign power and biopower have converged in Agamben's account, and sovereign power today rules on death while at the same time sustaining and regulating the conditions of biological life. We find this situation highlighted in the bioethical question par excellence – euthanasia. The decision of a doctor or a medical board to end the life of someone who is terminally ill – or of the government to allow the withdrawal of life support – has to be seen as a *political* decision, the decision made by a sovereign power who rules over life and death. By reducing this to ethical questions, bioethics simply obscures this hidden political dimension of sovereign power. Furthermore, debates in bioethics about the legitimacy or otherwise of euthanasia are eerily reminiscent of the practices and concerns of the Nazis: we have to remember that the Nazis, who widely practised euthanasia on the disabled and mentally ill, made all sorts of determinations about which lives were 'worth living' and which were not. Is there not a strange and disturbing parallel here with the discourse of bioethics today, in which philosophers – most notably Peter Singer – debate the merits of ending the life of a severely disabled child, a life that would not, by Singer's account, be worth living?[15]

This bureaucratisation of ethics – in which ethics becomes a normalising and regulatory discourse perpetuated by institutions – suggests that ethics has become the reigning ideology today. In other words, ethics operates as the ideological supplement to the state and to global capitalism, justifying and sustaining the practices of large institutions and corporations. Moreover, as I have already suggested, ethics obscures the political dimension of various social practices and identities. In a world increasingly saturated by ethics, there seems to be less room for politics – less scope to challenge dominant social practices and institutions at a more fundamental level.[16] Or perhaps it might be more precise to say that the reign of ethical ideology is a symptom of the shrinking of the political domain: the superabundance of ethics coincides with the dull mediatised politics of consensus, the inability to question the dogma of free market economics, and the eclipse of any real political alternative to global capitalism.

Badiou is also critical of this ethical ideology, suggesting that our time is marked by an overwhelming return to Kantian moral law. The modern form of Kantian ethics, Badiou argues, is the discourse of human rights, particularly as it is applied to the international sphere: for instance, we see military expeditions taken in the name of enforcing human rights, human rights thus operating as the ideological standard bearer of Western and particularly US imperialism.[17] While I think this argument is somewhat problematic – the US and Western powers in recent years have, as we have seen, openly transgressed and opted out of international human rights norms – there is no doubt that there is a certain ideology of 'human rights' and 'democracy' by which the West sustains itself in its smug satisfaction and its sense of superiority to those other 'less civilised' parts of the world where democracy, human rights and the rule of law 'are not respected'. While the discourse of human rights can be used as a means to resist and limit sovereign power, we have to recognise that it can also be perverted and co-opted into a hegemonic discourse which sustains the structures of global capitalism and Western imperialism: witness the way that this 'ethics of human rights' as Badiou refers to it, was used in part to justify the war on Iraq in 2003. According to Badiou, this liberal 'ethics of human rights' is problematic because it is premised on a universal law which bases itself around opposition to an Evil: in other words, it is a way of defining a consensus through its opposition to an indefinable Evil, which is usually projected onto those 'barbaric' and 'primitive' poorer countries. In this discourse, human rights become identified with the rights to non-Evil, and are based on a notion of the subject who is always at risk of being exposed to suffering and whose rights to non-suffering must be protected. The problem with this discourse, according to Badiou, is that the subject here is reduced to his 'animal substratum' – as the subject for whom the worst evil is to suffer pain – confining ethics to a paltry expression of pity for the 'suffering flesh'. This also has the effect of a kind of splitting, in which the good-Man/white-Man becomes the benefactor who alleviates the suffering of Third World sub-humanity. We can imagine here a figure like Gordon Brown or Tony Blair, with their contemptible, mealy-mouthed magnanimity towards poor African countries, once again playing the role of 'enlightened' colonial masters.

The second problem with this ethics of human rights, for Badiou, is that it attempts to ward off any sort of emancipatory project, any attempt at social transformation as a source of evil from which the worst consequences are likely to ensue:

> Such is the accusation so often repeated over the last fifteen years: every revolutionary project stigmatized as 'utopian' turns, we are told, into a totalitarian nightmare. Every will to inscribe an idea of justice or equality turns bad. Every collective will to the Good creates Evil.[18]

This ethical discourse is an ethics of finitude, a discourse that says it is better to avoid grand collective projects of emancipation because they always risk resulting in catastrophe; better to stick to finite projects aimed at avoiding suffering and enforcing human rights. For Badiou, this is a miserable ethics of resignation, an ethics of final reconciliation with the global hegemony of capitalism.

How should we respond to this resounding critique of ethics and the discourse of human rights? There is no doubt that the discourse of human rights has been subverted and manipulated by dominant powers, and is used as ideological window dressing for imperialism and global capitalism. Furthermore, it provides a kind of 'frame' through which we view, with a voyeuristic fascination, the violence and suffering of the Third World at a safe distance and with a comfortable sense of moral superiority. Badiou is right to suggest that humanitarian interventions, in their smug benevolence, conceal at the same time a

Ethics

contempt for the victims of poverty, famine and economic dislocation. And of course, here we should see these interventions – which are increasingly indistinguishable from military operations – as an example of a biopower exerted over populations reduced to 'bare life'. Furthermore, Badiou is right to argue that with this discourse politics is subordinated to ethics. What is needed in these Third World situations is not the 'benevolent' interventions and ethical pronouncements of wealthy Western countries, but rather authentic *political* projects of emancipation which emerge from within these situations themselves.[19] The Western discourse of ethical human rights seems to act to prevent this political dimension from emerging, thus preserving the status quo.

However, it is important here to separate the principles of human rights from the liberal-capitalist-imperialist framework in which they are currently articulated. In other words, in contrast to Badiou, I would suggest that human rights might have real emancipative and revolutionary potential, provided they can be disentangled from dominant global power structures and discourses in which their meaning is distorted and subverted. We have to recognise this two-sided nature of human rights discourse: while they appear as part of a dominant ideology, they also have the potential – if they are taken seriously – to undermine and destabilise this ideology. There is no reason why subjugated and exploited people around the world cannot invoke a universal conception of human rights in order to challenge and resist the power structures and economic relations which effectively deny them these rights. Furthermore, the content of human rights discourse can be deconstructed and thus expanded and rethought in all sorts of unpredictable and radical ways. I will say more about this later. However, what is important with the notion of human rights is its universality – the way that it offers an open universal politico-ethical horizon which people can refer to and draw upon in their struggles against domination.

Furthermore, I would also take issue with Badiou on the question of suffering, and the way this apparently serves as a basis for an ethics of human rights. While I agree with Badiou that Man as subject is precisely what transcends his biological substratum, and that ethics should therefore go beyond the mere alleviation of physical suffering, surely the alleviation of human suffering and misery – as well as the redress given to victims of genocide, ethnic cleansing, torture, economic apartheid and other crimes of the state – must at the same time be seen as *a* fundamental task of any politico-ethics. Behind Badiou's idea of Man as Immortal – a transcendent life beyond 'animal' concerns – there is a kind of Nietzschean pitilessness, almost a grand contempt, or at least disregard, for the 'smallness' of suffering. Certainly, a politico-ethics of emancipation must not dwell upon suffering; but at the same time, it cannot ignore it. Political solutions, rather than ethical hand-wringing, are of course the only way of addressing the causes of suffering. However, this also suggests that a radical politico-ethics must at the same time be concerned with the question of human

[*111*]

suffering, and must be motivated in some degree by a hatred of cruelty and injustice, and a pity for those who suffer.

The event of ethics

Badiou's gripe against ethical ideology is to do with its abstraction – an abstraction which leads to ideological conservatism, nihilism and the obstruction of radical politics. As an alternative to this, he proposes a radical revision of ethics: ethics must be understood in terms of a universal truth-event. As we saw in the preceding chapter, the truth-event, for Badiou, is what de-subjectifies the subject: it is a radical encounter with a universal truth which seizes hold of the subject, taking him 'out' of himself and disrupting his normal identity and social existence. Badiou sees ethics as a kind of fidelity to this truth-event – a willingness to think a situation according to the event which conditions it; to follow its path and affirm its consequences. In other words, ethics implies a perseverance of the subject in this truth event: 'Do all that you can in that which exceeds your perseverance. Persevere in the interruption. Seize in your being that which has seized and broken you.'[20] The typical sites of this ethic of truths, for Badiou, are *science*, *art*, *love* and *politics*. Ethics in such situations would be a willingness to think through the implications of a scientific breakthrough or recognise the novelty of an artistic innovation; to live one's life according to an amorous encounter or to proceed along a path invented by a revolution or insurrection, affirming the radical consequences of this event. What is important here is that this ethics of universal truth emerges from singular concrete situations rather than from abstract concerns about human rights and the categorical imperative. These situations are structured around a kind of void, and the event is what emerges from this void, while at the same time tracing its edges. We see that the event here forms the ontological ground for Badiou's notion of ethics: ethics does not depend on abstract deontological ethical imperatives, but rather on an encounter with a universal truth, and a fidelity to this event whose irruption disturbs the conditions of a normal situation, exposing the contingency of its foundations, the void upon which it rests.

What are we to make of this understanding of ethics, one that seems so different from the Aristotelian desire for the Good or the Kantian categorical imperative? Despite its idiosyncrasy, we can take from it a number of important consequences. First, ethics is a de-subjectifying experience: ethics is not based, in other words, on pre-given, essentialist tendencies in the subject or on some pre-ordained notion of the Good which the subject is supposed to follow. Rather, ethics is what radically disrupts the identity of the subject and takes him out of himself. Secondly, then, ethics takes the form of an event that irrupts in the stable normative order, throwing established forms of knowledge and ideas of the good into disarray; in this sense, it creates a space for ethical and, particularly, political experimentation. Thirdly, ethics is both universal and singular: while the truth-process which forms the ground for ethical experience is universal, the situations in which it emerges are singular and concrete. Again we see this theme of the universal-singular that I teased out in the previous chapter. While Badiou's intervention has certain problems, we can perhaps use it theorise the ontological conditions for a new radical politico-ethics.

Rorty and the ethics of postmodern irony

Another thinker who wants to free ethics from essential foundations – from established ideas about the good and the categorical imperative – is Richard Rorty. Yet, at the same time, we could not imagine two thinkers more different and radically opposed than Rorty and Badiou. For Rorty, the deconstruction of essential foundations leads not to an ethics of the infinite – the radical and universal truth-event as Badiou proposes – but, on the contrary, to an ethics of finitude: a recognition of the limits of language in understanding the world, and the limits of politics in changing it. Rorty would represent, perhaps even more than Lyotard, the postmodern 'age of the poets' which threatens to supplant philosophy and which Badiou so rails against.[21]

Like other thinkers broadly associated with the 'postmodern condition', Rorty recognises the breakdown of the social bond, the decline of metanarratives, the lack of absolute foundations and the plurality of language games that define the world. In this sense, for Rorty, it is impossible to see the world as an objective reality about which there is a stable agreement or consensus. The world is a contingent reality which is constructed by the sentences we use to describe it: the world is best understood in terms of the play of different metaphors.[22] For this reason, it is poetics, and particularly literature, which best defines the world, rather than science: the latter insists on an absolute truth, where the former plays with different modes of representation and experience. Because there is no universal understanding of truth in a contingent society – no categorical imperative or universal consensus – it is impossible to prescribe a particular understanding of morality or a right way to live our lives: we have to recognise that the individual in postmodern societies is engaged in a process of aesthetic self-creation which is entirely unique to him. Now the key ethical question for Rorty is how we reconcile this individual project of self-creation – a project which demands recognition and respect for difference – with the demand for some sort of public solidarity. Rorty's answer is to affirm a kind of split or separation between the two realms: a private, aesthetic realm of self-creation and 'postmodern irony', and a public realm of shared values, without there needing to be any correlation between the two. Moreover, according to Rorty, the only type of society in which this split is possible is a liberal society: a liberal society is one that recognises the contingency of its foundations, and which respects the right of individuals to pursue their own versions of the good life without enforcing any sort of collective or unifying principles upon them. A liberal society would be a society of 'strong poets'[23] – those who recognise the plurality of language games and the contingency of their own place in the world. At a public level, the function of liberal institutions would be to essentially leave people alone and to try to ameliorate different forms of suffering. The only solidarity necessary here is a broad recognition of a liberal 'we' – a shared acceptance of basic liberal principles.

Rorty is correct to recognise the absence of foundations that conditions contemporary society, as well as the contingency of social identities, ethical practices and political institutions. However, on this last point, his advocacy of a liberal polity is somewhat problematic. He seems to naturalise liberal society, or at least sees it as the highest point of conceptual development: 'Indeed, my hunch is that Western social and political thought may have had the last *conceptual* revolution it needs.'[24] This is because, in contrast to Foucault who unmasks the illiberal practices of liberal societies, Rorty believes that liberal societies, while they may be imperfect as they are, contain the institutions necessary for their own self-improvement. In other words, Rorty claims that liberalism forms the *ideal type* of polity – one in which 'postmodern ironists' can flourish – because it remains open to its own contingency, and is thus capable of changing and reforming in ways that other societies are not. However, are liberal societies really so open? While their institutions might be capable of certain political reforms, there does not seem much potential in liberal societies for broad social and economic transformation, for going beyond the capitalist paradigm. Indeed, it is such projects of economic and social transformation that Rorty remains suspicious of, and in his liberal utopia there is nothing to suggest any room for the redistribution of wealth and the promotion of economic equality. Furthermore, we find increasingly in liberal societies today a desire to anchor themselves in firm moral foundations – something that Rorty believes their virtue lies in avoiding. For instance, in the current conditions of the 'war on terror', not only do we see the resurgence of religious and conservative fundamentalism, but also a kind of liberal fundamentalism, found in the desire to not only root liberal societies in an explicit acceptance of liberal values, but also to impose these values on other people, in the conviction of their absolute moral and rational superiority. Thus we see, in the strange discourse of neoconservatism – many of whose exponents had their ideological origins in liberalism – a desire to extend the American liberal revolution to other parts of the world through the use of military power. Christopher Hitchens, a former Trotskyist, and now a forthright defender of the Bush Administration's foreign policy, particularly its intervention in Iraq, would be a good example of this. Furthermore, does not Rorty's notion of a 'liberal we' suggest a kind of liberal communitarianism that we see sustaining itself today through a racist opposition to the 'non-liberal' (Muslim) Other: that less enlightened, fundamentalist, obscurantist, women-oppressing, intolerant Other that is the object of so many liberal fantasies? Therefore, my problem with Rorty's argument is that, despite its anti-foundationalism, it ends up essentialising a liberal political paradigm – a paradigm which, contrary to what Rorty believes – is not all that open, or even all that 'liberal'.

At the very least, Rorty's ethics suggests a final reconciliation with liberal-capitalism, an ethics of quiet finitude and resignation – a shying away from collective projects of emancipation and social transformation for fear of their universality. For Rorty, contingency can only be realised and lived at the individual level, at the level of personal self-creation, and that is why he claims that there is no real alternative to liberalism. The problem here is two-fold, however. Firstly, the argument rests on the highly dubious idea that there can be a strict separation between private ethical life and public life – a compartmentalisation of identity which postmodernism itself, as well as other discourses like feminism, have challenged. Here one can say that postmodernism cannot successfully be articulated within a liberal paradigm – it is something which disrupts the neat separation of social roles and identities. Furthermore, there is a de-politicisation of the subject and ethics itself in Rorty: the subject has the freedom to reinvent himself in private life, to explore different modes of subjectivity, different ethical practices in the quest for self-perfection – a project which, as we have seen, seems perfectly suited to contemporary capitalism; however, in public life he must accept the liberal framework – he must not challenge its institutions or the social relations upon which it is based in any fundamental way. Moreover, there is no room for collective political projects in Rorty's postmodern liberal utopia: ethics is confined to the realm of the individual and to the simple 'respect for difference', and cannot become political ethics. Unlike Badiou, Rorty's notion of ethics does not provide any sort of basis for the emergence of emancipative politics and for collective political identities. The limitation of Rorty's understanding of ethics is that it equates the contingency of postmodernism with the private domain, seeing universality as a threat to contingency. This ends up, as we have seen, in a valorisation of the liberal project and the loss of any universal political dimension. By contrast, I would accept the premise of postmodern contingency, but would suggest that this can also appear on the side of the universal: as Badiou has shown, universality is a singular experience which emerges through a contingent event – in this sense it is the rarest thing of all.

The ethics of psychoanalysis

In contrast to Rorty's ethics of quiet finitude, Lacanian psychoanalysis suggests a notion of ethics that is more unconditional, radical and destabilising – more related, as we shall see, to the Kantian categorical injunction than the recognition of difference and the virtues of moderation. However, in psychoanalysis, the question of ethics is posed in an entirely different way to the traditional philosophical approaches: from a psychoanalytic perspective, ethics is not premised on the idea of an ideal or sovereign Good towards which we should strive. Psychoanalytic ethics is an ethics without a good that regulates conduct. In fact, the good is what stands in the way of desire, and therefore one of the purposes of psychoanalytic ethics must be to repudiate this ideal of the good: 'The sphere of the good erects a strong wall across the path of our desire.'[25] In contrast to traditional ethical thought, the ethics of psychoanalysis cannot be motivated by any quest to achieve a sense of harmony, balance or virtue in one's life – which were the traditional concerns of ethics. In this sense, Lacan echoes Freud's critique of morality, in which he saw morality as a repressive and coercive social force that produced neurosis and unconscious guilt, becoming internalised as the vindictive voice of the superego.[26]

However, neither Freud nor Lacan advocate the complete throwing off of moral limits and the reign of libertinage. For Freud, while morality is repressive, it plays at the same time a necessary role in guaranteeing civilisation.[27] For Lacan, the problem of transgressing the moral law is more complicated: transgressive enjoyment (*jouissance*) is only the *other side* of the moral law, and the desire to transgress moral law in the search for *jouissance* only reaffirms it. The libertine's quest for pleasure in opposition to moral law ends up in an internal deadlock in which internal prohibitions replace external ones. This critique of the libertine project is expanded in Lacan's radical reading of Kant with Sade. For Lacan, the Kantian moral law finds its paradoxical counterpart in the libertine transgressions of Sade: it is not merely that the coldness and austerity of the categorical imperative produces its own form of perverse and excessive enjoyment; it is also that excessive enjoyment itself becomes rigidified into its own cold, universal categorical imperative – an operation enacted in the sheer monotony encountered in the Sadeian boudoir. In other words, Sade unmasks the hidden enjoyment in Kantian law by holding up to it its dialectical mirror – a universal law of enjoyment: 'I have the right of enjoyment over your body, anyone can say to me, and I will exercise this right, without any limit stopping me in the capriciousness of the exactions that I might have the taste to satiate.'[28]

Lacan shows that the project of the libertines is a failure: 'The naturalist liberation of desire has failed historically.'[29] The increasingly desperate quest for enjoyment beyond the law only re-enacts the law, as the promised *jouissance* recedes further and further into the distance. Psychoanalytic ethics, while it is critical of the moral law, cannot, on the other hand, be simply an ethics of transgression, an ethics that seeks simply to liberate desire from the law. This insight has important implications for radical politics: an anti-authoritarian politics must always be aware of the limits of transgression, and the dangers of its own latent authoritarianism – of the new Master-in-waiting who lurks behind its libertarian desires.[30]

So if Lacan objects to the sovereign good and unmasks the perverse implications of the moral imperative, while at the same time resisting the lures of outright transgression and *jouissance*, then upon what terrain should we locate the ethics of psychoanalysis? Lacan's notion of ethics might be seen as a radical reformulation of Kant's categorical imperative, seeing ethics this time not as obedience to the moral law, but rather as acting in conformity with one's desire. The maxim for Lacanian ethics is, therefore: 'Have you acted in conformity with the desire that is in you?'[31] This question takes the form of an ethical judgement: it forces the subject to confront the question of his desire and the extent to which he might have already betrayed it. The figure who embodies pure desire, for Lacan, is Sophocles' character Antigone, who insists to the last – against the rational reasons to the contrary given by Creon, against the good of the city, and at the expense even of her own life – on proper burial rites for her brother. It is in this sense that *Antigone* 'reveals to us the line of sight that defines desire'.[32] The desire represented by the figure of Antigone is a desire that does not compromise, that is unconditional and which pits itself against what Lacan calls 'the service of the goods' – the smooth running of society and the normal conditions of existence. In this sense, the ethics of desire is one that goes beyond, and is at times in opposition to, the normal demands of daily life and established social norms and roles. This is not an ethics that seeks a comfortable or harmonious social existence: on the contrary, it is a radical ethics which obeys the law of desire, and which is on a different trajectory to that of the good. We can see here how different this notion of ethics is from that of Rorty: while both understandings of ethics insist on the importance of subjective desire, for Rorty this leads to a life of quietude and a comfortable reconciliation between private desire and the stability of the public liberal domain. By contrast, Lacan's notion of ethics is much more radical and unconditional, and thus more destabilising: it accepts no rapprochement with the social good, pursuing a path of desire which may lead to a disruption of the established social order. In this sense, Lacanian ethics is much closer to the theme of de-subjection that I have been pursuing in the previous chapter – it suggests a politics of contingency; an event whose unpredictability disrupts the established order.

However, while the ethics of desire, for Lacan, is not determined by considerations of the good – while it can find itself in opposition to the moral law – we should not see it as an injunction to transgress all limits. As we have seen, transgression only reaffirms the law. Rather, the ethics of desire seeks a suspension of this whole dialectic of transgression/law: unlike transgression, which aims at an imagined impossible *jouissance* beyond the moral law, desire exposes the emptiness, the void that really lies behind it. In this way, the ethics of desire resists closure, seeking to leave a space open for desire that really demands to *not* be satisfied. As Stavrakakis shows, psychoanalytic ethics does not try to master the real – the impossible dimension beyond the symbolic (and beyond moral law) – but simply to respect the dignity of its emptiness by *encircling* it.[33]

This last point, however, has been the site of some contention between certain Lacanian thinkers – particularly between Stavrakakis and Žižek. Stavrakakis has argued that this notion of encircling the real rather than attempting to grasp it, leads to a politico-ethics of hegemony and radical democracy, in which the key characteristic is its constitutive openness, its resistance to 'filling the gap' in the socio-symbolic order by concretising its foundations. By contrast, Žižek has interpreted Lacanian ethics in terms of an 'ethics of the act'. The act, as we mentioned in the last chapter, is an absolute decision which emerges *ex nihilo* and which retroactively constitutes its own foundations. Žižek has developed this notion of the psychoanalytic act into a kind of ethics of political decisionism – resulting in a politics that is not exactly democratic and which consolidates its position through openly authoritarian means. At issue in this debate is whether Lacanian ethics tends towards either a politics of finitude/negativity/lack or of the infinite/impossible. Žižek argues that Lacan's ethics shows that absolute acts – acts which are precisely impossible, which traverse the void – do indeed take place. Antigone's impossible demand – one that goes beyond the limits of the law – would be an example of this. Such acts have the dignity of a 'miraculous event' – something unforseen which, against all odds, does the impossible by completely re-inscribing the symbolic order. Furthermore, Žižek argues that such impossible acts also take place on the political field – a radical political act shows that '*only such an "impossible" gesture of pure expenditure can change the very coordinates of what is strategically possible within a historical constellation*'.[34] Stavrakakis, on the other hand, questions this idea of a miraculous event/impossible act, suggesting not only that this ignores the Lacanian insight that such acts emerge from finitude and lack, but also that it risks falling into the dangerous trap of transgression that Lacan warns us of.[35]

This question of finitude/lack vs. infinity in radical political ethics is an important one, and it forms one of the bases of current debates in continental political theory. It is also a question that I shall return to later when discussing the place of democracy in radical politics. At this stage, I would suggest that in this particular dispute over the Lacanian politico-ethics, both Stavrakakis and Žižek are correct in different ways and for different reasons: Stavrakakis is correct in drawing attention to Lacan's warnings about the dangers of transgression, of *going too far*; Žižek is also right to suggest that any real politics of emancipation must have a dimension of impossibility, of *demanding the impossible*, of fundamentally changing the coordinates of what is deemed to be politically possible. To give an example, formal left-wing political parties today see free-market global capitalism as an inevitability to which they have long since reconciled themselves – most of them no longer bothering even to ameliorate its effects through social democratic reforms. It is only when a political movement fundamentally challenges this system and proposes an alternative – when it demands the impossible, in other words – that this perceived inevitability begins to be questioned. It is worthwhile noting here that at the end of his article responding to Stavrakakis' critique, Žižek mentions the anti-globalisation movement as an example of a radical politics which is, precisely, doing the impossible – that is, challenging the global horizon of capitalism.[36] 'Miraculous events' in politics do indeed happen.

However, the problem I have with Žižek's take on Lacanian politico-ethics is not this desire to demand the impossible, but rather its overt authoritarianism – an authoritarianism which, I would suggest, is not a necessary component of radical politics, and indeed diminishes its emancipative force. As I have mentioned in the previous chapter, Žižek's ethics of the act often valorises a Leninist-style revolutionary politics of the vanguard, a politics that distinguishes itself from, in Žižek's eyes, 'bleeding heart liberals' by the willingness to assert the consequences of the revolutionary act, to consolidate the revolutionary regime through the ruthless exercise of power and the preparedness to use violence and terror against its opponents:

> The only 'realistic' prospect is to ground a new political universality by opting for the impossible, fully assuming the place of the exception, with no taboos, no apriori norms ('human rights', 'democracy'), respect for which would prevent us also from resignifying terror, the ruthless exercise of power, the spirit of sacrifice ... if this radical choice is decried by some bleeding-heart liberals as *Linksfaschismus*, so be it![37]

In other words, for Žižek, what is more important for a radical politics of universality than its destabilisation of the established political order, is its founding of a new order – something which can only be done, he claims, through authoritarian and possibly violent means, without regard to what most would consider to be ethical limits like respect for human rights. This is a politico-ethical position that almost revels in its ruthlessness, in its desire to exert power and violently transgress established norms and limits. What I would question here, firstly, is the idea that a universal politics of emancipation can be grounded in such measures: surely these authoritarian means stand at odds with the very idea of emancipation? Furthermore, such authoritarianism implies a vanguardist-style politics of a small revolutionary group seizing and maintaining power, a form of politics which would seem to have little to do with universality. Moreover, from an ethical point of view, Žižek really does succumb to the illusory and seductive lures of transgression: however, here we could say that in wanting to go too far – in wanting to transgress the ethical limits of human rights and democracy in a destructive whirl of violence and terror –

Žižek ends up by *not going far enough*. What I mean here is that the politics of authoritarianism and the ruthless exercise of power is really a *conservative-pragmatist* politics, a politics which seeks not to overthrow dominant power structures but to use them to exert power in a post-revolutionary situation.[38] The politics of emancipation, however, is not consolidated by such authoritarianism but *betrayed* by it.

It is here that Lacanian themes of finitude and lack become relevant. Finitude is not to be understood here in the same terms as Rorty's ethics of quiet resignation, from which any kind of emancipative politics is ruled out in advance. Rather, finitude should be seen in terms of a respecting certain limits – the limits of 'moderation' that Badiou has drawn attention to – instead of *passing to the act* as Žižek does. In other words, the Lacanian ethical injunction of *not giving way on one's desire* implies, at the same time, being able to take some degree of distance from it, rather than getting caught up in it. Žižek's ethics of the act gets caught up in an absolute revolutionary desire – leading only to a frenzied and violent authoritarianism, which in the end is deeply reactionary. Alenka Zupančič also points to certain limits that apply to Lacanian ethics: ethics is motivated by the Real – by the impossible dimension beyond the symbolic order – and yet ethical action cannot be the attempt to force an encounter with the Real:

> That is to say, we fall back into terror if we understand the term ethics to refer to an elaboration of a strategy designed to force the encounter with the Real, the Event, to happen: if we see it as a method for the production of the impossible.[39]

Is not Žižek's absolute act precisely the attempt to force an encounter with the Real, to produce the impossible in an artificial sense through the ruthless exercise of power; and is it any wonder, then, that this act is always accompanied by terror and violence?

Levinas, Derrida and the ethics of the Other

By dispensing with formal categories of the good, and by insisting on a kind of insurrectionary desire which defies social norms, Lacan has radicalised the understanding of ethics. However, as we have seen, this notion of ethics has to be accompanied by certain limits in order to prevent the desire for the impossible from descending into terror and violence. The catastrophe of revolutionary desire results not only from its betrayal and its turning towards reformism, but also from its potential to transgress all limits and to aim at consolidating itself in an absolute sense through authoritarian and terroristic means. In other words, the ethics of desire – while it pursues the impossible – must at the same time not try to concretise itself or establish an absolute ground for itself through the terrorism of the act, but rather sustain a certain space, a certain openness, and a certain constitutive distance between itself and the Real towards which it tends. In theorising this moment of openness which must define the ethical experience, we turn now to the project known as deconstruction.

Derrida's 'strategy' of deconstruction has always been understood as a certain way of reading texts, particularly philosophical texts, in order to uncover their *aporias* – in other words, their internal moments of self-contradiction and tension. Deconstruction is therefore a way of opening up a particular text to the moment of undecidability, where its consistency of meaning is suspended and new meanings and interpretations can emerge. It is a certain way of reading a text both *with and against* itself. In this way, deconstruction is aimed against the stabilisation and *closure* of meaning. However, this method of reading texts can also be seen as producing a certain ethical gesture: by interrogating philosophy in this way, deconstruction forces philosophy to confront its own internal structures of exclusion, its own discursive hierarchies in which one term is subordinated to another, as writing is to speech in Plato.[40] It is in this sense that, for Derrida, ethics cannot be reduced to morality – in other words to a series of established moral norms. Rather, ethics must involve a moment of openness, suspension and critical interrogation of this normative order: the question that ethics asks of morality is that if morality sees itself as absolute, can it still be moral?[41] This implies an ethics of openness – of *alterity*.

Derrida's ethics of alterity is influenced in large part by Emmanuel Levinas, who saw the ethical moment emerge from a point of exteriority which remained irreducible to the Same – this is the moment when the Same is called into question by the Other. According to Levinas, Western thought has been dominated by *logos* – by the idea of the knowing subject, the *ego*, the 'I' which remains identical to itself. It is through this sense of self-identity that we relate to the world, attempting to master and possess it, thus reducing the Other to the Same. However, there is a radical otherness which resists this 'imperialism of the same' and which remains absolutely Other, absolutely outside the experience of the Same. The ethical moment is when the 'I' recognises this Other, when he comes *face to face* with this Other – an experience in which his own self-identity is called into question:

> A calling into question of the same – which cannot occur within the egoistic spontaneity of the same – is brought about by the other. We name this calling into question of my spontaneity by the presence of the Other ethics. The strangeness of the Other, his irreducibility to the I, to my thoughts and my possessions, is precisely accomplished as a calling into question of my spontaneity, as ethics.[42]

Ethics is thus a radical experience of recognition, in which the 'I' recognises the Other in its strangeness and irreducibility and, more so, welcomes the Other. As long as the Other remains faceless or is not recognised, the ego is retained in its self-assurance – but the moment of recognition of the face of the Other shatters this sense of assurance and identity. One might think here of the way that in modern military operations – in which technology displaces hand to hand combat – killing becomes more efficient because the Other is faceless and anonymous: think of those countless faceless Afghans and Iraqis who have been killed anonymously in US military operations, operations which are fought with high-tech weapons such as laser-guided bombs and even military drones – unmanned, robotic planes which attack targets while being remote controlled thousands of miles away by some Pentagon technician. Here the (often civilian) victims of such attacks are precisely nameless and faceless – we do not usually even hear about their deaths. In this 'brave' new world of faceless warfare, such an ethical experience would be difficult to imagine. Indeed, more broadly, we can see the 'war on terror' as being based on an attempt to reduce the Other to anonymity: the Muslim Other has a face, but it is the violent, fanatical face that we have given him, the face behind which his Otherness is eclipsed. As Butler points out, we have no means even of mourning his death: in the 'war on terror', only 'our' deaths – the deaths of Westerners, the deaths of the 2,800 Americans killed in the WTC attacks, or the 52 Londoners killed in the underground bombings, can be mourned; while 'other lives will not find such fast and furious support and will not even qualify as grievable'.[43]

It is interesting to point out here the parallels between the Levinasian ethical relation, and the Lacanian encounter with the Real: both the Other for Levinas, and the Real for Lacan, occupy a position of radical exteriority to the ego, and the effects of the ego's encounter with this exteriority are traumatic in both cases. Moreover, it is this encounter with exteriority that constitutes the ethical dimension for both thinkers. However, the difference between the two approaches lies in this notion of the *absolutely Other*. For Lacan, there is no Other of the Other – that is, the symbolic order has no ultimate foundation outside itself, and thus its identity is split and inconsistent. For Levinas, on the other hand, the other presupposes an absolute 'identity' of Otherness, something which we can only understand as God.

However, despite the quasi-religious overtones of Levinas' thinking, this notion of the ethical relation as being mediated by an irreducible exteriority provides the basis for a radical new understanding of politico-ethics – one that is developed by Derrida. The ethics of the Other suggests that politics must always be mediated by an ethics which is *outside* it and which transcends it. In other words, political institutions, identities and practices can never form closed, all-encompassing systems; there is always an ethical moment which exceeds them and which points to their outside, opening them to a radical questioning and thus destabilising their foundations. Politics is always exposed to the ordeal of the ethical, to the eternal moment of questioning in which it is forced to confront its own exclusion of the Other. However, this ethical moment does not depoliticise politics or reduce it to impotence; rather, it demands of politics that it live up to a certain justice, thus opening it to the possibility of a just polity. As Simon Critchley argues, 'there must be a certain creative antagonism between ethics and politics which ensures that justice is done in the sight of the Other's face'.[44] Indeed, for Levinas, justice depends on an infinite responsibility to the Other, an unequal, infinite relationship that, at the same time, has the potential to lead to a more egalitarian polity:

> The equality of all is borne by my inequality, the surplus of my duties over my rights ... It is then not without importance to know if the egalitarian and just State in which man is fulfilled proceeds from a war of all against all, or from the irreducible responsibility of the one for the all, and if it can do without friendship and faces.[45]

In this way, the ethical relation, which produces an obligation of recognition and responsibility to the Other, can lead to a questioning of existing political institutions – especially the state: the question that is raised by Levinas here is whether the state is just or can ever be just. If the state is based on the premise of the war of all against all – as posited by traditional understandings of sovereignty – then surely it can never be just. Yet if the state is based on the infinite responsibility of the one for the all, then surely this would make problematic the very foundations of sovereignty which legitimise the state. I shall return to this question of sovereignty later, but the point here is that Levinasian ethics – because it submits politics to a kind of tribunal of justice – opens the possibility for a radical critique of political institutions and structures.

The idea that politics must be exposed to an ethics that is outside it, to a higher possibility of justice, has a certain Kantian ring to it – and it is certainly the case that there is a strong ethical injunction at work in the thinking of Levinas and Derrida. However, Derrida is critical of Kant's notion of moral duty and the categorical imperative which, he argues, turns ethics into a regulative and rationally calculable ideal, something that can be applied in an absolute sense to concrete situations.[46] Ethics and justice cannot be the simple application of a rule or the realisation of a norm, because this obscures the trial of undecidability which every ethical decision and every application of justice must experience. This notion of *undecidability* is crucial to Derrida's understanding of ethics and justice: it implies that we cannot rely on strict normative criteria to guide us in our decision – there is no absolute moral ground, no Kantian regulative ideal in which justice would be the mere application of a rule – and yet we *must* make ethical decisions. The ethical decision, in other words, must pass through this moment of undecidability in which there are no guarantees. The ethical decision, in this sense, is a *moment of madness* – a kind of leap into the unknown: indeed, the ethical moment can be seen precisely in this gap that exists between the decision and the normative order. This notion of ethics as making decisions without firm moral and rational criteria to guide us, does not amount to a kind of nihilism or a-morality, as many have alleged. On the contrary, as Derrida shows, if ethics were the mere application of a rule, then there could no longer be any conception of ethical responsibility, and thus no possibility of justice: 'the decision then no longer decides anything but simply gets deployed with the automatism attributable to machines'.[47]

Justice, human rights and hospitality 'to come'

The importance given in Derrida's thinking to the *decision* suggests that deconstruction not only has a strong ethical component but also a strong political dimension as well – contrary to what many critics have claimed. Not only is the question of the decision central to political theory, but it has become even more crucial to an understanding of the post-foundational political and social field: politics today involves making all sorts of decisions without guarantees, without firm normative criteria. In Derrida's earlier writings, which were devoted to the deconstruction of texts, there were broader, though less obvious, political implications: politics could be seen, from a deconstructive perspective, as a kind of 'text' itself, in which dominant institutions and practices are based on a series of discourses and rationalities which form our political identities, our perception of social relations and our understanding of the limits of what is possible in politics. Therefore, a deconstruction of these discourses and rationalities – an unmasking of their hidden contradictions and binary structures – could potentially lead to a rethinking of actual political institutions and practices, and a questioning of the assumptions and discursive myths from which they draw their authority and prestige. In this sense, the deconstructive enterprise can be seen as a kind of textual (and political) *anti-authoritarianism*.[48] However, Derrida's later writings have become more explicitly political, dealing with questions of human rights, sovereignty and terrorism. Here I will briefly examine three politico-ethical 'figures' in Derrida's thought, to show their relevance to radical politics today. Central to all these figures, as we shall see, is a deconstructive critique of authority – particularly the political principle of sovereignty.

For example, Derrida insists on a gap between justice and law: the law, as we have seen, is the application of a rule and, because of this, it occludes the dimension of personal responsibility which forms the basis of justice. Therefore, justice cannot be simply the application of a legal rule or norm: rather it must go through the ordeal of undecidability. In this sense, justice forms a kind of internal limit to the structure of law: it is what opens law to the other, to alterity, to the singularity of the decision that it cannot account for. While law is the application of the rule, justice is what continually reinvents the rule by applying it in different and unpredictable ways. Moreover, this operation unmasks the discursive violence which forms the underside of every legal decision. The law itself is based on a founding violence, which is both disavowed and, yet, enacted each time the law is applied. This founding or *originary* violence is what Derrida refers to as the 'mystical foundation of authority': the authority of the law is ultimately grounded in something that, at the same time, exceeds it, something that is, strictly speaking, *non-legal* because it had to exist prior to law – a violence without ground. As Derrida says: 'Since the origin of authority, the foundation or ground, the position of the law can't by definition rest on anything but themselves, they are themselves a violence without ground.'[49] Foucault, in a similar way as we have seen, exposes the violent origins of political institutions and laws, *the blood that has dried on the codes of law*. What is being revealed here is the aporetic character of the law itself. Justice has the paradoxical function of both affirming the law by acting in its name, and, at the same time, suspending the law by revealing the performative violence of the decision upon which it is ultimately based – thus opening the law to undecidability and allowing it to be interpreted in different and novel ways. Because justice performs a deconstructive operation upon the law in this sense, it cannot be deconstructed: justice, for Derrida, *is* deconstruction, or at least a fundamental condition for it.[50] Justice, in the sense that it goes beyond the structures of the law, is infinitely perfectible; justice is always 'to come', an event that 'exceeds calculation, rules, programs, anticipations …'[51]

It is this condition of infinite improvement, infinite perfectibility, that also informs Derrida's understanding of human rights, something that is closely bound up with the possibility of justice. As we have seen, Derrida insists on unconditional rights when it comes to resisting sovereignty and global hegemonies today. However, it would be a mistake to see this demand for human rights strictly in terms of the Kantian categorical imperative: this would reduce human rights to the application of a set of universal rules and norms, as in the law. Derrida also seeks to free the understanding of human rights from their traditional foundations in Enlightenment rationalist ideas about a universal human nature. A deconstructive approach reveals the historicity of human rights – the way they are constructed around a particular form of subjectivity and a particular, rather than universal, epistemological position. However, rather than this leading to the weakening of rights – as many, including Habermas have charged – it can actually lead to a fuller and more universal understanding of human rights. For Derrida, the supposed universality of human rights has been based on a series of discursive exclusions: traditionally, women, children, non-Western 'barbarians', the mentally ill etc, had been deprived of human rights in classical liberal discourse. By unmasking these exclusions, a deconstructive approach actually forces human rights to *live up to their own promise of universality*: it allows human rights to continue to be extended, as they have been historically, to a whole a series of previously excluded identities. In other words, by deconstructing the discursive limits of human rights, this approach shows that, like justice, human rights are infinitely perfectible and always 'to come': 'We are in need of them and they are in need, for there is always a lack, a shortfall, a falling short, an insufficiency; human rights are never sufficient.'[52] Here we see that, rather than a deconstructive/poststructuralist analysis depriving us of a universal dimension of human rights, it actually allows it to be realised.

Furthermore, according to Derrida, human rights must be freed from the category of the state and state sovereignty: human rights have traditionally been conditional upon one's citizenship in a nation; and even the Universal Declaration of Human Rights, while it was revolutionary in proposing that human rights would not be confined to national borders, was still dependent on the consent of nation states. However, there is an element of human rights discourse which situates itself in opposition to the state, and which provides a certain guarantee for a civil society that is beyond the state and which rallies against it. It is this anti-sovereign dimension of human rights that Derrida is interested in: he suggests that with the formation of institutions such as international courts of justice, and the concept of war crimes and crimes against humanity, it is in the 'name of human rights and their universality that the sovereign authority of the state is called into question'.[53] With the universalisation and globalisation of human rights – rights that are being invoked by so many radical political struggles around the world today – we are seeing the possibility of a global civil society emerging, one that increasingly presents itself as an alternative to the current global order of the 'security' state and neo-liberal economics. Here Derrida suggests that we must cultivate the Kantian tradition of cosmopolitanism, world citizenship and the idea of perpetual peace, while at the same time deconstructing its foundations, and revising and updating it.[54] In this way, deconstructive politico-ethics stands *with and against* Kant.

This cosmopolitan tradition that Derrida invokes suggests not only a principle of 'cosmopolitan right' – rights that are beyond the state and a condition for a global citizenship – but also a concept of 'hospitality'. For Kant, hospitality is not only a universal right but also an obligation. Derrida sees this right to hospitality as an idea with important ethical and political implications: refugees and asylum seekers around the world could lay claim to this universal right, thus imposing upon us – particularly in the wealthy West – an infinite obligation to show hospitality to these people without a home. Here again, in this notion of infinite responsibility to the other, the stranger, we can hear echoes of Levinas: indeed, as Derrida suggest, ethics – in this Levinasian sense that we have defined it here – *is* hospitality. However, in a typical deconstructive move, Derrida explores some of the aporias, contradictions and inconsistencies in this notion of hospitality. He shows, for instance, that the word hospitality is defined through its opposition to *hostility* – hostility to the stranger based on the friend/enemy distinction – and thus he refers to 'hosti-pitality' to show that the discourse of hospitality is always marked by the term it tries to distinguish itself from.[55] This points to the central contradiction or moment of undecidability that Derrida detects in the concept of hospitality: on the one hand, hospitality reaffirms the idea that one is *master* of one's house to which one welcomes the stranger – hospitality is thus always conditional on the will of the master. On the other hand, hospitality implies an unconditional right of the stranger, and an unconditional obligation placed on the master of the house, such that this position of mastery – of guarding the threshold and determining the conditions of the stranger's entry – is itself thrown into question. These two aspects of hospitality cannot easily be reconciled. To give an example, in Australia in the 2001 federal election campaign – an election that was held in the midst of (government manipulated) fears about asylum seekers and terrorism – one of the key slogans from the conservative party's successful election platform was: 'WE decide who comes into this country, and the circumstances in which they come!'[56] The implied meaning here was: 'we' – as a sovereign country – reserve the right to determine our own conditions of entry for those who want to come here; 'we' are a welcoming country, but there are limits to our welcome. A real, unconditional hospitality – as opposed to this mantra of national sovereignty and policed borders – is something that destabilises the very principle of state sovereignty itself, opening it up to the unlimited demand of the other: a true ethics of hospitality, Derrida argues, can never be conditional. It is in this context that Derrida talks about the possibility of re-establishing the ancient concept of 'cities of refuge' throughout the world – spaces which would be open to refugees and asylum seekers, and which would be beyond the sovereignty of the state. The need for such spaces, which are modelled on the city rather than the state, is critical today in the face of increasingly excessive and draconian restrictions that the state imposes on asylum seekers.[57] Like justice and human rights, moreover, this notion of hospitality and cosmopolitanism – which might one day take the form of cities of refuge – is always perfectible, and thus always open, always 'to come'.

From these interrelated politico-ethical figures we can draw upon a number of themes. Firstly, justice, human rights and cosmopolitanism/hospitality are all subject to a deconstructive analysis which seeks to interrogate their traditional foundations – whether it be a certain understanding of human nature or human essence, an immanent rationality or a universal moral imperative. Secondly, such a deconstruction, far from displacing and weakening these principles, opens them up to an even more radical universality – one of infinite perfectibility – in which they can be extended to ever more marginalised and currently excluded identities. Thirdly, these principles are always situated in opposition to state sovereignty and define a space beyond it – they are invoked against sovereignty and thus become increasingly important in the anti-sovereignist struggles of civil society. Fourthly, these ethical principles can only be fully understood against a background of globalisation: globalisation, while it is highly ambiguous in its effects, is increasingly providing the horizon through which these principles can be realised, albeit only imperfectly. Globalisation is a process which leads to a weakening of the traditional model of the nation state, and because of this, it is defining a space in which new understandings of global justice, global human rights and global hospitality can arise.

The anti-sovereign aspect of these ethical figures that Derrida constructs, highlights the anti-authoritarian dimension that I see as central to any radical political ethics – indeed, we might say, to any notion of ethics at all. It is also for this reason that I see Derrida's politico-ethics as more compelling than either Rorty's ethics of 'postmodern irony', or Žižek's psychoanalytic 'ethics of the act': the former cannot mount any effective challenge to liberal polity and capitalism, and cannot serve as a basis for a collective, universal politico-ethical experience; while the latter – aside from questions relating to how closely it actually conforms to Lacan's psychoanalytic notion of the ethics – ends up, in an absolute desire to transgress moral norms and concretise emancipative universality, in a ruthless vanguard politics of pragmatism and authoritarianism. Yet, to what extent does Derrida's politico-ethics live up to the universal political event that Badiou saw as arising from singular situations, the event which, in the wake of the breakdown of moral and rational metanarratives, forms perhaps the only ontological ground upon which ethics may be considered? While in contrast to Badiou, I would insist that human rights form an important component of any radical political ethics, I have also suggested, along with Derrida, that they must be reformulated. To this end, we could say that the 'perfectibility' of justice and human rights does not mean they exist as abstract Kantian norms according to which every situation is judged and falls short; but rather that these norms themselves are always insufficient for grasping concrete situations – they are always lacking, always perfectible, always 'to come'. As such, they exist as an immanent potentiality within radical political situations. Furthermore, they can be reinterpreted and used in unpredictable ways, particularly in ways that question and resist the authority of the sovereign institutions which have now become the official transmitters of 'ethics discourse'. Moreover, notions such as justice, human rights and hospitality open onto the possibility of a universal politico-ethical experience: as we see, their universality is invoked by increasingly global struggles against domination and inequality.

However, on this last point, we would have to ensure that the supranational political and human rights institutions that Derrida draws upon as possible examples of a new polity, do not simply repeat the gesture of sovereignty. This would have to involve the invention of new forms of politics which avoid or go beyond sovereignty, institutionalism and authoritarianism, and this raises the question of democracy. In what sense can democracy serve as the basis for this new politics of universal emancipation – or, another way of formulating this question might be *is democracy the only ethical form of polity?* This will be examined in the next chapter.

Notes

1 See Foucault, 'Preface to *Anti-Oedipus*', *Essential Works*, pp. 106–110.
2 J.-F. Lyotard and J.-L. Thebaud, *Just Gaming*, trans. W. Godzich (Minneapolis: University of Minnesota Press, 1985), p. 16.
3 Lyotard and Thebaud, *Just Gaming*, p. 26.
4 I. Kant, *Critique of Practical Reason*, trans. T. Kingsmill Abbot (London: Longmans, 1963) p. 38.
5 Moreover, the US Attorney General has redefined torture in such a way – as having to involve either death or 'significant organ failure' – as to make it unintelligible.
6 See A. Dershowitz, 'Tortured reasoning', in S. Levinson (ed.) *Torture: A Collection* (USA: Oxford University Press, 2004). See also Dershowitz's essay 'Rules of war enable terror', in which he argues that the current Geneva Conventions on the treatment of prisoners are outdated and have become an impediment to the 'war on terror': <www.aish.com/jewishissues/middleeast/Rules_of_War_Enable_Terror.asp>; as well as A. Dershowitz, *Why Terrorism Works* (Melbourne: Scribe Publications, 2003).
7 See S. Žižek, *Welcome to the Desert of the Real: Five Essays on September 11 and Related Dates*, (London: Verso, 2002), pp. 102–104.
8 In John Gray's satirical essay 'Torture: a modest proposal', he envisions a nightmarish scenario in which judicial torture becomes totally legitimised and accepted, in which universities would offer courses on torturing skills, and where torturers would have access to psychotherapists who would help them overcome their 'negative self-image'. Torture would become a hideous categorical imperative, a kind of Sadeian right to torture: 'In fact, in a truly liberal society, terrorists have the inalienable right to be tortured.' See *Heresies: Against Progress and Other Illusions* (London: Granta Books, 2004), pp. 132–138.
9 See Jacques Derrida in G. Borradori, *Philosophy in a Time of Terror: Dialogues with Jurgen Habermas and Jacques Derrida* (Chicago: University of Chicago Press, 2004), p. 132 (original emphasis).
10 Foucault, 'Useless to revolt?', *Essential Works*, pp. 449–453, p. 453.
11 Foucault, 'Useless to revolt?', *Essential Works*, p. 453.
12 See Žižek, *The Ticklish Subject*, p. 345.
13 See J. Lacan, 'A theoretical introduction to the functions of psychoanalysis in criminology', *JPCS: Journal for the Psychoanalysis of Culture and Society*, 1: 2 (1996): 13–25, p. 15.
14 B. Noys, *The Culture of Death* (New York: Berg, 2005), pp. 77–79.
15 I share many of the concerns here raised by people such as Noys, Agamben and Badiou on the question of euthanasia – although at the same time, I would defend the right of people to end their own lives in an assisted way in order to avoid intense pain and suffering. What I see as more at issue here is the danger of euthanasia being determined and administered by the state.
16 See also C. Mouffe, 'The ethics of democracy', in *The Democratic Paradox* (London: Verso, 2000), pp. 131–140.
17 Badiou, *Ethics*, p. 2.
18 Badiou, *Ethics*, p. 13.

19 Badiou, *Ethics*, p. 13.
20 Badiou, *Ethics*, p. 47.
21 See Badiou, *Manifesto for Philosophy*, pp. 69–78.
22 Richard Rorty, *Contingency, Irony and Solidarity* (Cambridge: Cambridge University Press, 1989), p. 5.
23 Rorty, *Contingency, Irony and Solidarity*, p. 53.
24 Rorty, *Contingency, Irony and Solidarity*, p. 63.
25 J. Lacan, *The Ethics of Psychoanalysis 1959–1960: The Seminar of Jacques Lacan, Book VII*, ed. J.-A. Miller, trans. D. Porter (London: Routledge, 1992), p. 230.
26 See S. Freud, 'The Ego and the Id', *The Freud Reader*, ed. P. Gay (London: Vintage, 1995), pp. 628–658, p. 655.
27 See Freud, 'The future of an illusion', *The Freud Reader*, pp. 685–721, p. 690.
28 Jacques Lacan, 'Kant with Sade', *October*, 51 (1989): 55–95, p. 58
29 Lacan, *The Ethics of Psychoanalysis*, p. 4.
30 Lacan's suspicions about radical politics were expressed in his infamous warning to the student protestors of May 1968 in Paris: 'Revolutionary aspirations have only one possibility: always to end up in the discourse of the master. Experience has proven this. What you aspire to as revolutionaries is a master. You will have one!' (Cited in Stavrakakis, *Lacan and the Political*, p. 12). I have also explored some of these ambiguities in 'Interrogating the master: Lacan and radical politics', *Psychoanalysis, Culture and Society*, 9 (2004): 298–314.
31 Lacan, *The Ethics of Psychoanalysis*, p. 314.
32 Lacan, *The Ethics of Psychoanalysis*, p. 247.
33 Stavrakakis, *Lacan and the Political*, p. 130.
34 Slavoj Žižek, '"What some would call …": a response to Yannis Stavrakakis', *UMBR(a)* 1 (2003): 131–135, p. 133 (original emphasis).
35 See Yannis Stavrakakis, 'The lure of Antigone: aporias of the ethics of the political', *UMBR(a)*, 1 (2003): 117–129.
36 See Žižek, '"What some would call …"', p. 135.
37 Laclau, Butler and Žižek, *Contingency, Hegemony, Universality*, p. 326.
38 Here I have often been struck by Žižek's advocacy of ruthless pragmatism in politics, and especially his admiration for conservatives' apparent willingness to 'get their hands dirty'. See Rex Butler and Scott Stephens' article 'Slavoj Žižek's Third Way', in which they suggest that Žižek's politics can be seen, in a paradoxical way, as a kind of liberal conservatism which would be akin to Tony Blair's 'Third Way' project: <www.lacan.com/zizway.htm>. Žižek expresses his admiration for the pragmatism and 'honesty' of Third Way politics: '… what I find honest about the Third Wayists is that at least they openly show their cards. They don't bluff in the sense of relying on some fetishistic notion of the left …'. See S. Žižek and G. Daly, *Conversations with Žižek* (Cambridge: Polity Press, 2004), p. 146.
39 A. Zupančič, *Ethics of the Real: Kant, Lacan* (London: Verso, 2000), p. 236.
40 See J. Derrida, *Dissemination*, trans. B. Johnson (Chicago: University of Chicago Press, 1981), p. 148.
41 See R. Kearney, 'Derrida's ethical re-turn', in G. B. Madison (ed.) *Working Through Derrida* (Illinois: Northwestern University Press, 1993).
42 E. Levinas, *Totality and Infinity: An Essay on Exteriority*, trans. A. Lingis (Pittsburgh: Duquesne University Press, 1969), p. 43.
43 Butler, *Precarious Life*, p. 32.
44 Simon Critchley, *The Ethics of Deconstruction: Derrida and Levinas* (Oxford: Blackwell, 1992), p. 233.

45 E. Levinas, *Otherwise than Being or Beyond Essence*, trans. A. Lingis (The Hague: Martinus Nijhoff Publishers, 1981), p. 161.
46 See Derrida in Borradori, *Philosophy in a Time of Terror*, pp. 134–135.
47 Derrida in Borradori, *Philosophy in a Time of Terror*, p. 134.
48 John Caputo has suggested that Derrida's thinking can be seen as a kind of 'responsible anarchy'. See John Caputo, 'Beyond aestheticism: Derrida's responsible anarchy', *Research in Phenomenology*, 19 (1988): 59–73.
49 Derrida, 'Force of law', p. 14.
50 See J. Derrida, *Deconstruction in a Nutshell: A Conversation with Jacques Derrida*, ed. J. Caputo (New York: Fordham University Press, 1997), p. 16.
51 Derrida, 'Force of law', p. 27.
52 Derrida in Borradori, *Philosophy in a Time of Terror*, p. 132.
53 Derrida in Borradori, *Philosophy in a Time of Terror*, p. 132.
54 Derrida in Borradori, *Philosophy in a Time of Terror*, p. 130. Here, also, James Brasset and Federico Merke suggest that deconstructive strategies can be used not only to destabilise the traditional theoretical categories and concepts of International Relations discourse, but also to rethink existing international institutions and relationships that are based on these categories. See 'Just deconstruction? Derrida and global ethics', in P. Hayden and C. el-Ojeili (eds) *Confronting Globalization: Humanity, Justice and the Renewal of Politics* (New York: Palgrave, 2005), pp. 50–67.
55 See J. Derrida, 'Hostipitality', trans. B. Stocker, *Angelaki*, 5:2 (December 2000): 3–18, p. 5.
56 This was a slogan taken from a speech on Australia's refugee and border protection policy given by the incumbent Prime Minister John Howard.
57 See J. Derrida, *On Cosmopolitanism and Forgiveness*, trans. M. Dooley and M. Hughes (London: Routledge, 2001), pp. 1–24.

5

Democracy

IN THE PRECEDING chapter I tried to construct a radical understanding of ethics, founding it not on some pre-given notion of the good or a rational consensus, but rather on the singularity of an event which disrupts this consensus. Furthermore, I suggested that ethics must contain an anti-authoritarian dimension which situates itself in opposition to established political institutions and practices. Ethics, in other words, is what opens political institutions to the other that they exclude, revealing the undecidability of their own foundations through which the dull visage of the sovereign appears.

The question which immediately presents itself here is that of the relationship between ethics and democracy. In other words, should democracy be seen as simply another polity or regime that must be subject to an ethical interrogation of its limits and foundations; or should it be seen as a mode of politics which incorporates this ethical interrogation into its own structures, and which remains open to the other as a consequence of its perpetual indeterminacy? That is to say, to what extent can democracy be seen as either a totalising form of politics or one which remains open to difference and undecidability; does democracy seek absolute foundations or is it founded irretrievably on their absence; is democracy simply another guise for sovereignty and inequality, or is it a political logic which radically throws them into question? To some extent, though, this question is badly posed: I shall suggest here that both dimensions are present in democracy, and that it remains in tension with itself. The chapter will explore this constitutive tension central to democracy and, through this, will investigate the theoretical conditions for democracy's renewal and radicalisation.

The crisis of democracy

It is now a commonplace to say that democracy today is in dire need of renewal, and that its triumph – symbolised by the eclipse of the Communist systems –

has now coincided with its global crisis. The enthusiasm which initially greeted the democratic revolutions in Eastern Europe in the late 1980s/early 1990s quickly turned to bewilderment and consternation as what ensued – economic dislocation, oligarchic crony capitalism and virulent nationalism – made a mockery of Fukuyama's liberal democratic dreams. The more the liberal democratic capitalist form was universalised, the more its own hidden truth of violence, dislocation and communitarian identification revealed itself. The rise of religious fundamentalism around the world is not to be seen as simply the last bastion of obscurantism, the last hurdle to be overcome before the eternal reign of the liberal democratic peace, but rather as a contradiction that emerges from within the logic of global postmodern capitalism itself and the liberal democratic paradigm through which it is being foisted on the entire planet.[1] So what have we to show for our liberal democratic experiment?: an ex-KGB man is once again in the Kremlin, evoking the authoritarian dreams of old but with the official democratic stamp of approval (albeit wearing a bit thin these days) especially as he is 'a strong ally in the war on terror'; the contestation of the liberal democratic 'consensus' now takes the form not only of nationalist strife and fundamentalist terror, but also, as if in a kind of dialectical *Aufheben*, of fundamentalist democracy, in which the democratic aspiration is not for liberal institutions but for Sharia law.

One could be forgiven, then, for being disenchanted with democracy at the moment. It appears to be little more than a kind of global brand or logo which every dictator around the world likes to drape himself in. The recent elections in Belarus saw the incumbent president getting over eighty per cent of the vote, having learnt a valuable lesson from the West about the political efficacy of using the spectre of 'terrorism' as a way of discouraging dissent and protest. Democracy is now a universal standard of legitimacy for every regime – it is impossible to not be, formally at least, a democrat, and there is now a global injunction to join the democratic 'family of nations'. And yet the standards for democratic legitimacy seem to be impossibly *low* – Afghanistan and Iraq, while there is Islamic religious law in the former and civil war in the latter, are now said to be 'burgeoning democracies'. The recent case of a man in Afghanistan who was facing the death penalty for the crime of apostasy caused considerable embarrassment to the Western nations who so 'selflessly' got rid of the Taliban regime so that democracy and freedom could flourish in its place.

It seems clear that the global democratic project is really a global imperialist project, in which Western and particularly American hegemony is ruthlessly asserted around the world through the use of military force. 'Democracy' is the ideology of this hegemonic power, its standard bearer, operating as a pretext for violent regime change and the brutal coercion of less powerful countries. Democracy is, as Badiou points out, a way of organising a consensus around this imperialist project – a consensus which is sustained by war.[2] The 'war on terror' therefore styles itself as a war designed to spread democracy around the world, or at least to defend democratic 'values' against what Tony Blair and George Bush are both fond of calling a 'hate filled ideology'. However, it would seem that for these ideologues of the global imperial democratic project, democracy equates simply with the free market, and perhaps more so, with US economic interests, and that democratic interventions around the world are a way of stabilising global capitalism, which essentially boils down to making the world safe for American corporations. Moreover, the absurdity of this conviction that democracy, even of the limited American kind, can be imposed through military force, finds its ultimate answer in the catastrophe that is Iraq – not only in its blood-filled streets but also in the torture chambers of Abu Ghraib, whose perverse goings on were a kind of *mise en scène* of this democratic farce.

And what of democracy closer to home? In some ways it fares little better. Perhaps the only consolation for those around the world who suffer from the excesses of the Western imperial democratic project is that in the West itself democracy takes a similarly depleted, impoverished and hypocritical form. For years, political scientists and commentators have been lamenting falling levels of voter turnout and the consequent decline in democratic legitimacy; but on the other hand, can anyone really blame people for not having the slightest interest in the sham that passes for democratic politics today? The ideological convergence between mainstream political parties, the consequent lack of any meaningful political choice, the spin and media management, all combine to turn democracy into a kind of simulacra of politics: a media-driven, opinion poll-obsessed orgy of mediocrity, in which voting – while symbolised as the highest democratic act – becomes a meaningless ritual to be performed every few years to elect a new set of masters. The entity known as 'the people' in modern democracies simply does not exist beyond a constructed mediatised image, a simulacrum brought into being and given meaning through endless opinion polls and voter surveys. The 'issues' are constructed for us in advance by the corporate-media machine which operates in a kind of seamless circuit with politicians, policy makers, image consultants and media minders – a circuit to whose functioning 'the people' appear to be increasingly irrelevant. Politicians like Silvio Berlusconi embody, in an exaggerated form, this ultimate convergence between politics and the media, getting around the problem of media management by simply becoming the media.

Moreover, can we not perceive the face of tyranny behind this democratic media spectacle? It is with some desperation that Western democratic leaders try to distinguish themselves from those authoritarian regimes 'out there' when it is becoming increasingly clear that authoritarianism is also to be found 'in here'. A new paradigm is emerging of the security state, in which liberal democracies are transforming themselves – in the very name of protecting democracy – into authoritarian and surveillance regimes in which democratic limits and rights are

[*134*]

increasingly restricted and violated. The whole series of 'anti-terrorist' laws and measures that have been implemented in recent years – everything from the expansion of surveillance powers to the permanent detention without trial of terrorist suspects – shows that we can no longer speak with any intelligibility about the difference between *actually existing* democratic and authoritarian systems. There is a blurring of the distinction here – democracy slides into authoritarianism under the guise of 'security', and governments not only restrict democratic rights but appear to be increasingly unaccountable. The fact that in 2003, governments around the world ignored the protests of millions of their citizens against the war in Iraq, and that the British government actually used this as an excuse to ban protests within a 1km radius of Westminster, shows what democracy has become today in the era of the 'war on terror'. The only recognisable features of a modern democracy now are a parliament, which is quite often dominated by one side of politics, and a neo-liberal market, about which there is little disagreement, in any case, on *either* side of politics. Badiou has preferred to call modern democracy 'capitalist parliamentarianism'[3] and I think this is a good name for it.

We should concede, however, that democracy – despite its manufactured, contrived and depleted nature today – still has some surprises in store for us. The election of Hamas in Palestine, and the left-wing ballot box revolutions in Venezuela and Bolivia – while very different phenomena – still show that occasionally democracy has some life in it, and that at times democracy can go against the wishes of the global democratic imperialist consensus, throwing in its face its own ideological discourse, as if to say *if you are serious about spreading democracy around the world today, then you must accept its consequences.* So while democracy can generally be said to be in a state of crisis at the moment, unpredictable events which occur through the democratic system allow us to reflect more deeply on what democracy actually means today and how it might be renewed.

My analysis of democracy will not start with the assumption that democracy actually exists today – I am not sure that it does – but rather with the question of whether or not democracy today is possible. In other words, the re-evaluation and possible renewal of democracy must start with a questioning of democracy, a questioning not only of its existence but also its desirability and relevance for radical politics. Badiou and Žižek are two thinkers who throw down the gauntlet here and openly challenge the value of democracy – although they reach somewhat different conclusions. Both thinkers denounce what they see as a kind of ideological injunction that exists today to be a democrat: they argue that the consensus on democracy has become so pronounced – particularly on the Left after the collapse of Communist systems – that today it is practically impossible to not be a democrat. The democratic consensus has become totalitarian in form, imposing upon everyone the demand to be a democrat, to respect the rules and procedures of democracy. As Badiou says:

It is forbidden, as it were, not to be a democrat. More precisely, it stands to reason that humanity aspires to democracy, and any subjectivity suspected of not being democratic is deemed pathological. At best it refers to a patient re-education, at worst the right of military intervention by democratic paratroopers.[4]

However, the problem with this democratic consensus is that it has become a barrier to radical political thought and action. In other words, accepting democracy now equates with accepting the liberal-parliamentary regime and the capitalist system – to such an extent that any questioning of this system, any talk of an alternative to liberal capitalism, is automatically ruled out in advance as 'undemocratic' and potentially totalitarian. In this discursive paradigm, any sort of politics of emancipation and social transformation is seen as potentially leading to the gulag. Indeed, Žižek sees in this a new kind of 'Denkverbot', a fundamental prohibition on thinking, an ideological constraint that wards off any radical critique of the current global order.[5] The triumph of the democratic consensus for both thinkers therefore translates into a miserable politics of finitude and resignation in which the dream of emancipation has given way to the acceptance of the contours of the global capitalism system. Indeed, it is precisely *because* of this general consensus over democracy today that, as Badiou argues, democracy should be questioned – indeed it is the first task of philosophy to scrutinise what appears to us as normal and automatically legitimate.[6]

Both Badiou and Žižek subject democracy to a critical scrutiny, yet with different results. Žižek seems to dismiss democracy altogether in favour, as we have seen, of a Leninist authoritarian style of politics, seeing this as the only way of breaking out of the ideological straightjacket of liberal capitalism. Badiou, on the other hand, is more nuanced in his treatment of democracy, suggesting that democracy can be relevant to radical politics only if it can be detached from the framework of the state: 'So can "democracy" be relevant? Yes I shall say so, *as long as "democracy" is grasped in a sense other than a form of the State.*'[7] In other words, democracy is generally conceived as a political system or regime – a series of political institutions which would be distinguished, in the Aristotelian schema, from other types of political regimes. However, this conception always limits democracy to a form of the state, and it is precisely this link which deprives democracy of its radical and emancipative potential and contributes to the watered down 'bourgeois-liberal' version of democracy that we have today.

I find Badiou's treatment of democracy far more fruitful than Žižek's wholesale dismissal of the concept, and will suggest that the radical potential of democracy has not been exhausted, despite the malaise that democracy currently finds itself in. To this end, I will try to disengage the concept of democracy from that of the state, and explore what democratic politics beyond the state might mean.

Postmodernity and democracy

However, we must first examine more rigorously the impact of the postmodern condition on democracy. While Žižek tends to associate postmodernism with the triumph of the democratic consensus, the relationship between them is in fact far more ambiguous. The collapse of the metanarrative identified by Lyotard, and the pluralisation of social spheres, identities and lifestyles, has in fact posed major problems for any consideration of democracy. Democracy, in other words, can no longer be seen as a universal aspiration of people every-where, and indeed, it is quite clear that many people around the world reject democracy in favour of fundamentalism, or seek to articulate fundamentalist beliefs and practices within a democratic framework – thus we have, for instance, emerging 'Sharia democracies' in places like Afghanistan which are a long way removed from the Western concept of democracy. Because post-modernity is characterised by the breaking down of the social link and the fragmentation of the cultural, social and political field, not only does this jeop-ardise a collective or universal dimension upon which democracy ultimately depends, but it also leads, as I have argued before, to new conservative and fundamentalist forces which try to restore, in a paranoid way, some imaginary social 'lifeworld' and, in doing so, also threaten to eclipse the democratic horizon. However, as I have pointed out, these forces at the same time use democracy to further their anti-democratic agenda: the electoral success of the Far Right in France and elsewhere, as well as of Hamas in Palestine and even Christian conservative forces in the United States, can all be seen as examples of this.

What place, then, does the concept of democracy have in the conditions of postmodernity? While I would accept that postmodernity poses a threat to democracy, I do not agree with those like Thomas Pangle who argue that post-modern theory makes the thinking of democracy impossible. Pangle believes that for the democratic project to be resurrected, it has to be based on the firm grounds of reason and rationality, grounds which postmodern theory, in its 'nihilism', jeopardises.[8] Here I shall take a different position, and argue that postmodernity, while it unsettles the epistemological foundations upon which is usually conceived, allows, in doing so, for a radical rethinking of democracy.

For instance, Lyotard argues that democracy in conditions of postmodernity can no longer have the status of a grand narrative – in other words, it can no longer see itself as the ultimate political form and highest human aspiration. Democracy can no longer be placed in a universal discourse of emancipation along with liberal notions of freedom and the rights of man. Indeed, as Lyotard argues, the 1789 French Revolutionary Declaration of the Rights of Man and the Citizen was a universalising and totalising doctrine because it relied on an 'imperialist' principle of legitimation – an abstract, universal idea of Man – and thus imposed upon the people, its addressee, an artificial unity.[9] In other words, for Lyotard, 'the people' – the addressee of any democratic declaration – does not exist other than as a heterogeneous concatenation of entities and differences, and yet by referring to 'the people', democratic declarations attempt to create a unified representative fiction out of this which cannot be sustained. Such declarations, furthermore, hide a central ambiguity between 'the people' as a universal category and 'the people' as citizens of the more narrow category of the nation state. Lastly, democratic declarations also hide the sovereign illegitimacy of their own foundations: not only is revolutionary authority declared by the representatives of the 'people', but this authority had to be self-authorising because it started to make this declaration before having been authorised to do so. In other words, every democratic identity is always haunted by the paradox of sovereignty: on what does sovereignty – even democratic sovereignty – base itself, if not on an illegitimate act of self-authorisation, an act which is ultimately at odds with the very principle of democracy itself? The ambiguous relationship between democracy and national citizenship, and between democracy and sovereignty, are two important problems that I shall return to later.

Lyotard, however, while he rejects the idea of democracy as a grand narrative, does not necessarily dismiss democracy entirely. Indeed, he sees in democracy a deliberative function which reveals the *differend*, the incommensurable difference and heterogeneity of 'phrase regimes': 'in the deliberative politics of modern democracies, the differend is exposed, even though the transcendental appearance of a single finality that would bring it to resolution persists in helping forget the differend, in making it bearable'.[10] In other words, while democratic deliberation aims at producing consensus between interlocutors – a situation in which the differend is silenced and excluded – it only ends up revealing its impossibility. Any consensus that is achieved is not based on rational agreement but simply the silencing or marginalisation of another point of view, and the decision that follows deliberation, while it appears to be the logical outcome of preceding discussions, actually follows no preceding rules. For Lyotard, then, the deliberative process of democracy should not be aimed at reaching a final consensus but should simply allow the differend to appear: 'The deliberative is more "fragile" than the narrative, it lets abysses be perceived that separate genres of discourse from each other and even phrase regimens from each other, the abysses that threaten the "social bond".'[11] The role of democracy in postmodernity, according to Lyotard, is not to try to restore the social bond through building consensus, but rather to simply testify to its fragmentation, to reveal the incommensurability or 'abysses' that appear between discourses and speaking positions. For Lyotard, then, the conditions of postmodernity force us to question the accepted foundations of democracy – the universal ideals of the rights of man, the sovereignty of the people and the legitimacy of consensus. Instead, democracy – or at least the deliberative procedures inherent in it –

derives its legitimation from simply bearing witness to the incommensurability of differences, the incommensurability which at the same time jeopardises any firm grounds for political legitimacy.

In a similar manner, William Connolly talks about unearthing, through a Nietzschean genealogical approach, the 'building stones' that are part of democracy but which are buried under notions of identity, consensus, legitimacy and the common good. In other words, there is a tension in democracy between on the one hand, its indeterminacy, its acceptance of contingency and its potential to question established discourses, institutions and practices; and on the other, the ideas of consensus and identity in which democracy is usually grounded and which limit its more radical tendencies. Democracy as an expression of a social ontology of 'discordant discordances' stands at odds with the usual understanding of it as being based on some pre-established notion of the 'common good'.[12] Like Lyotard, Connolly accepts the theoretical conditions of postmodernity – difference, heterogeneity and the contingency of identity – and calls for a form of democracy which respects difference and which incorporates a Nietzschean *pathos of distance*, where spaces are opened for individual autonomy. In order to do this, democracy must become *agonistic* – in other words, rather than seeking to impose a collective unity upon a plurality of differences, democratic politics must situate itself around an ethic of contestability which remains open to the contingency of identity, and through which the tension between identity and difference is continually worked through and negotiated without the guarantee or even the desire for final reconciliation. An agonistic democracy would involve a pluralistic field of relations in which differences would be respected rather than eliminated:

> A democracy infused with a spirit of agonism is one in which divergent orientations to the mysteries of existence find overt expression in public life. Spaces for difference are to be established through the play of political contestation. Distance becomes politicized in a world where other, topographical sources of distance have been closed up.[13]

However, the possibility of this agonistic openness to difference emerging in democracy is at the same time limited and threatened by a number of factors and tendencies, according to Connolly. Democracy often works against this ethos of pluralisation: it can become a way of organising and channelling collective resentments against those who are different, as the recognition of the contingency of identity and the way that difference contaminates it becomes too much to bear. Thus we see a growing conservatism in the electorate translating into a democratic populism which takes as its target perhaps the unemployed, or the 'illegal' immigrant or the Muslim. One needs to look no further than the astonishing electoral success of Far Right anti-immigrant political parties in Europe to see evidence of this. So while, on the one hand, democracy can open up spaces for difference and the agonistic contestation of identities, it can also shut these spaces down and seek to eliminate or marginalise difference in order to bolster a hegemonic (usually national) identity. Furthermore, what ties individual and collective identities together is the sovereign territorial state, but this is the institution which, according to Connolly, at the same time limits democracy. This occurs not only through the imposition of constraints on democratic contestation in the name of, for instance, 'national security', but also through tying democracy to a territorial location and to a narrowly defined concept of national citizenship. However Connolly argues – and here I agree with him – that globalisation and what he calls 'late modern [or postmodern] time', have combined to make this national democratic space more and more untenable: 'late modern time' is a time without a corresponding political space. He therefore calls for a reconfiguration of the democratic space beyond the territorial limits of the nation state: a nonterritorial democratic space would involve transnational activists and networks of regional actors organising their activities across national borders. Instead of calling for simply a *globalisation of democracy* – a call which could, in a perverse way, come from the lips of George W. Bush himself, and which can merely serve as the ideological guise for the ruthless pursuit of national interest – what is being invoked here is something far more radical, something which jeopardises the very idea of national sovereignty itself: a politics of *nonterritorial democratisation of global issues.*[14]

This idea of freeing democracy from the territoriality of the nation state, and extending the democratic space to global issues and concerns, is an extremely interesting one for radical politics and I shall return to it later. Indeed, the strength of Connolly's analysis lies in its attempt to think democratic politics beyond the sovereignty of the nation state, seeing this as something which ultimately restricts democracy: '[T]o confine the ethos of democracy to the state today is to convert the state to the penitentiary of democracy.'[15] Lyotard, too, as we have seen, reveals the tension that exists between democracy and sovereignty – not only in the way that sovereignty illegitimately authorises itself through founding democratic declarations, but also in the way that it imposes an artificial unity on the people, one that, after the universal fictions of the rights of Man have fallen away, usually boils down to a national collective identity. Both thinkers therefore unmask the aporias of democracy – the way that democracy is threatened and limited by the sovereign and collective identities in which it is usually conceived. The indeterminacy and ethos of contestability that is at the heart of democracy is at the same time closed down, or at least threatened, by the collective, unifying and consensus building imperative, and by the essential identities such as the 'common good' and the 'universal rights of Man' upon which democracy is usually founded.

Lyotard and Connolly both emphasise the indeterminate and ethically open dimension of democracy that I outlined at the start of the chapter, an aspect that is in tension with the opposed tendency of democracy to ground itself in absolute foundations and universal narratives. They have shown that post-modernity – with its pluralised social spheres, incommensurable discourses and perspectives, and contingent identities – demands a rethinking of democracy with a renewed focus on the first dimension rather than the second. In other words, if democracy is to remain relevant in postmodernity, it must eschew essential foundations and open itself to contingency, indeterminacy and, above all, difference.

In pointing to the need for democracy to remain open to difference and pluralism – and in showing, as Connolly does, how democracy might be recon-figured for this purpose – these two thinkers have made an important contribution to the theorisation of democratic politics. However, it could be argued that their conception of democracy is somewhat limited in the sense that it is perhaps *too* concerned with difference and incommensurability, with carving out spaces for individuality and autonomy, and neglects the collective, universal dimension which is equally important to democratic politics. For instance, the emphasis in Lyotard's and Connolly's accounts of democracy seems to be entirely on individual difference and autonomy, rather than on equality, and this strikes me as a rather narrow way of thinking about democ-racy, especially as in most understandings the principle of political equality is primary. It is not that political, social and even economic equality is excluded from their notion of democracy, but rather that democracy's main function or virtue is seen to be the respect for difference and preservation of the pathos of distance in which individuality can flourish. It is not that democracy should *not* be concerned with individual autonomy, but surely its egalitarian dimension is equally important and should not be neglected. In Connolly's account at least, this focus on difference and autonomy is due to his Nietzschean influence. Indeed, in a self-consciously Nietzschean rebuttal to imaginary interlocutors who might insist on the need for further reductions of economic inequality and greater levels of community in an already democratic agonistic society, Connolly detects in such 'democratic idealism' a hidden *ressentiment*. In other words, Connolly is suggesting that behind such a demand for greater equality there might lurk a totalising desire for unity and identity, and a secret desire for *revenge* against those who have more wealth, who possess an '*impermissible* priv-ilege'.[16] Connolly is telling us to be aware of the *ressentiment* that at times hides behind radical democratic demands for greater equality – but this overt Nietzscheanism seems to sit uneasily with the very idea of democracy. My point is that Nietzsche, with his suspicion of equality – which he saw as an example of 'herd morality' – and his outright hostility towards demands for social, political and economic equality, and indeed the whole radical political tradition in which such demands were articulated, strikes me as a somewhat odd figure from which to draw inspiration in theorising a 'radical' conception of democracy. Connolly is at great pains to point out that he is using Nietzsche in an idiosyncratic manner, picking out certain aspects or strains of his thought and reading them against his more anti-democratic tendencies – and this is certainly legitimate. However, my question to Connolly would be: to what extent does the emphasis on difference in your notion of agonistic democracy reflect, even if in a veiled or extremely oblique form, this Nietzschean suspicion of equality? In other words, to what extent does this reverence for difference and the pathos of distance that characterise agonistic democracy slide into inequality, or operate as a mask for it?

So while I certainly accept the need for democracy to remain open to difference and contain an ethos of pluralisation, it must also be based around a strong *ethos of egalitarianism*. I am not sure that a model of democracy almost entirely focussed on difference and pluralisation provides sufficient space for equality, or has the potential to extend it beyond a very basic idea of political equality. Moreover, while it is important that democracy creates spaces for individual autonomy, it is equally important that it allows some sort of collective dimension to appear. Indeed, we might say that any conceptualisation of democracy – no matter how pluralistic or agonistic – would still depend on some sort of notion of a universal ground through which these individual spaces are constituted. I would argue here for a democracy without absolute foundations – without the necessity for it to be grounded, for instance, in some essential human desire or aspiration. However, democracy must still retain a collective dimension – no matter how open and undefined – which can be invoked and extended by all those struggling for democratic rights or for political, social and economic justice.

The attempt to theorise democracy without essential foundations can also be found in the project of 'deliberative democracy'. Deliberative democratic theorists like Habermas and Seyla Benhabib have sought to develop an understanding of democracy that is based not on moral grounds or a substantive notion of community, but rather on a democratic consensus achieved through rational deliberation. We know that Lyotard also speaks of the importance of the deliberative function of democracy, but he rejects any notion of consensus that might be achieved through it. For the deliberative democracy theorists on the other hand, the achievement of a consensus is seen as the goal of democratic discussion. I have already explored in previous chapters Habermas' notion of the ideal speech situation – there is a prior agreement about the procedures for deliberation, so that any agreement which emerges from it can be said to be legitimate according the rules of rational communication. This becomes the basis for a proceduralist or discourse model of democracy, which Habermas sees as superior to both the liberal and republican models of democracy: the liberal paradigm, with its emphasis on individual negative rights and a market-based model of democracy, leaves no room for a normative core upon which would be based a public use of reason; while the republican paradigm, with its strong emphasis on a substantive civic community and the public use of reason, at the same time overloads politics with ethics and reduces public communication to communitarianism. Rather, according to Habermas: 'Discourse theory has the success of deliberative politics depend not on a collectively acting citizenry but on the institutionalisation of the corresponding procedures and conditions of communication.'[17]

This idea is developed by Benhabib, who argues that any notion of democratic legitimacy must ultimately be based on an unconstrained communication on matters of common concern. In other words, democracy is essentially an arrangement that allows common interests to be attained through a process of collective and rational deliberation among free and equal participants. This deliberative understanding of democracy is based on an agreement about the discursive rules and procedures for communication, such as norms of equality and symmetry, the right to question assigned topics of conversation and the right to initiate arguments about these very rules themselves.[18] Such procedures and rules bestow legitimacy and rationality on collective democratic decision making because agreements are reached under conditions which allow the maximum amount of debate, deliberation and questioning.

However, while this deliberative model of democracy has the virtue of going beyond both the narrow liberal conception of democratic politics as well as the communitarianism at the heart of the republican model, it still presupposes a notion of uninterrupted and undistorted deliberation which, as I have suggested before, ignores not only ideological dissimulation and power effects, but, more fundamentally, the structural impossibility of stable meaning and open communication. It assumes that the terrain of public communication is an open, neutral space free from distortion and irrationality. Moreover, it substitutes one form of ultimate foundation for another – that of an assumed universal rationality. However, it is precisely the universality of this rationality that cannot be simply assumed: the rational form of deliberation has to be seen, as Lyotard would say, as only one genre or phrase regimen amongst others, and to see it as universal turns it into a totalising metanarrative in which other phrase regimens are elided and swallowed up. The idea of the rational consensus could only emerge, then, through the discursive exclusion of other positions and perspectives which would be branded as 'irrational'. In other words, while the deliberative democracy model claims to be open to difference and plurality – setting down the rules by which a rational agreement can be reached between conflicting positions – the very form that these rules and procedures take ends up excluding difference and plurality in advance and imposing certain restrictions on this supposedly free process of communication. As Chantal Mouffe argues:

> What is misguided is the search for a final rational resolution. Not only can it not succeed, but moreover it leads to putting undue constraints on the polit-

ical debate. Such a search should be recognised for what it really is, another attempt at insulating politics from the effects of the pluralism of value ... [19]

So we might say that while Connolly and Lyotard are too concerned with pluralism in their conceptions of democracy – seeing the respect for difference, pluralism and individual autonomy as the central virtue of democracy – deliberative democratic theorists like Habermas and Benhabib do not take pluralism seriously enough, trying to hide it behind an all-encompassing rational consensus which forms the basis of democratic decision making.

Too much consensus!

Moreover, we should perhaps question the desirability of the democratic consensus. Perhaps the problem with what passes for democracy today is not its inability to form a consensus between different positions and perspectives, but on the contrary its excessive readiness to do so. Modern democracies are characterised not by too little consensus and agreement but by *too much* – by an excessive, stifling consensus. The dominant ideology of modern democracies today is that which announces the very eclipse of ideological conflicts between Left and Right, which claims to be 'post-ideological' and to be about solving society's problems in a rational, 'common sense' way without the constraints of ideology. The idea of the social-democratic 'Third Way', which claims to seek a 'middle road' between socialism and capitalism and which purports to represent the 'radical centre' of political opinion, would be paradigmatic of the 'post-ideological' consensus. Of course we should recognise that this so called era of 'post-ideological' consensus simply means that the ideology of neo-liberal markets has become so entrenched, so sedimented, so accepted as economic orthodoxy by both sides of politics, that we no longer recognise it as ideology as such. The 'post-ideological' consensus is simply a neo-liberal ideological consensus, and the so called 'Third Way' was never really a third way at all, but simply a way of disguising the formal Left's capitulation to neo-liberalism by providing it with some flimsy social democratic window dressing.[20] Now we could say that after people have come to realise the fraudulence of the Third Way project, a new consensus has been emerging around the idea of 'security' – we see both sides of politics largely converging around the imperative of 'security' and in support of anti-terrorist legislation.

Far from this new consensus style of politics being a sign of the maturity of democracy, it is a sign of its degradation and immanent collapse. We are dealing here with a new mutation of democracy, in which the triumph of 'democratic consensus' coincides with, and is symptomatic of, the complete eclipse of real democracy. Indeed, Rancière has suggested that the very term 'consensus democracy' is a contradiction – one can either have consensus or democracy – and has proposed instead to call it *postdemocracy*.[21] According to Rancière, the global triumph of democracy during the 1990s which came with the collapse of the Communist regimes, at the same time coincided with a kind of shrinking of the democratic space: democracy has not only given up on the people – on the idea of popular sovereignty and real democracy – but this has also led, paradoxically, to the erosion of the power of even the formal parliamentary mechanisms of representation. Power in modern postdemocracies increasingly rests with unelected and unaccountable experts, technocrats and committees. The idea of consensus increasingly effaces democracy itself, because, as Rancière argues, democracy is based on a fundamental dispute or disagreement between the *part of no part* – the part that is whole – and the police order which excludes or does not count this part. In this sense, the people or the democratic subject is not some sociological category to be prodded and poked by public opinion experts and pollsters, but rather a kind of fractured or partial space of subjectification; it refers not to 'mainstream opinion' but, on the contrary, to an excluded part, the part that is 'miscounted', that demands to be included by claiming to be whole. We can see how different this understanding of democracy is from that of the prevailing ideology of consensus, which only sees the people in terms of 'mainstream opinion' – an entity that is continually polled, studied and counted. For Rancière, the people is precisely what disturbs this counting and the consensus which supposedly ensues from it; it is the part that is excluded from 'mainstream public opinion', that is not counted. The democratic subject is a kind of permanent fissure in any consensus.

However, this democratic subject – the place of this fundamental disagreement of the people – is precisely what is made invisible in contemporary postdemocracies. The politics of dispute and disagreement is replaced by consensus, by a 'reasonable' politics of negotiation. In this model, decisions are made on the most efficient way of distributing social goods. Thus, the democratic subject is transformed into a consumer of government services, and, according to the rational choice theories of democracy, a consumer also in the democratic marketplace who selects the party that most closely corresponds with his 'preferences'.[22] In this paradigm, disputes that arise are immediately translated into problems to be solved by experts and technicians: look at the way, for instance, that the riots that took place in Paris in November 2005 were immediately interpreted by a whole army of sociologists, experts and TV panellists into a series of 'issues' like high youth unemployment and social marginalisation, issues which might be solved by 'well-targeted' government policies and programmes. Postdemocracy, according to Rancière, is therefore a kind of utopian vision of democracy – a seamless process for the aggregation of interests and the parcelling out of social goods, one that is free of conflict: 'The utopia of postdemocracy is that of an uninterrupted count that presents the total of "public opinion" as identical to the body of the people.' In other words, 'the people' only exist in postdemocracy as a kind of artificial body, a simulacrum that is created by opinion polls and public opinion experts. Here, the people 'are always both totally present and totally absent at once. They are entirely caught in the structure of the visible where everything is on show and where there is thus no longer any place for appearance.'[23]

From this great, mediatised democratic spectacle, the real democratic subject is foreclosed. However, we know from Lacan that *what is foreclosed from the symbolic returns in the real* – and thus we see all around us violent explosions of 'the people', such as the 2005 Paris riots; but also the emergence of new forms of anti-immigrant racism. In the latter case, however, racism emerges not only from the foreclosure of the people and the disappearance of the space in which disputes can be heard, but rather from the specific form this takes in post-democracies. 'Public opinion' – or the entity which stands in for the people – is transposed onto a notion of community, which consensus democracies are now said to represent: how often have we heard this communitarian refrain from politicians – the whole mantra about 'listening to the community', about the need for the 'respect of communities', 'community protection' from 'anti-social behaviour' etc? However, this figure of the community is artificial, as any real sense of community life had long since been eroded by neo-liberal market policies. Given these factors, then, it is perhaps not entirely surprising that the excluded – the unemployed, for instance, or the working class – at times might vent their frustration at being excluded against those who are even more excluded, against those 'outsiders' who are seen to threaten their already tenuous sense of community identity. For Rancière, then: 'The new racism of advanced societies thus owes its singularity to being the point of intersection for all forms of the community's identity with itself that go to define the consensus model.'[24] Anti-immigrant racism results from the way that postdemocracy takes as its central representative figure not the people but the 'community' – basing consensus on 'mainstream community views'. Moreover, postdemocracies aim to manage such outbursts by simply incorporating them into itself, so that we now have the major political parties – both left and right – now proposing ever more draconian border security measures, and promising to 'get tough' on 'illegal' migration.

We should acknowledge, of course, that this notion of postdemocracy or 'consensus democracy' is a long way from what the deliberative democracy theorists envisage as a genuine rational democratic consensus – one that would, in theory, reflect a diversity of different viewpoints and perspectives. However, the vision of postdemocracy painted here nevertheless alerts us to some of the dangers inherent in consensus – the way that consensus can simply operate as a mask for the exclusion of certain perspectives, those that might challenge, for instance, the legitimacy of free market dogma. In other words, one could say that, ultimately, consensus is incompatible with democracy. Rather than seeking a rational consensus – which as Mouffe correctly suggests is a flight from pluralism – perhaps democracies must find a way of building pluralism into their very structures, or of allowing the genuine disagreements of the people that Rancière talks about, to be staged.

The democratic revolution

The conclusions reached in the previous sections have highlighted the need to rethink democracy. Rather than reject the concept of democracy itself – as Žižek does – I would suggest, along with Rancière, that democracy must be distinguished from postdemocracy.[25] The failings of the latter do not necessarily condemn the former. In other words, we need to return to democracy itself and find ways in which it might be reactivated and renewed, so that it can provide a genuine radical alternative to the depleted and impoverished form of politics that takes its name today. There is a radical potential in democracy that has not been realised, that cannot be exhausted by democracy's modern expressions. The principle central to democracy – that of the *rule of everyone by everyone* – is still radical today, yet it needs to be renewed. As certain theorists of radical democracy have suggested, we need to reactivate the democratic revolution: in the words of C. D. Lummis, 'Understood *radically*, it [democracy] contains a promise yet to be fulfilled.'[26]

However, what exactly is meant here by the 'democratic revolution'? According to Claude Lefort, democracy has to be seen as a particular form of the social, in which the orders of power, knowledge and law – which had been previously held together and incorporated symbolically within the single body of the prince in aristocratic societies – are dis-incorporated and radically separated. In other words, the emergence of democracy created a crisis in the preceding symbolic order, producing a place of power which – while it had been previously occupied by the figure of the prince – was henceforth *empty*: 'The locus of power becomes an empty place.'[27] Because the exercise of power in democracy is periodically redistributed through elections, then the place of power is occupied only temporarily, and no identity – whether an individual or political party – can become consubstantial with it. In other words, the emergence of democracy is revolutionary, according to Lefort, because it introduces into the body of the social a fundamental indeterminacy. Democracy is characterised by the *dissolution of the markers of certainty*:

> Modern democratic society seems to me, in fact, like a society in which power, law and knowledge are exposed to a radical indetermination, a society that has become the theatre of an uncontrollable adventure, so that what is instituted never becomes established.[28]

So, according to Lefort, the democratic revolution opens the political and social field to a radical contingency – democracy makes visible, and indeed institutionalises, the absence of ultimate foundations and the severing of the social bond, thus exposing society to an indeterminacy in which power relationships are always unstable and reversible.

To some extent, I accept this argument – undoubtedly, modern democracy is an advance on the *ancien régime* in which power relationships were much more stable and hierarchical and were not subject to redistribution through voting. In this sense, the advent of even modern representative democracy is certainly a significant and radical development. However, Lefort's argument also tends to ignore many of the limitations of modern democracies: the way that power can also become entrenched in certain institutions and elites; the way that democracy is at the same time undermined by social and economic inequality and corporate power; the ideological domination which legitimises the capitalist system and which is perpetuated by the media; the general mediatisation of politics which turns democracy into a simulacrum of itself; and the rise of the tyranny of democratic consensus. Here we could also point to the security state and new forms of power and surveillance that emerge through the democratic system. All of these factors suggest that democratic societies are perhaps not quite as open and indeterminate as Lefort imagines; that the orders of power, knowledge and law are indeed bound up and re-articulated through, for instance, 'anti-terrorist' measures in which law no longer checks sovereign power, and in which surveillance and information-gathering techniques make possible an undreamt of level of knowledge about society.

The problem here is that Lefort bases his conception of democracy on a formal differentiation from other political systems, especially totalitarianism: while totalitarianism emerges out of a crisis in democratic societies, it is sharply distinguished from the symbolic order of democracy in the way that it seeks to reincorporate society into a single entity and reunite the orders of power/knowledge/law. However, is this distinction between democracy and totalitarianism so clear in reality? I have pointed to all sorts of ways in which democratic societies – particularly under contemporary conditions of the 'war on terror' – move imperceptibly towards greater authoritarianism and social control. It is not so much that they have passed from democracy into totalitarianism, but that state security and surveillance measures, as well as more pervasive forms of ideological control which operate through the market, produce a 'zone of indistinction' – as Agamben would say – in which this division between democracy and totalitarianism is no longer meaningful.[29] This has become more than ever the case in the wake of the collapse of the 'totalitarian' regimes in Eastern Europe. It would seem that democracies – now without any alternative system to measure themselves by and without any natural competitors – can undergo all sorts of strange and authoritarian mutations while still claiming to be democracies: indeed, one could say that they now exercise even greater levels of control over their citizens than those crumbling bureaucratic monoliths of the Soviet era.

Lefort also considers the question of the permanence of the *theologico-politi-*

cal – in other words, the left-over trace of religion that might still haunt the structures of modern democracy – coming to the conclusion that with the advent of democracy and the formal separation of Church and State, the theological and the political have become radically and irretrievably divorced.[30] However, has not Lefort been too hasty here? It would appear that modern democracies are still haunted by the ghost of religion, that the theological stain is far from having been removed from democratic politics: do we not see, with the emergence of fundamentalist and neo-conservative forces in modern democracies, the continual overlapping between religious and political discourse – not only in the 'faith-based' policies of the Bush administration, but also in the way that politicians today increasingly make references to their personal faith or talk about the importance of God in their lives? Tony Blair, in a recent interview, said that God alone would judge him on his decision to go to war in Iraq: which is a profoundly anti-democratic statement, implying that the people do not figure at all in his decisions – only his personal relationship with God – and almost hearkening back to the old doctrine of the divine right of kings. It would seem that modern democracy has not shaken off the theological baggage that permanently limits and threatens it, and which binds it to sovereignty.

The point here is that while Lefort's analysis shows the radical potential of democracy, it also neglects the ways in which this radical potential is at the same time constrained, not only by the informal structures of power that exist in modern democratic societies – the media, the capitalist economy, the applications of surveillance technology – but also by the persistence of sovereignty and its theological stain. The reason for this oversight on Lefort's part is that he reduces democracy to a particular institutional form – that of *liberal democracy*. In other words, what he is talking about with the emergence of the modern democracy is the emergence of liberal representative democracy, which combines the principle of popular sovereignty with a certain institutional arrangement, defined by the separation of the orders of power, knowledge and law. As Ernesto Laclau has pointed out, the empty place of power which Lefort locates at the heart of modern democracies is not completely empty or neutral but takes a particular form: 'The difficulty with Lefort's analysis of democracy is that it is concentrated exclusively on liberal-democratic *regimes*, and does not pay due attention to the construction of popular-democratic *subjects*.'[31] The focus of Lefort's conception of democracy, in other words, is on a particular series of institutional and power arrangements that could be said to characterise liberal democracies – perhaps to the neglect, as Laclau suggests, of what is really at the heart of democracy: the democratic subject and the construction of the popular will. In other words, in Lefort's account democracy is always attached to a regime, a series of institutions and a form of state which, I would argue, limits it.

The tension highlighted by Lefort's treatment of democracy – between the radical and anti-sovereign potential of democracy and the liberal institutional regime in which it is articulated – again reflects the ambiguity one inevitably encounters when approaching the question of democracy: is democracy to be seen as an ethically and constitutively open and contingent form of politics, or is it grounded in a series of sedimented practices and institutions? Lefort's analysis reflects both dimensions here: on the one hand, democracy is seen in terms of a revolutionary destabilisation of existing power relations and social hierarchies; but on the other, the very form taken by this destabilising force fixes it within a certain institutional arrangement and symbolic framework that at the same time limits it. For instance, there seems to be little room in Lefort's model for forms of direct democracy which would bypass representative and liberal institutions.

Democracy without foundations

Nevertheless, the importance of the democratic revolution as described by Lefort should not be lost on us: by making the absence of foundations visible and by subjecting the social body to indeterminacy and contingency, the democratic revolution contains a real emancipative force, one that can actually work against existing political institutions and power relations. A project of radical democracy would therefore seek to harness and deepen this democratic revolution, extending it from beyond the political domain into the social and economic domains.

There are many different understandings of radical democracy, but the one that I would like to focus on here is that which is introduced by Laclau and Mouffe in their work *Hegemony and Socialist Strategy*, and which is subsequently developed by Mouffe in later writings. According to Laclau and Mouffe, the democratic imaginary, instituted by the democratic revolution, can provide the Left with a new emancipative horizon, one that has become more significant today since the collapse of the Communist systems. The democratic imaginary is one that transcends both Marxist totalitarianism and wishy washy social democracy, allowing radical rearticulations of liberty and equality and, through this, the displacement of democratic rights to the ever widening arena of social struggles and antagonisms characteristic of postmodernity. For instance, feminist, anti-racist and ecological struggles, and the struggles for autonomy of ethnic and cultural minorities, can all be seen as democratic struggles which are invoking new rights as well as challenging new relations of domination.[32] In other words, democracy should not be confined to a narrow idea of political equality, or to series of institutional arrangements, or even to a certain regime of liberal rights: the democratic imaginary cannot be contained within these discursive and institutional limits, and spills over into other arenas of social and economic struggle. As Mouffe says, 'The problem therefore is not with the ideals of modern democracy, but the fact that its principles are a long way from being implemented, even in societies that lay claim to them.'[33]

According to Mouffe, furthermore, the way to deepen and radicalise democracy is to recognise its paradox – that is, the way that modern liberal democracy rests on a fundamental and constitutive tension between the *liberal* principle of the institutional protection of individual rights and the *democratic* principle of popular sovereignty and political equality. While these two are often conflated, they emerge from different traditions, and it is only a matter of historical contingency that they have been brought together.[34] Recognising the permanent tension and incompatibility that exists between these principles allows liberty and equality, individual rights and popular sovereignty, to be articulated in new and innovative ways and to be extended to different identities and social struggles.

Moreover, the existence of these different identities and struggles means that the principle of pluralism must be built into the very structure of democracy itself. Here it is important to stress that Mouffe is not talking about the simple empirical 'fact' of pluralism, but rather the principle of pluralism and difference itself. To see this principle as constitutive of democracy itself would mean that democracy can no longer be understood as being based on essential foundations or stable fixed identities, but would, rather, be structurally open to different articulations and would eschew the idea of a perfect harmony or reconciliation at the level of social relations and identities. As Mouffe argues, the problem with both deliberative and liberal theories of democracy is precisely that they seek this reconciliation in the form of a rational consensus. Such a reconciliation, however, is not only impossible, but also threatens the pluralism and contestation of interests which is constitutive of democracy itself:

> Indeed, such an illusion carries implicitly the desire for a reconciled society where pluralism would have been superseded. When it is conceived in such a way, pluralist democracy becomes a 'self-refuting ideal' because the very moment of its realization would coincide with its disintegration.[35]

Moreover, the illusion of harmony or final reconciliation can also be seen as a way of excluding the dimension of the 'passions' from politics. According to Mouffe, the desire for consensus is really an attempt to foreclose or make invisible the antagonism – or in Rancière's terms, the disagreement of the people – which is actually constitutive of democracy. In the universal rational consensus, the more passionate or visceral forms of politics simply have no place, and would be branded as 'irrational' – and we have seen that, as a result of this exclusion, they often return in more violent and destructive anti-democratic forms. Therefore, some sort of space must be provided in which these antagonisms can be staged or played out. As Mouffe suggests, the principle of contestation must be incorporated into democratic politics. However, rather than a simple relationship of antagonism, in which one's opponent is seen as an enemy to be eliminated, Mouffe proposes a relationship of *agonistic pluralism,* where the other is seen as a worthy adversary whose difference is respected and whose right to disagree is considered inviolable.[36] We can see in this agonistic model of democracy clear parallels with Connolly's democratic ethos of pluralisation, in which the boundaries of identity are contested and in which spaces for individual difference and autonomy are guaranteed.

However, there is also a difference between the two approaches. Connolly seems to think that this ethos of pluralisation is a sufficient basis for democracy, whereas Mouffe seeks to ground her notion of democracy on some understanding of a democratic community and citizenship. Here Mouffe rejects what she sees as the false dichotomy between the liberal emphasis on individual rights and freedoms, and the communitarian emphasis on a substantive community identity and ethics: the liberal approach allows only a limited notion of community and citizenship, and neglects the socially situated nature of the individual; while the communitarians, on the other hand, tend to sacrifice individual rights and freedoms on the altar of community. Instead, Mouffe turns to the republican tradition with its notions of 'civic virtue' and shared civic values. Rather than a substantive notion of a common good and a fixed community identity, a basis for a democratic citizenship could be established through shared democratic values and practices, a common language of civil intercourse. Here she refers to Michael Oakeshott's idea of *respublica* as a 'practice of civility' which specifies a series of rules and conditions for performances, as a possible way of conceptualising this democratic 'being-in-common'.[37] However, the contours of the democratic citizenship would be also defined through a relationship of antagonism – or 'agonism' – towards what is outside it, in the sense that the limits of any identity can only be constituted through its exclusion of a particular element. Mouffe draws on Carl Schmitt's friend/enemy distinction in order to show that a democratic 'we' can only be defined through its common opposition to a 'them'. Indeed, Mouffe argues that democracy – if it is to avoid essentialist foundations in abstract notions of a common good or a common humanity – can only be understood through this logic of inclusion/exclusion; 'the people' is constituted as a democratic subject through the establishment of a boundary or frontier defining the limits of democratic citizenship.[38] However, this frontier would not be fixed, and would always be open to renegotiation and to different articulations.

I largely agree with Mouffe's reformulation of democracy and her attempt to deepen and expand the democratic revolution through the displacement of rights beyond the liberal-capitalist paradigm. Her model of democratic agonism has clear advantages over those previously discussed, particularly as a way of thinking individual rights collectively, so that the principles of equality and liberty are not sacrificed to one another. Democracy must be seen as a way of bringing together, in new and innovative ways, these unconditional principles of equality and liberty. Furthermore, Mouffe shows that democracy can be conceptualised without essential foundations: without recourse, on the one hand, to a substantive idea of community identity and a common good proposed by communitarians; and on the other, the universal rational consensus suggested by both liberals and deliberative democratic theorists. Mouffe largely bypasses these two alternatives by constructing her conception of democracy around the principle of agonistic pluralism – as Connolly does. However, she also goes beyond this by proposing a notion of citizenship – seen in terms of a shared democratic language and a series of practices. In this sense, Mouffe's notion of democracy largely conforms to the theoretical conditions of postmodernity without, at the same time, sacrificing the idea of a collective and universal dimension upon which any understanding of democracy – especially more radical understandings – must be based.

However, there are also a number of limitations with this model. Firstly, it could be argued that Mouffe tends to overemphasise the distinction and incompatibility that she sees existing between the principles of individual rights and freedom and those of democracy and political equality. While it is true that such principles emerge from different philosophical traditions, Mouffe's analysis tends to neglect the way that many of what are now considered to be fundamental 'liberal' rights – like freedom of assembly, for instance – did not come from liberalism at all. On the contrary, such rights were won through democratic and socialist struggles during the nineteenth century, and were initially regarded as anathema by liberals. What I am suggesting here is that this distinction that Mouffe draws between the liberal traditions of rights and individual freedoms, and the democratic tradition of popular sovereignty – a distinction which she sees as the basis of the 'democratic paradox' – is in fact less clear-cut than she supposes, and has been subject to historical contamination. For instance, it is difficult in many cases to distinguish between liberal rights and democratic rights, and when we think about the initially limited understanding of rights proposed by liberalism – rights that were restricted to property owning males for instance – and, furthermore, the way that the language of rights was expanded through democratic struggles, it becomes impossible to determine which rights belong to the liberal tradition and which belong to the democratic tradition. Indeed, it would seem that the democratic impulse has in the past proved a much more viable and radical vehicle for rights and liberties than liberalism. So while I would certainly agree with Mouffe that there is a distinction, and even an incompatibility, between liberalism and democracy, I do *not* see this as translating into an incompatibility between individual rights and freedoms and democracy – between liberty and equality. Furthermore, I would suggest that the very idea of a distinction between them is itself part of the language of liberalism and reflects many of the liberal suspicions about democracy and popular sovereignty. In other words, to insist, as Mouffe does, on a fundamental incompatibility between 'liberal' rights and freedoms and democratic popular sovereignty, seems to privilege a liberal understanding of democracy: to believe that the liberal tradition of individual rights acts as a check on the democratic principle of political equality risks situating democracy on a liberal theoretical terrain, a terrain that democracy must transcend if it is to become radicalised. I am not suggesting here that individual rights are not important, or are secondary to the principle of popular sovereignty – quite the contrary. What I *am* saying, however, is that individual rights and freedoms can only really be thought and extended on a democratic rather than liberal terrain. While Mouffe argues for a constitutive antagonism between liberty and equality, I would argue for a constitutive *contamination* between them – a contamination that can only be realised through democracy rather than liberalism. Here I think, for instance, that Étienne Balibar's idea of *equaliberty* – the idea that liberty is not thinkable without equality and equality is not thinkable without liberty[39] – is perhaps closer to a radical idea of democracy than Mouffe's notion of the 'democratic paradox'.

My second concern about Mouffe's model of democracy relates to the implications of the Schmittian 'friend/enemy' distinction upon which she bases her idea of democratic citizenship. Again highlighting the tension that she sees as existing between individual rights and democracy, Mouffe draws on Schmitt's contention that democracy implies the idea of an equality between citizens of a specific demos, an equality which cannot be extended to those beyond the boundaries of this community. These more universal notions of the 'equality of humanity' are part of an abstract liberal humanism according to Schmitt, something which is not compatible with democracy. In other words, for Schmitt, democracy and equality belong to citizens of the demos – and the demos can only be thought through a demarcation which separates it from those outside – foreigners, aliens, non-citizens.[40] While Mouffe is of course wary of the reactionary implications of Schmitt's thought, and is, in certain places, very critical of it, she nevertheless takes his central idea that democracy and political equality are only realisable through this logic of inclusion/exclusion. Indeed, she uses this argument to criticise ideas about a cosmopolitan global citizenship which would transcend national boundaries. Such ideas, she contends, come from an abstract liberal universalism which only entrenches the current global liberal order: 'We should be aware that without a demos to which they belong, those cosmopolitan citizen pilgrims would in fact have lost the possibility of exercising their democratic rights of law-making.'[41] Mouffe is partly right in the sense that global democratic institutions are not sufficiently developed – if they exist at all – to allow any substantively democratic notion of global citizenship today, and that this would simply abandon the global citizen to a limited notion of human rights and to relying on relatively weak transnational legal institutions to enforce them. However, this criticism at the same time seems to ignore the emergence of what many people see as a movement for global democracy and justice: the 'anti-globalisation' movement suggests new forms of democratic identity and decision making which are increasingly transnational in nature. I will say more about this movement in the following chapter, but it is surprising that Mouffe's analysis seems to ignore the possibility that 'the people', or some notion of democratic citizenship, could be constituted globally and beyond the borders of the nation state. Moreover, the global sense of citizenship which is potentially emerging through such movements is not confined to an abstract liberalism and to a limited conception of human rights, as Mouffe seems to predict: on the contrary, it is precisely what challenges the global liberal order through the demand for a more substantive understanding of rights – the right, for instance, to exercise greater democratic control over the global economy. Mouffe's mistake is to equate the possibility of a global citizenship with the entrenchment of the global liberal economic order and the loss of democracy; yet we see precisely the opposite occurring – not only the challenging of the global 'free-market' order but also the expansion of democracy through this emerging notion of global citizenship. I am not suggesting, by any means, that the idea of a global citizenship is unproblematic – not only is its realisation highly tenuous, but the very concept of citizenship would have to be radically rethought. However, it seems to me that globalisation, while in certain instances posing a threat to democracy – particularly that which is practised within national borders – is also opening up new possibilities for transnational democratic identity.

Moreover, Schmitt's friend/enemy distinction raises deeper questions about 'the people' and its other. That is to say, if the demos – the democratic 'us' – is constituted through a relation of inclusion/exclusion, who exactly is the 'them'? While Mouffe makes it clear that the frontier that delineates democratic citizenship is a discursive one, and, moreover, one that is shiftable and renegotiable, it seems to ignore, at the same time, the way that modern democracies constitute themselves through *real* structures of exclusion – the exclusion, for instance, of refugees and 'illegal' migrants from the concept of national democratic citizenship. In other words, it is not entirely clear what sort of place the refugee or the figure of the absolute outsider has, if any, in Mouffe's concept of democratic citizenship, particularly as this would seem, following Schmitt, to be only realisable within a national space. In other words, to what extent can this discursive inclusion/exclusion or friend/enemy antagonism translate into real relations of exclusion, in which the figure of the outsider is eliminated from the public space? We see the way, for instance, that democratic identity today increasingly seeks to define itself in opposition to its 'intolerant', 'anti-democratic', 'fundamentalist' other – embodied in the figure of the Muslim.

Democracy and sovereignty

The question that looms up before us, then, is whether it is possible to have a notion of democracy that is not based on a relation of exclusion, on the friend/enemy distinction. I have already hinted at the need to extend the idea of democracy and political rights from beyond the borders of the nation state, to include those who are currently excluded – in particular to refugees and other stateless people around the world. Indeed, we could say that the existence of these stateless people, and their growing demands for rights and recognition, suggests new understandings of political space and political belonging that no longer conform to the national space. However, a further consideration is that the friend/enemy distinction always invokes the dimension of sovereignty: for Schmitt, sovereignty is the ability to rule on the exception, the moment which defines the political space on the basis of a constitutive exclusion. The position of sovereignty is not made entirely explicit in Mouffe's account of democracy, but it seems clear that that moment of exclusion through which democratic citizenship is defined and the contours of 'the people' emerge, necessarily involves the sovereign decision.

Here I want to propose a radically anti-Schmittian understanding of democracy – one that is *not* based on the moment of exception, on the sovereign decision which lays down the limits of the political through the possibility of their suspension and which establishes divisions between friend/enemy, us and them. My contention here is that democracy is ultimately incompatible with sovereignty, and that, for democracy to be realised today, for democracy to be radicalised and renewed, we must find ways of detaching it from sovereignty.

Before exploring this seemingly impossible task, I must first define what I mean by democracy. It should be clear by now that democracy cannot be thought of as a form of the state: that is to say, democracy is not a regime or a series of political institutions – such as parliament or constitution. Such a definition not only confines democracy to the limited liberal capitalist form that prevails today but, more fundamentally, ties it to the principle of state sovereignty which permanently threatens it. Rather, democracy must be thought of in terms of a *collective autonomy* in which liberty can only be realised in conditions of equality and equality in conditions of liberty. At the heart of democracy, then, I see a fundamental link between liberty and equality – and it is this link which, at the same time, makes democracy ultimately incompatible with sovereignty, particularly that which is enshrined in the modern state. This was something that was fundamentally grasped by the anarchist Mikhail Bakunin:

> [E]quality of *political rights*, or *a democratic State*, constitute in themselves the most glaring contradiction in terms. The State, or political right, denotes force, authority, predominance; it presupposes inequality in fact. Where all rule, there are no more ruled, and there is no State. Where all equally enjoy

the same human rights, there all political right loses its reason for being. Political right connotes privilege, and where all are privileged, there privilege vanishes, and along with it goes political right. Therefore the terms *'democratic State'* and *'equality of political rights'* denote no less than the destruction of the State and the abolition of all political right.[42]

In other words, the equality of political rights entailed by democracy is fundamentally incompatible with *political right* – the principle of sovereignty which grants authority over these rights to the state. At its most basic level, political equality can only exist in tension with a right that stands above society and determines the conditions under which this political equality can be exercised. Political equality, if taken seriously and understood radically, can only mean the abolition of sovereignty. So it is not only that democracy cannot be contained within the borders of the nation state, but that the equality of wills and rights implied by democracy means that it is ultimately irreconcilable with any state, with any form of sovereignty. Even the sovereignty that is now deploying itself beyond national borders is being met with anti-sovereign democratic struggles that challenge its legitimacy.

Democracy to come

This incompatibility – or at least fundamental tension – between democracy and sovereignty is also something that concerns Derrida. However, as he points out, it is not a matter of simply choosing between democracy and sovereignty, but rather of exploring the *aporetic* structure of democracy itself in order to uncover its moments of tension with sovereignty and, through this, to find ways of detaching democracy from state sovereignty and of thinking democracy beyond its limits. For Derrida, the democratic revolution has largely left sovereignty unchallenged; indeed we could say that the democratic revolution has actually reinforced sovereignty by providing it with the cloak of legitimacy. In contrast to Lefort, who insists on the irreversible separation of the religious and the secular as a result of the democratic revolution, Derrida highlights the theological stain that continues to haunt modern democracies and which is to be found in the *ontotheological* nature of sovereignty itself: the sovereign is simply the secular image of God, embodying the same idea of the One, the point of unicity, indivisibility and absolute authority – the authority that is grounded in itself alone.[43] This theological dimension of sovereignty can be found throughout the whole tradition of the philosophy of sovereignty, from Hobbes and Bodin, to Rousseau and Schmitt – and the democratic revolution, by leaving the position of sovereignty essentially unchallenged, has only reaffirmed it. However, the paradox is that this idea of sovereignty as a single, indivisible moment of authority, while it forms the basis of democracy, is also fundamentally at odds with it. In a deconstructive reading of Rousseau, Derrida shows that Rousseau's idea of a democracy of *gods* which would have no need of government suggests *a more than one* – a plurality or multiplicity of wills – that announces the possibility of democracy, and at the same time challenges the indivisibility of God and, therefore, of sovereignty itself.[44] Another aporia is revealed in tension that exists between the idea of *kratos* or force expressed in the idea of democratic freedom – freedom implying here a kind of mastery and the power of decision – and the uncontrolled, unruly, *unmasterable* freedom of the demos that Plato and Aristotle found so abhorrent. Therefore, there is in democracy the idea not only of sovereign determinacy and decision, but also a freedom and indeterminacy, a freedom which opens democracy to the historical contingency of its own conditions, allowing it to be interrogated and taken in new and unpredictable directions.

Again what is revealed here is the double-sided nature of democracy that I referred to before – democracy as a form of polity, a stable, fixed series of institutions, discourses and practices; and democracy as an open, contingent form of politics which eschews its grounding in a stable polity. It is this second aspect of democracy that Derrida emphasises here, seeing it as being at odds with sovereignty. In other words, there is a dimension of democracy that allows all forms of polity – including democracy itself – to be questioned and challenged, and it is here that Derrida would agree with Lefort about the fundamental indeterminacy central to democratic societies: democracy is 'the only name of a regime, or quasi regime, open to its own historical transformation, to taking up its intrinsic plasticity and its interminable self-criticizability, one might even say its interminable analysis'.[45] However, this openness of democracy to criticism is always potentially dangerous: does it not suggest a certain self-destructiveness, a certain suicidal quality in democracy itself? Here Derrida refers to the *autoimmunity* of democracy – the way that democracy has a tendency not only towards self-destruction, but to destroying itself in the name of protecting itself. Two examples illustrate this logic of autoimmunity: the 1992 elections in Algeria, which saw the government suspending the democratic system itself because it looked like the fundamentalist Islamist bloc would gain power – showing the way that anti-democratic forces can use the democratic system to gain power (here we could point to numerous other examples of ultra-conservative and religious fundamentalist parties, who want to limit democratic and human rights, participating in democratic elections – such as Hamas in Palestine, for instance); and, secondly, the way that governments, in the name of protecting and securing their democracies from outside terrorist forces that threaten it, introduce measures and laws which undermine democracy from within. Both examples show the fragility of democracy and the fundamental risk of leaving itself open to those who challenge it.

However, for democracy to *be* democracy it must take this risk – as we have seen, to try to immunise democracy against such challenges itself destroys it. It is on this undecidable and inherently risky ground that Derrida poses the question of the *democracy to come*. Democracy to come can be seen as an unforseen event – an event which comes from the outside, but at the same time emerges from the radical potential of democracy itself, urging democracy to live up to its own promise, its own *perfectibility*. It is in this sense that, as Derrida says: 'we do not yet know what democracy will have meant nor what it is'.[46] Democracy is what cannot be represented, what cannot be satisfied by a number of minimum conditions or embodied in a certain regime – democracy always points to a horizon beyond, to the future; it is always 'to come'. It is for this reason that it is impossible. However, this impossibility does not mean that we should give up on democracy – on its promise of perfect liberty with perfect equality. On the contrary, it means we should never be satisfied with existing forms taken by democracy and should always be working towards its perfectibility.

Let us examine in greater detail this figure of democracy to come, for I would suggest that it provides a new, radical way of thinking about democratic politics – one that, importantly, allows democracy to work itself out of the grasp of sovereignty. Democracy to come, according to Derrida, can be understood in a number of different yet related ways: 1) as a call for a militant political critique which protests against every attack on democracy, every attempt to disguise a shortfall in existing democracy, and every attempt to use the term democracy rhetorically to cover up or legitimise the worst kinds of abuses and inequalities; 2) the coming of an event which is totally unforseen, an irruption which cannot be limited by existing systems or contained within the borders of the nation state; 3) the extension of democracy beyond the borders of nation state sovereignty and national citizenship – the creation of an international juridico-political space in which sovereignty is continually challenged and divided; 4) the conjunction of democracy with justice, so that the democracy to come is also a *justice to come*; 5) rather than a regulative idea which democracy must live up to, or a right to defer to some point in the future, democracy to come is an unconditional injunction and a singular urgency – it is always invoking a *here and now*.[47]

Democracy to come must therefore be seen alongside of, and at the same time as the basic condition for, Derrida's other ethical figures discussed in the last chapter – justice, hospitality and human rights. Like these figures, democracy to come invokes an infinite perfectibility – so that any kind of inequality or limitation of rights is incompatible with the democratic promise. This suggests an extension of democracy and rights to the social and economic realms as well as a continual interrogation of every existing situation that passes itself off as democratic. Furthermore, this infinite perfectibility is only possible, paradoxically, if democracy is considered without essential foundations and its absolute historicity is asserted. Like these other ethical figures, democracy to come is *universalisable* precisely because its assumed universality can be deconstructed:

in other words, the only way the concept of democracy can be extended beyond its existing limits is if it can be freed from its supposed universal foundations – in, for instance, human nature, or a rational consensus, or national citizenship. For instance, to see democracy as a natural human aspiration – as George Bush does, or claims to do – is to promote one particular model of democracy around the world, which, as we all know, is really the promotion of one particular set of national interests around the world. To see democracy, on the other hand, as deconstructible and therefore universalisable, could mean the extension of the concept of democracy beyond the boundaries of nation state sovereignty and the creation of, as Derrida suggests, a genuinely international juridico-political space in which the supremacy of narrow national interest would be challenged. Here we should note the way that the United States, for all its rhetoric about the promotion of democracy and human rights abroad, has been consistently opposed to any possibility of an international human rights structure – and has exempted itself not only from many existing conventions but also from the jurisdiction of the International Criminal Court.

The democracy to come should therefore be seen, above all, as a singular event – an event through which a genuine and radical political universality can emerge. In this sense, the event owes its legacy to the Enlightenment, or at least to a particular tradition of reason that emerged from the Enlightenment. Derrida seeks to utilise this tradition of critical reason not only against the technical deployments of scientific reason that abound today, but also against what can only be seen as the irrationalism or unreasonableness of the reason of state (*raison d'etat*). In other words, we should submit to critical reason all those abuses of power that are justified in the name of the reason of state or the fundamental prerogative of the sovereign. In this sense, reason should be understood as unconditional, which means that it cannot be appropriated by sovereign power or even by calculable knowledge. Rather, the unconditionality of reason is that which allows each singularity to be related to the universalisable: 'it will have to require or postulate a universal beyond all relativism, culturalism, ethnocentrism, and especially nationalism'.[48] So we see here, as we did with the democracy to come, the motif of a singular event which opens onto an unconditional universality.

Moreover, what is made problematic in these figures of *reason to come* and the *democracy to come* is the position of sovereignty itself. These figures are to be seen as anti-authoritarian, anti-sovereign figures, and the singular event from which they emerge is one in which sovereignty is fundamentally challenged. Through these figures, Derrida wants to separate unconditionality from sovereignty, which, as we know, itself claims an unconditionality – the right to decide on the exception: what would unconditionality look like without sovereignty, without an absolute, indivisible point of authority? For Derrida, drawing on Walter Benjamin, unconditionality without sovereignty could be only understood in terms of another kind of theology; but unlike the one that presupposes an absolute and indivisible God which, as we have seen, translates into the absolute indivisible nature of sovereignty, this would be a fragile, vulnerable god and a weak force – a *force without power*. Here Derrida speaks of a *messianicity without messianism*.[49] The democracy to come, for instance, can be understood in terms of a messianic promise – not like the messianic tones with which George Bush speaks of America's democratic promise to the world, in which the word democracy is taken to new levels of degradation, but rather as a kind of solicitation, in the name of democracy, which the weak of this world make upon the strong. We might think here of those mothers and grandmothers of the Asociacon Madres de Plaza (The Mothers of the Disappeared) who, since 1976, have continued to gather silently in a Buenos Aires plaza to protest the 'disappearance' of their sons and daughters at the hands of the government during Argentina's 'dirty war', and to demand justice. Or we might think of the Zapatista woman dying of cancer who led a protest march from Chiapas to Mexico City to demand justice for the indigenous and landless peasants of Mexico; or those relatives – again mostly women – of the 8,000 Bosnians who were massacred in Srebrenica, who carry banners bearing their names and gather outside the International Court of Justice in the Hague; or even Cindy Sheehan in the United States, whose son was killed in Iraq, and who persists in protesting outside George Bush's ranch in Texas, reigniting the anti-war movement in that country and bringing considerable embarrassment to the Administration. These silent solicitations of justice made by those who are weak, who have no power, constitute at the same time a force which knocks persistently on the doors of the bastions of the strong, and which quietly lays siege to sovereignty, confronting its hegemony in the name of something more unconditional, more universal.

Democracy and globalisation

The notion of democracy to come – understood as an event and a messianicity without messianism – can be seen as an attempt to free democracy from sovereignty. Sovereignty is the rule of the strong and, as such, necessarily constitutes an abuse of power; democracy, on the other hand – if it can be understood at all – suggests a certain unconditional liberty and equality in which this rule of the strong is fundamentally called into question. Moreover, new possibilities of detaching democracy from sovereignty, or at least of making problematic their relationship, are presenting themselves as a result of globalisation. We have already pointed to the way that globalisation is creating conditions for a new international juridico-political space in which national sovereignty is in certain ways superseded. However, at the same time we should certainly not be too sanguine about the democratic prospects of globalisation: while globalisation is

undermining nation state sovereignty, it is also leading to the paranoid rein-
forcement of national borders; economic globalisation is not only entrenching
poverty and inequality around the world but also corporate and financial power
structures which themselves pose a significant threat to democracy, even of the
limited national kind; and, furthermore, we should also recognise that national
communities can actually serve as sites for a resurgence of democracy as a
bulwark against these global economic power structures – witness the case of
Venezuela, for instance, in which a form of populist democracy increasingly
presents itself as a site of resistance to the neo-liberal economic policies that are
being foisted on Latin and South America, as well as to the global hegemony of
the United States.

Nevertheless, the reality is that globalisation is leading to a weakening of the
traditional concept of national sovereignty and, thus, to a situation in which the
idea of the national community as the only site of democratic decision making
needs to be rethought. New international and transnational organisations and
legal frameworks are emerging which, while not exactly democratic, at least
present the possibility for their future democratisation. Activists have suggested
a number of reforms which would perhaps go some way towards establishing an
initial basis for a democratic global order: for instance, a Peoples' Assembly
which would supplement the General Assembly of the United Nations, and
whose model of democratic representation would be population districts that
would cut across national borders; the extension of the jurisdiction of international legal and human rights institutions such as the ICC; the implementation
of the Tobin Tax, a tax on global financial transactions; as well as the elimination of controls on international property such as patents.[50] However, these
measures, while significant in themselves, should be seen as ultimately limited
and imperfect approaches to democracy. The democracy to come would suggest
the possibility of completely new and innovative ways of thinking about and
implementing democracy globally, ways that we perhaps cannot yet grasp.
Whatever the case, a global form of democracy can only emerge, as Hardt and
Negri suggest, through some unprecedented political intervention or, as they
put it 'an audacious act of political imagination'.[51] In similar terms, following
Derrida, we could say that democracy can only be understood as a wholly
unforeseeable, singular and contingent *event*.

In this chapter I have considered how democracy might be rethought according to the theoretical conditions of postmodernity – conditions which entail the
breakdown of metanarratives and essential foundations. In exploring a number
of different approaches here – including agonistic democracy and deliberative
democracy – I have argued that a radical renewal of the democratic revolution
would have to involve the attempt to detach democracy not only from the
limited liberal-capitalist-parliamentary form in which it is expressed today, but
from the very principle of sovereignty itself. Once democracy is thought beyond

the limits of sovereignty, this opens it to all sorts of radical re-articulations, including forms of transnational democracy which go beyond the boundaries of the nation state and which are actually emerging everywhere today in the form of global struggles for rights, justice and equality. Above all, democracy is understood here in terms of a singular and contingent event – an event which opens onto a new dimension of universality.

However, it is perhaps because democracy is detached from sovereignty in this way, and taken so far from traditional understandings of political regimes, that there appears a certain ambiguity or even reticence regarding the very word 'democracy': Derrida, in an interview, said about democracy, '[A]s a term it's not sacred. I can, some day or other, say "No", it's not the right term. The situation allows or demands that we use another term ...'[52] What might this other term be however? Let us take a risk here and suggest that if democracy is seen here as a form of radical politics which takes as its horizon the goal of perfect liberty with perfect equality, a horizon in which state sovereignty is fundamentally called into question, that this 'other term' for democracy might be *anarchism*. I shall consider this possibility in the following chapter.

Notes

1 A similar point has also been made by Žižek. See 'For a leftist reappropriation of the European legacy', *Journal of Political Ideologies*, 3/1 (1998): 63–78.

2 See A. Badiou, 'Democratic materialism and the materialist dialectic', *Radical Philosophy*, 130 (March/April 2005): 20–24.

3 See Badiou, *Metapolitics*, p. 84

4 Badiou, *Metapolitics*, p. 78.

5 See S. Žižek, 'Repeating Lenin', <www.lacan.com/replenin.htm>.

6 Badiou, *Metapolitics*, p. 78.

7 Badiou, *Metapolitics*, p. 85 (original emphasis).

8 See T.L. Pangle, *The Ennobling of Democracy: The Challenge of the Postmodern Age* (Baltimore: The Johns Hopkins University Press, 1992), pp. 5–6.

9 Lyotard, *The Differend*, p. 145.

10 Lyotard, *The Differend*, p. 147.

11 Lyotard, *The Differend*, p. 150.

12 W.E. Connolly, *Identity/Difference: Democratic Negotiations of the Political Paradox* (Ithaca: Cornell University Press, 1991), p. 190.

13 Connolly, *Identity/Difference*, p. 211.

14 Connolly, *Identity/Difference*, p. 218.

15 Connolly, *Identity/Difference*, p. 220.

16 See Connolly, *Identity/Difference*, p. 194.

17 J. Habermas, 'Three normative models of democracy', in S. Benhabib (ed.) *Democracy and Difference: Contesting the Boundaries of the Political* (Princeton New Jersey: Princeton University Press, 1996), pp. 21–30, p. 27.

18 S. Benhabib, 'Toward a deliberative model of democratic legitimacy', *Democracy and Difference*, pp. 67–94, p. 70.

19 Chantal Mouffe, *The Democratic Paradox* (London: Verso, 2000), p. 93.

20 However, in the case of the New Labour travesty in the UK, even this window dressing has now fallen away – the party now tries to stitch up its image by drawing on the worst kind of conservative communitarianism, having moved so far to the right that now the Conservative Party has realised that its best chance in beating it is to outflank it from the left! The new Conservative leader is a sort of 'Tony Blair lite' – trying to appear more humane on issues such as the treatment of asylum seekers.
21 Rancière, *Disagreement*, p. 95.
22 See for instance, A. Downs, *An Economic Theory of Democracy* (New York: Harper & Row, 1957).
23 Rancière, *Disagreement*, p. 103.
24 Rancière, *Disagreement*, p. 120.
25 This distinction is also insisted on by Yannis Stavrakakis. See 'Re-activating the democratic revolution: the politics of transformation beyond reoccupation and conformism', *Parallax*, 9:2 (2003): 56–71.
26 C. D. Lummis, *Radical Democracy* (Ithaca: Cornell University Press, 1996), p. 15.
27 C. Lefort, *Democracy and Political Theory*, trans. D. Macey (Cambridge: Polity Press, 1988), p. 17.
28 C. Lefort, *The Political Forms of Modern Society: Bureaucracy, Democracy, Totalitarianism* (Cambridge: Polity Press, 1986), p. 305.
29 Similar criticisms were made in response to Lefort's paper 'The Question of Democracy' delivered at the Centre for Philosophical Research on the Political at the Ecole Normale Superieure in Paris in 1982 – including those from Philipe Lacoue-Labarth and Jean-Luc Nancy, who suggested that a kind of 'soft' invisible totalitarianism was operating in Western democracies in the form of techno-scientific ideology. See discussion of this debate in Critchley, *The Ethics of Deconstruction*, pp. 207–212.
30 See Lefort, *Democracy and Political Theory*, p. 255.
31 Ernesto Laclau, *On Populist Reason* (London: Verso, 2005), p. 166.
32 See E. Laclau and C. Mouffe, *Hegemony and Socialist Strategy: Towards a Radical Democratic Politics*, 2nd edn, (London: Verso, 2001), p. 159.
33 C. Mouffe, 'Preface: Democratic Politics Today', in C. Mouffe (ed.), *Dimensions of Radical Democracy: Pluralism, Citizenship, Community* (London: Verso, 1992), pp. 1–14, p. 1.
34 See Mouffe, *The Democratic Paradox*, pp. 2–5.
35 Mouffe, *The Democratic Paradox*, p. 32.
36 Mouffe, *The Democratic Paradox*, pp. 101–102
37 C. Mouffe, 'Democratic Citizenship and Political Community', *Dimensions of Radical Democracy*, pp. 225–239, pp. 232–233.
38 See Mouffe, *The Democratic Paradox*, pp. 36–59.
39 See E. Balibar, 'Ambiguous universality,' *Differences: A Journal of Feminist Cultural Studies*, 7:1 (1995): 48–72, p. 72.
40 See Mouffe, *The Democratic Paradox*, pp. 40–41.
41 Mouffe, *The Democratic Paradox*, p. 42.
42 M. Bakunin, *Political Philosophy: Scientific Anarchism*, ed. G. P. Maximoff (London: Free Press of Glencoe, 1984), pp. 222–233.
43 See J. Caputo, 'Without sovereignty, without being: unconditionality, the coming God and Derrida's democracy to come', *Journal for Cultural and Religious Theory*, 4:3 (August 2003): 9–26.
44 Derrida, *Rogues*, p. 75.
45 Derrida, *Rogues*, p. 25.

46 Derrida, *Rogues*, p. 9.
47 Derrida, *Rogues*, pp. 86–90.
48 Derrida, *Rogues*, p. 149.
49 Derrida, *Rogues*, p. xiv.
50 See M. Hardt and A. Negri, *Multitude: War and Democracy in the Age of Empire* (New York: Penguin, 2004), pp. 290–303.
51 Hardt and Negri, *Multitude*, p. 308.
52 See J. Derrida, *Negotiations: Interventions and Interviews, 1971–2001*, ed. and trans. E. Rottenburg (Stanford: Stanford University Press, 2002), p. 181.

6

Radical politics today

IN THE PREVIOUS chapter, I explored a number of different approaches to the question of democracy. I suggested that democracy – if it is to be taken seriously today – must be thought beyond the political limits of the nation state, and beyond even the theoretical limits of sovereignty itself. As a form of politics which takes *equaliberty* as its horizon, democracy can no longer be confined to the state, a political category which, in the very name of democracy, crushes its aspirations and denies its radical potential. Perhaps the anti-democratic 'security' measures employed by the state in recent years have the effect not only of radicalising democratic struggles, but this, combined with the political, economic and social transformations that go by the name of 'globalisation', is also creating the conditions for new transnational forms of radical democratic politics.

In this chapter I will examine the conditions for radical politics today against the background of a rapacious globalising capitalism and an increasingly aggressive and authoritarian state sovereignty. The various struggles, activist networks and protest movements that come under the rather inadequate heading of the 'anti-globalisation' movement,[1] can be seen as an example of a new form of radical politics that calls into question the current state capitalist global order and the neo-liberal ideology which animates it. Moreover, this 'movement' or 'movement of movements' – as activists like to refer to it – represents new forms of political subjectivity, ethics and practice that go beyond both the class paradigms of Marxism and the identity politics of the 'new social movements'. In this sense, it can be seen as a form of 'postfoundational' politics which articulates universal concerns and issues in radically new and non-essentialist ways. Here I will show how the different theoretical approaches discussed in previous chapters can inform our understanding of this movement, as well showing how this movement can in turn advance contemporary radical political theory and help us resolve some of the tensions central to it. Furthermore, I will explore the link between this new radical politics and anarchism: the anti-authoritarian and anti-capitalist tendencies of this movement, as well as its non-hierarchical practices and modes of organisation, not only reflect – even if 'unconsciously' – many of the key principles of anarchism, but also highlight the political relevance today of both anarchist and poststructuralist theory, two perspectives which themselves converge in a number of important respects.

Capitalism, globalisation and postmodernity

Globalisation, as hackneyed and clichéd a term as it is, is at the centre of radical political concerns today. The transnationalising tendencies of capitalism – the dizzying flows of capital investment and technology across national borders, the concomitant transformations of national economies and the emergence of new transnational centres of power – are not only creating new antagonisms around issues such as environmental destruction, worsening labour conditions and the dispossession of indigenous people, but are also presenting new opportunities for international cross-border activism as well as for the emergence of a global 'civil society'. While these are commonplace observations in most studies of the politics of globalisation,[2] these factors also force us to rethink many key aspects of radical political theory. This refers not only to the fact that radical political struggles can no longer be confined to national spaces and concerns, but also to the new forms of identification and activism central to these struggles. I will explore this in greater detail later; however, it is clear that capitalist globalisation increasingly forms the horizon of radical politics today. So far in the book, I have touched on a number of different aspects of this horizon: the emergence of global 'security' networks which increasingly go beyond the borders of the nation state; the corporate and financial centres of global power – multinational corporations and institutions such as the IMF, WTO and the World Bank; as well the possibility of transnational juridico-political spaces and global understandings of human rights and the democracy to come.

In this context we must also consider the question of postmodernity, which has thus far formed the major *theoretical* horizon and problematic of this book. Postmodernity can be seen as forming the epistemological matrix of globalisation. I am not suggesting here simply that postmodernity is a historical period which coincides with the emergence of a globalised capitalist economy, but rather that the 'postmodern' condition of knowledge that Lyotard reported on in the early 1980s – characterised by the transformation of capitalism into a post-industrial or post-Fordist mode of production and the proliferation of new computer and information technologies – corresponds to the very conditions of globalised capitalism. Furthermore, the fragmentation of the social bond and the destabilisation of existing identities and structures associated with the postmodern condition, is one of the main tendencies inherent in globalisation: the

[*167*]

transnationalisation of capitalism results in the loss of existing social and cultural practices, and the displacement of traditional local and community identities. There would seem to be a postmodernising tendency inherent in the logic of global capitalism – a tendency towards destabilisation, fragmentation and flux. Indeed, Marx recognised as much when over a century ago in the *Communist Manifesto*, he talked about the way that capitalism itself leads to the sweeping away of 'all fixed, fast frozen relations'.[3] Postmodernism and global capitalism, it would seem, have a similarly *deterritorialising* effect.

However, as Deleuze and Guattari pointed out, for every deterritorialisation there is also a *reterritorialisation*. In other words, while capitalism releases flows of flux and becoming, it also 'codes' these back into its own structures and into those of the state. I have also highlighted a similar tendency in postmodernity itself: while it leads to the fragmentation of existing identities and structures, and the severing of the social bond, it also produces, in a paradoxical fashion, the opposed and paranoid desire to restore or reaffirm the social bond at all costs, to cling onto some imaginary identity or life world. The rise of neo-conservative doctrines, religious fundamentalism and virulent nationalism and xenophobia can all be seen as examples of this reterritorialising tendency. In an era that promises us unlimited *jouissance* and total liberation – from our bodies and identities – we see instead, on this 'open' landscape of postmodernity, the old figures of family, religion and nation; the hybridised, disembodied post-modern subject of cyberspace seems to find his paradoxical double in the figure of the suicide bomber who reasserts the corporeality of his body, and so on.

I would suggest that a similar phenomenon can be found in the logic of capitalist globalisation: where, for instance, the promise of global free trade seems to find its answer in economic colonialism and the exploitation of poor countries by rich countries; where the promise of a universal liberal peace ends up in a situation of total and permanent war; where the promise of a world without borders leads to the strengthening of old borders and the emergence of new ones, both between and within national territories. Globalisation, rather than leading to the emergence of a new supranational global Empire without boundaries, as Hardt and Negri contend, is producing new borders everywhere – from the increasingly heavily policed borders of the nation state, to the springing up everywhere of the gated communities of the rich with their well-defended walls and security systems to keep out the poor. On the terrain of capitalist globalisation we find reterritorialising forces everywhere – the supposedly free circulation of goods, labour and capital seems to lead only to new barriers, divisions and communitarian identifications; the nationalism and anti-immigrant racism present in so many societies today has to be seen to be as much a symptom of globalisation as free trade agreements and 'cultural exchanges'. The economic interconnectedness of the world seems to be resulting in growing disconnectedness and outright hatred. Social conservatism, religious fundamentalism and even Islamist terrorism emerge as reactions to the perceived loss of 'traditional' values and ways of life that comes with globalisation.

We have to insist, then, that capitalist globalisation is an inherently paradoxical process, one that is producing contradictions everywhere. It would seem, for instance, that while capitalist globalisation is leading to a weakening of national economies and, thus, a transformation of the national state structure, there is also an aggressive reassertion of both a nationalism detached from the state and a state detached from the nation. The nation state is undergoing a kind of convulsion in which it is pulled in contradictory directions by the forces of global capitalism. On the one hand, the state now exists to serve the interests of global capitalism, deregulating its national economy and opening it to foreign investment, and this often creates nationalist antagonisms and conservative populist movements opposed to globalisation. On the other hand, the state itself often has to appeal to nationalist and even isolationist tendencies in order to do so. Thus we see the state playing on fears about terrorism and national security, and appealing to the worst anti-immigrant and xenophobic sentiments – the recent controversies in the United States about port security and illegal immigration serve to illustrate this.

Of course, we could point to other, potentially more serious contradictions inherent in capitalist globalisation: a global economy which is increasingly dependent on oil is plundering to the point of exhaustion its existing oil reserves; the broader problem of environmental devastation and global warming, in which the avariciousness of capitalism and its perpetual quest for commodities and profit is at the same time destroying the material basis of its very existence; the promise of greater prosperity for all has only produced greater inequalities and, in many cases, worsening poverty; the economic 'freedom' of neo-liberalism brings with it greater restrictions on personal and political freedom, as well as perpetual surveillance and social and moral disciplining; global capitalism is increasingly articulated through a global state of war which, while it is designed to stabilise the structures of capitalism, is only making it more unstable and volatile. It remains to be seen whether such contradictions will lead to the demise of capitalism, as Marx believed about the contradictions of the nineteenth-century capitalism: capitalism as an economic logic has a remarkable tendency, as Deleuze observed, to perpetuate itself even through its own contradictions, and to incorporate these into its structures.[4] However, the point is that these contradictions are producing growing political antagonisms and forms of resistance which may in the future have the potential to radically transform the global capitalist system.

Global resistance

While there had been growing dissent and resistance to capitalist globalisation throughout the 1980s and 1990s – particularly in the global South – it was not until the 'event' of 1999, which saw unprecedented and unexpected demonstrations outside the WTO meeting in Seattle, that one could talk about an anti-globalisation *movement*. Here the disparate struggles against capitalist globalisation became more focussed, and the antagonisms created by it exploded in a spectacular fashion across our political horizon. Symbolised in this event was a global rejection of the hegemonic neo-liberal consensus and its vision for the world, a resounding signal to their global masters that many people around the world – even those in wealthy Western countries – did not accept the 'wisdom' of free markets. Moreover, aside from the spectacle and drama of the demonstrations themselves, and their global visibility, the real importance of 'The Battle of Seattle' lay in the new forms of politics that it gave rise to.

The Seattle demonstrations could be seen as a reassertion, primarily, of a democratic political space – a space that was in danger of being entirely eclipsed by the global neo-liberal project.[5] Perhaps the single most important concern addressed by these protests, the concern that brought together all these different groups – trade unionists, environmentalists, anarchists and even Church groups – was the deeply undemocratic nature of capitalist globalisation: the way that economic decisions – decisions which affected everyone – were made by politico-economic elites with little or no democratic accountability. The protests were an expression of outrage at the way that corporate dictatorships, global financial institutions, and the governments that collude with them, are able to determine the economic, political, social and environmental future of the planet; and that the only consolation for ordinary people was some paltry concession to parliamentary democracy, whose limitations I have already commented on. What was being challenged here in these protests – even if only symbolically – was the emergent new economic and political order whose influence was starting to be felt around the world: the obscure sources of private power and concentrated wealth; the legal frameworks which were enshrining the rights to exploitation; the global institutions which represented the interests of the rich and powerful; the privatisation and labour-market 'flexibility' programmes that were being foisted on countries everywhere; the political influence of multinational corporations, particularly over the governments of poorer countries. These elements increasingly defined a process of capitalist globalisation that was seen as being entirely beyond the control of ordinary people. Therefore the demonstrations could be seen as an expression of opposition to this democratic deficit – and an attempt to claw back some form of democratic power, to define a political space that could not be bought and sold but which properly belonged to the people.[6] The demonstrations at Seattle therefore showed that the demand for democracy could not be confined to the formal political realm: what was being expressed here was not only a demand for some form of economic democracy – some kind of democratic say over global and national economic decision making – but also the potential for *another* form of democracy, a collective or mass democracy that went beyond formal representative channels of the state.

This new democratic politics was to be found in the very structure and practices of the anti-globalisation movement itself. At the Seattle demonstrations, and in subsequent mass gatherings at Genoa, Prague, Davos, Cancun and Gleneagles, new forms of democratic decision making were evident in the organisational structure and activities of the various affinity groups involved. Indeed, one of the most remarkable and innovative aspects of this movement was that it was a movement without a leader – without a dominant Party to represent it or a centralised decision-making body to direct it. Rather, decision making was, in many instances, democratic, participative and decentralised: decisions were made about issues, aims and tactics in a non-hierarchical, non-authoritarian fashion and at a grass roots level. Indeed, the forms of direct democracy employed by different groups has been seen by various commentators as a kind of anarchist politics in action.[7] As I suggested in the last chapter, democracy, if it is taken beyond the representative forms of the party and the state, might be seen as a form of anarchism in which the collective autonomy of the people prevails over institutionalised forms of sovereignty. I shall say more about this later; however, it is clear that what was emerging here was a new, radical form of politics which rejected formal party politics, and in whose organisational structure power was decentralised and dispersed. Instead of the traditional working-class mass movements which were directed by a central party apparatus, what could be seen in aspects of the anti-globalisation demonstrations was a new form of direct democracy, in which different affinity groups and organisations mobilised collectively while retaining their autonomy.

This combination of collective action and autonomy was perhaps the most striking and important feature of this new form of politics. What was remarkable about these demonstrations was the sheer diversity of different groups, identities and interests involved: environmentalists, anarchist affinity groups, NGOs, human rights groups, anti-corporate campaigners, Marxists, consumer groups, indigenous land rights activists, anti-racists, peace campaigners, as well as ordinary men and women concerned about particular issues or simply about the general course of capitalist globalisation. While the demonstrations also involved trade unions and labour organisations, the agenda of the movement was not dominated by them – and in this sense it could no longer be seen as a working-class movement in the traditional sense. Indeed, 'class', as a category, would no longer be appropriate to define the subjectivity of the movement – it was more like a heterogeneous mass.

Moreover, the issues represented there were no longer the traditional economic issues of working-class movements: while the background that was being contested was the globalising capitalist economy, this functioned more as

[*171*]

a kind of 'empty signifier' – as Laclau would put it – which had different resonances for different groups: for environmentalists it meant environmental devastation; for trade unions and labour organisations it meant declining working standards and labour rights, as well as casualisation and job losses; for indigenous groups it meant the loss of traditional lands or the corporate takeover of traditional farming techniques; for human rights groups it meant the collusion between multinational corporations and authoritarian governments, and so on. In other words, while the background upon which these issues were constructed and these struggles took place was an economic one, the way in which they were articulated was *political*: capitalist globalisation antagonised different people for different reasons, and their opposition to 'global capitalism' was not something that grew organically out of its economic processes or that could be automatically assumed – who would have imagined that Church groups would join socialists and Marxists in contesting global capitalism? – but was, rather, based on a political and discursive link that they were able to draw between a particular issue and a general economic form.

The discursive construction of links across different issues and concerns points to a further crucial dimension of the movement: that while it was made up of diverse groups and identities, it could no longer be seen as another form of identity politics. Instead of different groups and identities simply demanding recognition and autonomy, and articulating purely particularistic concerns, one of the important characteristics of the movement was the way that all sorts of 'transversal' alliances were formed between different groups and a common ground was articulated between different concerns. While there was often no clear consensus formed on the general aims of the Seattle demonstrations, nevertheless, broad coalitions were built between different groups, groups who would otherwise have little in common: the 'teamster/turtle' alliance formed between workers and environmentalists; or the loose coalitions between different grass roots affinity groups such as the Direct Action Network, People's Global Action (PGA) and ATTAC. We can point to a new kind of 'network' activism in which semiformal and informal links are developed between different groups in ways that are often unpredictable, eschewing any direct centralised political control and direction.[8]

The 'transversality' of the movement could also be seen in the various transnational links formed between activists all over the world. While there are of course significant differences that exist between the causes of those in the global North and those of the South, there have been numerous examples of transnational and cross-border activism: news of the Seattle demonstrations, for instance, was greeted with strikes, protests and port blockades around the world in a show of solidarity. We could also point to the cross-border campaign organised between workers and labour organisations in the United States and Mexico to fight for the rights of the *maquiladora* workers along the Mexican borderland. Here there was a realisation that the manufacturing workers from the United States and Mexico shared a common fate; that despite the differences that existed between them, their future livelihood was bound up together through their mutual implication in the free trade policies of the North American Free Trade Agreement. We could also mention the informal coalitions and alliances that have been formed – largely via the internet – between the Zapatistas in Chiapas and activists in the United States and Europe. There are, of course, different degrees of transnationality: many activist groups have no or very weak and informal transnational ties, whereas others have developed more extensive and formalised links.[9] However, what seems to be emerging here is the genuine possibility of a *global* movement of opposition to global capitalism. Not only have significant connections been established between activists in different parts of the world, but movements in poorer countries – such the Zapatistas and Sem Terra or landless movement in Brazil (MST) – have often been leading the way in counter-globalisation struggles, developing new and innovative models of direct action activism that have been adapted and modified in the global North.

The different forms of activism displayed by the anti-globalisation movement are another important feature of this new radical politics. Aside from the large set-piece demonstrations that have taken place around the meetings of the WTO, G8 and WEF, there is also a diverse array of often quite spectacular and highly creative direct action techniques which employ different strategies of parody and the reclamation of physical spaces. While violent confrontations with police and the destruction of property are no doubt legitimate in many cases, one of the problems is that, apart from the negative media attention, it tends to provoke, in a predictable fashion, even greater violence from the system it challenges. Hence, as David Graeber shows, many activists have been trying to develop new forms of civil disobedience, tactics which are highly symbolic and effective, and yet which avoid actual violence – a kind of 'non-violent warfare' as he calls it. Such protest techniques include: the *tute bianche* or 'white overalls', whose members dress in padded foam armour and form a kind of phalanx which pushes its way through police barricades; giant puppet shows; and the occupation of space by groups such as Reclaim the Streets in order to hold impromptu parties and festivals.[10]

Richard Day divides direct action activism into a number of broader politico-theoretical strategies. Zero participation, as the name suggests, is a kind of 'lifestyle' anarchism which involves 'dropping out' of normal social and economic practices such as work, and the building of alternative communities and ways of living. Cultural subversion or *detournement*, which originated with Situationism, involves techniques such as 'ad-busting' as a way of subverting dominant capitalist messages and drawing attention to the contemporary society the spectacle through the staging of alternative spectacles.[11] There are also forms of non-violent direct action which involve property damage and economic sabotage, such as destroying GM crop fields and computer hacking or 'hacktivism'. Another strategy involves not only occupying public spaces but also reinventing them as 'autonomous zones'. The central idea with these occupations is that an autonomous space can be created that is beyond the immediate control of the state and in which new forms of social interaction and new non-authoritarian and non-exploitative ways of living can be fostered. Here Day also points to food cooperatives, squatting and Independent Media Centres. Behind such experiments is the idea that rather than confronting global capitalism and the state head on, the best way to overcome them is to work around them, to gradually take over spaces and build a new society from the ground up, within the shell of the current one.

The new radical politics

I have suggested, then, that the anti-globalisation movement represents a new form of radical politics, involving new causes – or at least a new rearticulation of old causes – new modes of identification, and new forms of organisation, mobilisation and direct action. How are we to understand the theoretical significance of its emergence?

We can point here to three historical configurations or 'stages' of radical politics. The first stage would be the great working-class struggles from the mid-nineteenth century to the mid-twentieth century: even though many of these struggles were quite diverse, they could generally be grouped under the dominant Marxist subjectivity of the proletariat, understood as both an actual socio-economic category and a revolutionary identity. Moreover, the issues concerned in these struggles were largely economic, generated by, in many societies, rapid industrialisation and the social dislocations this wrought: capitalism was seen either as an economic system whose contradictions would create the conditions for its own revolutionary transformation, or as a system which could be reformed and from which material concessions could be wrung – such as the improvement of pay and conditions, the reduction of the working week, and so forth. Furthermore, the organisational form taken by this mode of politics was the centralised and disciplined mass party and trade union, or in the Bolsheviks' case, the small revolutionary vanguard party. The dominant form of mobilisation, moreover, was either the idea of the revolutionary seizure of the state apparatus or the general strike.

The second stage was that of the New Left and the New Social Movements, beginning from the period of the 1960s and continuing until the late 1980s. Due to transformations in the capitalist economy from industrial to post-industrial modes of production and to the relative levels of material comfort achieved, at least by some, in Western societies, new demands and struggles started to spring up over issues such as the environment, personal autonomy, gender, sexuality and ethnic and cultural identity. New forms of political organisation, based on grass roots decision making and direct action, replaced the more formal and centralised representative structures of traditional Left politics.

However, while there was a certain radical potential in many of these struggles, they ultimately produced a form of politics based on the assertion of a particular identity and the demand that it be recognised in its specificity and particularity: certain strands of feminism, as well as the struggles of gays and cultural and ethnic minorities might be seen as examples of this.[12] This sort of politics of difference, however, no longer represents any real threat to the capitalist system. Indeed, as thinkers like Žižek have observed, 'liberal multiculturalism' or the demand that different identities be recognised and 'respected', far from being subversive today, actually serves as the ideological supplement of contemporary global capitalism.[13] According to Žižek, the demand for cultural autonomy and the recognition of different identities has become part of a global capitalist system which, rather than suppressing differences, actually operates through the logic of difference, officially tolerating and even eliciting it. In seeking out and politicising newer and more hidden arenas of discrimination, sexism and homophobia, identity politics implicitly recognises the inevitability and even legitimacy of the global capitalist system, and thus operates as a way of sustaining a more fundamental prohibition on politicising global capitalism itself. There is, in other words, a kind of hidden conservatism underneath the extravagance of claims about institutional homophobia and sexism, and of demands, for instance, for the institutional recognition and representation of ever more marginal and specific sexual identities – Gay-Lesbian-Bisexual-Transgender-Intersex, etc.

This focus on ever more minute differences and ever more specific forms of discrimination indicates a kind of exhaustion of identity politics and the politics of difference. The politics of difference has for the most part reached its historical, theoretical and political limit. In drawing on a certain interpretation of postmodern theory – particularly that of Lyotard – and in rejecting, as it was no doubt right to do, the universalism of the Enlightenment humanist conception of Man, it has fallen into another form of essentialism: the *essentialism of difference*. In other words, by insisting, in a narcissistic fashion, on the differences between identities – on their specific properties and particular characteristics – identity politics has failed to recognise the instability of identity itself, and therefore the undecidability of differences.

Politically, this form of politics is no longer subversive or radical, not only fitting hand-in-glove with the multicultural logic of globalised capitalism, but also invoking the state apparatus at every turn – an apparatus which, in many Western countries at least, is only too happy to grant concessions, to recognise differences, to rule out sexual discrimination and sexual harassment in the workplace, to increase the number of female MPs, to criminalise racial vilification and hate speech, to grant same-sex partners the right to inherit property or even marry in civil unions, and so on. The willingness with which the state is prepared to implement such measures highlights the ultimately conservative nature of these demands – the sense in which they do not present any fundamental challenge to the state-capitalist system, and indeed allow the state to actually expand its bureaucratic and policing apparatus into different areas of social life, private morality and interpersonal relations.

Dissatisfaction and disillusionment with the reformist limitations of identity politics has lead to the emergence of new forms of radical politics – exemplified by the anti-globalisation movement. Here we can point to a new configuration or 'third stage' of radical politics, which differs from the first two stages in crucial ways. As I have already shown, this form of politics differs from the Marxist working-class struggle: it is no longer based on the central subjectivity of the proletariat and, therefore, even though traditional working-class organisations are involved in important ways in these struggles, the movement is no longer intelligible under the rubric of class struggle. It is no doubt an anti-capitalist struggle, but not in the classical Marxist sense: rather, global capitalism operates as an open horizon which is interpreted politically rather than simply economically, and which is understood by different people in different ways. Moreover, it is no longer based on the Marxist model of political mobilisation – that of the centrally organised mass party – but rather embodies, as we have seen, a 'network' activism of loose affinity groups and diverse organisations engaged in both traditional demonstrations and more innovative forms of direct action.

However, while the anti-globalisation movement draws on certain aspects of identity politics – basing its struggles on grass roots organisations rather than political parties – it also goes beyond this logic. Firstly, it re-politicises capitalism: global capitalism becomes once again the universal problematic from which different issues emerge, and the universal terrain upon which different struggles take place. In the words of Žižek: 'It is not only the so-called Seattle movement; there are other signals that demonstrate that – how shall I put it? – capitalism is becoming a problem again.'[14] However, I would not agree with Žižek that this signals a return to a Marxist politics in which issues such as racism and cultural autonomy are no longer important. These still remain important concerns, but they are no longer seen in isolation and are refracted back through the general problematic of globalised capitalism. Moreover, these concerns become increasingly bound up with other more 'economic' concerns such as labour rights, economic exploitation, wealth inequality and corporate greed. The way in which these different struggles relate to global capitalism depends on a political articulation, on constructing a discursive link between a specific issue and a more general problematic. So the anti-globalisation movement is a movement which fundamentally questions the structure of global capitalism, calling for either major reforms – aimed at the redistribution of wealth and the limitation of corporate power – or for a total transformation of the system itself. In this sense, it goes beyond the more limited and narrow ambitions of identity politics.

Furthermore, counter-globalisation politics also radically challenges the state: even though there are certain reformist trends within the movement – particularly amongst the NGOs who are prepared to work with governments through more formal channels – many activists are entirely opposed to working through state institutions, and refuse participation in representative party politics. More generally, the state represents, for many activists, an institution which fundamentally supports the global capitalist system, providing it with stability and protecting private property through the use of coercive force. The massive police presence at demonstrations – especially at Genoa where close to a billion dollars was spent on security, and where the Italian police actually shot and killed an unarmed protester at point blank range – shows the lengths to which the state will go to protect the interests of the rich and powerful. Increasingly, the state and capitalism are coming to be seen as part of the same problem – the two sides of the same hegemonic structure. Indeed, the state, in its new post-September 11 'security' mode – where democratic rights are being increasingly restricted and where anti-terrorist laws are increasingly being targeted at anti-globalisation activists –appears as a ruthless and violent machine which seeks to protect the interests of global capitalism at any cost. From the anti-globalisation and also the anti-war demonstrations – two causes which have become in many ways coextensive – there has emerged an idea of a civil society and a form of politics that is not only beyond the control of the state, but which is increasingly calling into question its very legitimacy. In a world darkened and made opaque under the looming shadow of the state, there are forces which increasingly contest its authority and carve out a political space beyond its grasp.

While anti-globalisation politics differs from identity politics in its more rigorous contestation of both capitalism and the state, it also differs fundamentally from it on the question of identity itself. We can point here to a new relation to identity, a new relationship between politics and identity: instead of a politics of identity, we can talk here about a politics of 'disidentification'. Here radical politics has entered a new configuration in which political subjectivity is defined in different ways: it is no longer about the assertion of a particular identity and the demand for recognition; rather, there is a kind of removal, or as Badiou would put it, a 'subtraction', of the self from established identities and subject positions – a subjectification which is at the same time a rupturing of subjectivity. I have discussed this in Chapter 3, outlining a number of different theoretical perspectives which converge around this idea of political subjectification as a destabilisation of existing identities. However, when I speak about a politics of 'disidentification', we should be clear that this does not mean that all identities and all differences are swallowed up or eclipsed. Instead, it means a new way of relating to one's identity and to those of others, one that is based no longer on the assertion of a difference or particularity but rather on the attempt to find points in common with others – to establish some kind of collective ground. Thus we see in anti-globalisation demonstrations, different groups and identities represented – workers, indigenous groups, feminists, sexual minorities – but the way of relating to this identity is completely different to previous struggles: what we see is a kind of *contamination* of different identities and concerns which results from a disengagement from one's own particular position. There is a realisation that global capitalism, while it affects different people in different ways, nevertheless affects *everyone* – and therefore that everyone shares a common enemy and engages with a common problem. While identity and diversity continue to be important, there is also the willingness to establish links between differences – and even to overcome differences: in this sense, identity and diversity no longer operate as impediments to the realisation of a collective political project.[15]

A poststructuralist politics in action?

This move that I have charted beyond Marxist class politics and identity politics, suggests that a new theoretical 'paradigm' might be needed to interpret anti-globalisation politics. My contention here is that poststructuralism, rather than Marxism and liberal pluralism, would be the most appropriate 'prism' – if we can call it that – through which to view the movement. I do not mean to suggest here that poststructuralist theory can be unproblematically applied to counter-globalisation politics: there will always be a gap between theory and practice. However, at the same time, this does not mean that political practice remains unintelligible from the point of view of theory, or that theory can have little to say about politics 'on the ground' as many activists claim. Perhaps we could say, though, that in the case of this new radical politics – as with many other political innovations – theory has lagged behind practice.

Indeed, there is a surprising reticence about anti-globalisation politics on the part of many of the contemporary theorists I have discussed. While this new politics emerged after the time of Foucault, Deleuze and Lyotard, there has also been a general silence about it from more recent thinkers: Žižek and Laclau only make passing reference to the anti-globalisation movement, for instance, while Badiou seems to be utterly scathing of it. The theorists who write most about this form of politics are Hardt and Negri, and yet their approach to it is highly problematic for reasons I shall discuss below. However, despite this general lack of engagement, there are clear points of proximity with poststructuralist theory.

Where might these points of proximity lie? Anti-globalisation struggles represent a form of radical politics which rejects institutional and formal party politics, as well as the idea of a revolutionary vanguard party. In this sense, it seems to reflect the theoretical move away from Marxism and Communism that characterised much poststructuralist thought. As Foucault observed, until the late 1960s in Europe, a certain interpretation of radical politics was dominant: that which was laid down by the formal Communist Parties and which was sanctioned by the official Marxist-Leninist line. But then, as a consequence of a series of major events, that politico-ideological hegemony started to break down:

> Krushchev, Budapest: the political justifications crumbled. De-Stalinization, the 'crisis of Marxism': the theoretical legitimation became blurred. And the opposition to the Algerian War formed a historical meeting point from which, in contrast to the Resistance, the Party would be strikingly absent. No more law on the Left: the Left could emerge.[16]

This new Left that emerged from May '68 was a post-Marxist Left, or at least a Left which questioned many of the central tenets of Marxist-Leninist theory, particularly the central importance of the Party, the truth of the dialectic and historical materialism, and the universal and essential status of the proletariat.[17] The intellectual heterogeneity of the post-Marxist Left, reflected in more contemporary thinkers like Laclau, Badiou and even Žižek (whether he admits to it or not) is something that seems to find its concrete articulation in the anti-globalisation movement.

Furthermore, there is a new relationship between the universal and the particular: anti-globalisation politics takes as its universal horizon anti-capitalism or the opposition to the global neo-liberal project. Gobalised capitalism functions, in this sense, as a common enemy which unites disparate struggles in a contingent way. To understand the processes of articulation at work in the construction of this unity, one could turn to the poststructuralist logic of discourse analysis. Central here is the notion of a particular element or signifier that comes to stand in for a plurality of different struggles, providing them with a common frontier through which they become intelligible. According to Laclau, for instance, the social field is characterised by an irreducible heterogeneity of elements – a central and constitutive lack which unsettles every attempt to impose a stable unifying meaning or identity on society.[18] It is important to emphasise here that this field of heterogeneity is not a field of absolute difference and incommensurability, but rather an *uneven* field in which meaning is fixed, partially and temporarily, at certain points. Jacques Lacan calls these *points de capiton* or 'anchoring points': while signifying systems which constitute meaning are characterised by the metaphoric and metonymic movements between signifiers, so that meaning is never wholly determined or complete – which is why we are always engaged in searching after an impossible fullness of meaning – nevertheless, there are 'master signifiers' in this chain which, at certain privileged 'nodal points' anchor the signifier to signified, thus allowing meaning to be partially fixed.[19] This idea of anchoring or 'quilting' points may be applied directly to the politico-ideological field. We see that our understanding of politics, the way we constitute our political identities, is ultimately dependent upon ideological and discursive systems of meaning through which we make sense of our world. The breaking down of metanarratives and essentialist identities that characterises postmodernity has meant that politics is ultimately an indeterminate and contingent enterprise because social and political meanings are never entirely fixed or stable. However, the other side to this is that meanings and identities are also *partially* fixed: certain key signifiers operate in the contemporary political world which organise meaning. For instance, Žižek talks about the way that 'Communism' functions as an ideological quilting point around which different representations are constituted:

> If we 'quilt' the floating signifiers through 'Communism', for instance, 'class struggle' confers a precise and fixed signification to all other elements: to democracy (so called 'real-democracy' as opposed to 'bourgeois formal democracy' as a legal form of exploitation); to feminism (the exploitation of women as resulting from the class-conditioned division of labour); to ecologism (the destruction of natural resources as a logical consequence of profit-oriented capitalist production); to the peace movement (the principle danger to peace is adventuristic imperialism), and so on.[20]

Can we not see exactly this quilting logic at work in anti-globalisation struggles, where the signifier 'anti-capitalism' is no longer fixed to any specific content but, rather, operates as a medium through which different struggles are refracted, bestowing upon them a certain meaning and intelligibility and providing a contingent ground upon which they can be brought together? Here anti-capitalism acts as a universal frontier that unites this heterogeneous field of antagonisms, issues and ideologies – environmental, labour, feminism, human rights, corporate greed, global poverty and inequality, democracy, anti-war, Marxist, anarchist – fixing upon them a common, albeit contingent, identity through the construction of a common enemy.

For these reasons, then, I would argue that the anti-globalisation struggle(s) can be seen as a form of post-foundational or poststructuralist politics: as I have shown, there is no essential or organic foundation uniting these disparate identities and struggles – only a contingent one; the 'identity' of the anti-globalisation movement is not determined in advance and cannot be seen as emerging, in a strictly dialectical fashion, as an inevitable consequence of the dynamics of global capitalism. Any 'identity' or unity that is established is done so through a *synthetic* process, where activists construct alliances between different identities and demands. In this sense, it is a form of politics which is no longer bound up in a single metanarrative – that of working-class emancipation, for instance. However, rather than there being instead simply a plurality of incommensurable 'little narratives' (*petit recit*) as Lyotard would put it, there is, in the anti-globalisation politics, a *contamination* of identities and narratives. In other words, there is a movement beyond identity and particularity – an attempt to find what people have in common and to establish a collective ground.

Therefore, when I suggest that the anti-globalisation movement can be seen as an instance of a poststructuralist political logic, I am emphasising a certain moment or tendency in poststructuralist thought – that which is based around the idea of an *unstable universality* rather than simply the logic of difference. In this book, I have attempted to draw out a certain movement within poststructuralist thought beyond the thematic of difference and incommensurability to one where some form of universality is possible. However, this universal dimension is still theorised through the absence of stable foundations and essentialist identities and, therefore, *within* the epistemological conditions of postmodernity. Here I think we can talk about a *postmodern universality*.

Unstable universality and the construction of 'the people'

The major theoretical figure or motif that I have tried to tease out from a number of different thinkers – including Derrida, Laclau, Žižek, Rancière, Badiou – has been the notion of a universal singularity/singular universality. The central theme here is that a universal political dimension can only emerge in a contingent way through an event, an event which is singular and wholly unpredictable. There is a kind of irruption of the political, in which singular events seem to symbolise the very universality of politics itself: this might be understood as the 'democracy to come' for Derrida; the hegemonic articulation of the universal and particular for Laclau; the emergence of 'the people' for Rancière; or the moment of political subjectification for Badiou.

I would suggest that elements of this can be found in the anti-globalisation movement. Its emergence in 1999 can be seen as an event of unparalleled significance: it seemed to come from nowhere and took everyone by surprise, including activists themselves. It represented, as I have suggested, a new moment of political universality, one that had been buried for so long under the hegemony of neo-liberal economics on the one hand, and an impotent and largely conservative identity politics on the other. Moreover, there was a different articulation of political universality here: one that did not swallow up difference in a universal identity, or drown out universality in a sea of differences, but, rather, produced a different mediation between them. For this reason, anti-globalisation politics can be seen in terms of a political singularity – a contamination of difference and universality.

However, in considering the relationship between singularity and universality, a more difficult question arises: to what extent can the anti-globalisation movement be seen as an instance of 'the people'? In other words, in having defined, as I have hoped to do in this book, some sort of universal dimension or collective political space, it remains to be considered what form of radical subjectivity can emerge from this space. Therefore, the question of 'the people' is really central to radical politics today, especially at a time when the Marxist category of the proletariat has fallen by the wayside and the politics of identity has led us to a dead-end. Which political agent, which revolutionary subjectivity, is to take their place? This highlights one of the major debates taking place today in continental and poststructuralist political theory: whether the central figure in contemporary political struggles is *the people* or *the multitude*.[21] This is largely a debate between, on the one side, thinkers like Laclau and Rancière – who want to retain the central category of 'the people' – and, on the other, Hart and Negri, who claim that the people as a political subjectivity has been superseded by the multitude. This also relates to the question of how to define politics: is politics the immanent expression of some economic logic or essence, or is it about the articulation and constitution of identities and demands? Let us examine the different sides of this debate.

Hardt and Negri, in their works *Empire* and *Multitude*, have argued that within the global Empire of capital, there is the growing hegemony of what they call 'immaterial labour' – labour that is increasingly aimed at producing information, knowledge, images rather than, say, cars and refrigerators. Immaterial labour is not just a mode of economic production, but also a form of *biopolitical* production in which new social relationships and new forms of life are created through new networks of communication and common knowledge. While these 'things' are produced under conditions of capitalism and private ownership, they are increasingly difficult to commodify and tend towards a 'being-in-common'. In other words, what is emerging with this form of production is a new mode of subjectivity defined by the possibility of a 'becoming-common' of labour. This commonality, which Hardt and Negri term the multitude, is a class concept, but one that is different from the Marxist notion of the proletariat: it refers to all those who work under Empire, not simply, or even primarily, blue collar workers. Its existence, moreover, is based on a becoming or immanent potential, rather than being defined by a strictly empirical existence; and it represents an irreducible multiplicity – a combination of collectivity and plurality – rather than a unified identity like 'the people'. This immanent multiplicity has a tendency to converge into a common organism, a singularity, which will one day turn against Empire and emancipate itself:

> When the flesh of the multitude is imprisoned and transformed into the body of global capital, it finds itself both within and against the processes of capitalist globalisation. The biopolitical production of the multitude, however, tends to mobilise what it shares in common and what it produces in common against the imperial power of global capital. In time, developing its productive

figure based on the common, the multitude can move through the Empire and come out the other side, to express itself autonomously and rule itself.[22]

There are a number of interesting themes here, themes which would appear to be reflected in certain key aspects of the anti-globalisation struggles I have described. There is the idea, firstly, that globalisation – whether understood through the figure of Empire or not – is creating opportunities for a new radical politics, and even a new political commonality – something which I think is true. Indeed, Hardt and Negri themselves see the anti-globalisation movement as indicating a new mode of political organisation, based on affinity, collaborative relationships and decentralised networks of communication. Secondly, their idea that the multitude can no longer conform to the traditional Marxist concept of the proletariat also seems to correspond to the anti-globalisation movement. Furthermore, there is also the idea that the multitude is a singular political formation that can no longer be defined through the representative structures of capitalism or the state, and which seeks to emancipate itself from both. Again, this can be said about the anti-globalisation movement.

However, there are also a number of problems with this notion of the multitude. For instance, there is some question over how coherent and inclusive the concept of the multitude actually is. Hardt and Negri argue that the conditions for this new subjectivity are being created by a 'becoming-common' of labour: in other words, people are increasingly working under the same conditions of production within Empire and are therefore melding into a commonality, defined by new affective relationships and networks of communication. However, surely this ignores the major divisions that continue to exist in the conditions of labour between a salaried white collar worker in the West, and someone whose daily survival depends upon searching for scraps in garbage dumps in the slums of the global South. To what extent can we speak of any commonality between such radically different forms of 'work', such radically different experiences of oneself, one's body and one's existence? These two people live not within the same Empire but in *totally different worlds*. In the case of the white collar worker, who perhaps works in the services sector, one can indeed speak of 'immaterial labour'; while the slum dweller in the Third World is completely removed from this experience. The two share no common language. While it is true that 'immaterial' biopolitical production is increasingly penetrating the global South – one thinks here of the uncanny figure of the call centre worker in India – there are still major economic and social divisions in conditions of work, and therefore in the social relationships and forms of communication that flow from this. While capitalist globalisation is a process that is affecting the entire world, it is at the same time creating savage divisions between people and continents, offering some in the West an unprecedented degree of material comfort, while consigning others in the global South to a crushing poverty and a radical exclusion from the market and from global circuits of production. To what extent, then, is it possible to talk about a new commonality defined by one's incorporation into Empire and 'immaterial labour'? Given these disparities and socio-economic divisions, would the multitude not be a highly fractured, divided body – or perhaps even a body from which are excluded those subjectivities that cannot be defined by immaterial labour, or indeed by any form of labour at all?[23]

This highlights the problem of trying to construct a 'general will' across such radically different forms of life and experience. However, the difference here between Hardt and Negri's approach and mine is that I would emphasise the need to painstakingly build transnational political alliances between people in the global North and South – something which we can already seen signs of, albeit in a limited form, in the anti-globalisation movement; whereas Hardt and Negri seem to assume that such a unity is already immanent within the productive dynamics of global capital, and therefore that the formation of the multitude is an inevitable and permanent potentiality. While I would accept that the processes of capitalist globalisation, although they are producing divisions everywhere, are also at the same time creating new opportunities for transnational alliances, there is nothing inevitable about this process. Any sort of transnational movement has to be *constructed* politically.

The problem, then, with Hardt and Negri's notion of the multitude is that it seems in some senses to be nothing more than a dressed up version of the Marxist theory of proletarian emancipation. The multitude is something that develops organically through the dynamics of Empire and the hegemony of 'immaterial labour', just as, for Marx, the proletariat and proletarian class consciousness emerged according to the dynamics of industrial capitalism. In each scenario, moreover, this agency harnesses the economic forces of capitalism in order to transform them and create a new series of social relationships. In other words, there is an *immanentism* in Hardt and Negri's analysis which seems to parallel Marxian economism: both suggest a kind of organic or automatic process in which a new revolutionary class develops through the capitalist dynamic, until it eventually transcends it through a general revolt. What is lacking here in this understanding of the multitude is any notion of *political articulation* – in other words, any explanation of how this multitude comes together and why it revolts. There is only an assumed unity and an assumed 'natural' propensity to revolt. As Laclau points out, however, in his criticism of Hardt and Negri, we cannot simply assume that people will naturally rebel against the totality of global capitalism. What is needed is a more sophisticated understanding of why people resist and how they come to take up a position of resistance – and yet this is precisely what is lacking in Hardt and Negri's account. In the words of Laclau, 'we have the complete eclipse of politics'.[24]

In opposition to this notion of the immanent multitude, then, Laclau emphasises the discursive logics of articulation that go into the construction of 'the people'. In his discussion of populism – which is a collective form of politics in which the figure of 'the people' is central – he shows that this figure is not an empirical reality or an essence that emerges teleologically through the development of social and economic forces; rather, it is a political and discursive construct which emerges through the articulation of 'chains of equivalence' between different socio-political *demands*. In other words, we can presuppose no natural or essential unity between different identities, demands and antagonisms that emerge all around us on the political field: this unity has to be constructed in a contingent way around some sort of common political frontier. In my analysis – and this is something Laclau recognises as well – the frontier that is increasingly emerging is that of global capitalism. However, the broadening of this political and economic ground, according to Laclau, makes the processes by which collective identities are constructed much more difficult: in other words, because global capitalism is creating everywhere new antagonisms and moments of social, cultural, political and economic dislocation, it means that the anti-globalisation movement has to construct alliances between ever more heterogeneous social demands and identities. In particular, I would suggest that the anti-globalisation movement needs to construct alliances and forms of solidarity across national boundaries and develop a new *internationalist populism* – a project which is surely fraught with difficulties, given the traditional attachment of 'the people' to a national identity.[25] The important thing here, however, is that there is no immanent process at work in the formation of this unity, as Hardt and Negri suggest: the moment of political unity between identities, and the demands upon which this unity is constructed, are *exterior* to capitalism. Laclau gives an example: 'The demand for higher wages does not derive from the logic of capitalist relations, but interrupts that logic in terms that are alien to it – those of a discourse concerning justice, for example'.[26] We could say, then, that 'the people' is external to global capitalism. This does not mean, of course, that those who make up the people, those who take part in anti-globalisation activities, are somehow removed from capitalist processes – this would be impossible – but simply that, in doing so, they occupy a political dimension which cannot be wholly subsumed or explained by economic processes.

We find a similar theme in Rancière, who sees politics in terms of a certain space of subjectification, in which there is a break with the established order of roles, parts and identities. The 'place' of the people refers to a kind of structural gap between an excluded part and the established order from which it is excluded. This excluded part, as we have seen, not only demands to be part of the whole, but claims that it *is* the whole, that its demand represents the interests of the whole community. Understood in this sense, anti-globalisation struggles could be seen as the movement of those who are excluded from the 'success story' of global capitalism, the global poor, those who, in both the global North and South, are downtrodden, unemployed or underemployed, exploited, marginalised, or oppressed by the state – as well as those who place themselves in solidarity with them. This is not a movement of a single part, but rather a movement of *parts* – parts that claim to be whole, that represent their struggle as the struggle of all humanity. This implies a different understanding of radical subjectivity to Hardt and Negri's multitude: the multitude is immanent to capitalism and Empire – it is something that emerges from *within* its dynamics. This is not to say, of course, that the multitude is not oppressed and exploited by capitalism, but rather that it is at the same time immersed within it, creating the conditions for its autonomy and emancipation through its everyday labour. By contrast, 'the people' would be those who define themselves as *excluded* from the system, as having no place within the system. The multitude defines itself through its labour – it would identify itself as 'worker', signifying its place within capitalism, even though this refers to an almost universal range of work. 'The people', on the other hand, would define itself as something completely different – as a kind of radical *surplus* or excess that cannot be incorporated into the system.

Towards a new international

What I am trying to arrive at, through these various formulations of 'the people', is an alternative understanding of subjectification which *takes its distance* from economic processes and which points to an autonomous political dimension. I am not suggesting here that the political has nothing to do with the economic, or that the economy does not structure the ultimate horizon in which political events take place – simply that the moment of the political, and the subjectivities which arises from it, cannot be *determined* by the economy. This is the major difference, as I see it, between the people and the multitude. The people refers to a moment of political subjectification which is not determined by economic processes but which, on the contrary, involves a separation or 'subtraction' from the economic domain. The reason for insisting on this moment of separation is that to see a politics of resistance as wholly immanent to the structure one resists – as Hardt and Negri do with regards to the multitude and 'immaterial labour' – is to remain caught up in this structure. Here Badiou makes an interesting point, saying in an interview:

> Objective Marxist analysis is an excellent, even indispensable, practice but it's impossible to develop a politics of emancipation as a consequence of this analysis. Those who do so find themselves on the side of the totality and of its movement, hence on the side of the actually dominant power. To my mind, the 'anti-globalisation' movements, or the Italian autonomists who follow the analyses of Toni Negri, for example, are only the most spectacular face of

recent adaptations to domination. Their undifferentiated 'movementism' integrates smoothly with the necessary adjustments of capital, and in my view does not constitute any really independent space.[27]

In other words, according to Badiou, emancipatory politics cannot be wholly derived from an analysis of the capitalist economic system – it must go beyond this and define for itself a space outside this system and its processes. Radical politics must involve a kind of break or subtraction from the dominant structure that it seeks to emancipate itself from, and therefore cannot be explained or derived simply from its internal workings. Marxism, for instance, might provide an effective analysis of the capitalist economy and therefore of the backdrop against which a politics of emancipation can take place, but it cannot, on its own terms, account for the event of politics – the unpredictable moment in which the political irrupts into our social and economic space. As for those that Badiou calls the 'movementists' and 'followers of Negri', not only can they not define an independent space for politics, but they are secretly enthralled with the processes of global capitalism itself: in other words, those who celebrate the motifs – inspired in part by Deleuze, and also by Spinoza – of rhizomatic networks of communication, the becoming-common of immaterial labour, hybrid identities, biopolitical production and so on, are only mirroring the language of global capitalism itself, with its instantaneous flows of communication, capital and technology, its giddying whirls of investment, its unstoppable production, its energy and dynamism in which, as Marx would say, *everything that is solid melts into the air*. We can see this fetishisation of capitalism clearly in Hardt and Negri, whose thesis is basically the Marxist one – that capitalism (and Empire) is itself an emancipatory, revolutionising force whose processes only need to be harnessed by the multitude.

Here we could also point out the difficulties in Hardt and Negri's application of the category of biopolitics, in which production in Empire is increasingly aimed at the production of new forms of social life. This understanding of biopolitics is largely influenced by the Italian autonomists – those like Paolo Virno, who emphasise the potentially liberating aspects of social labour and see biopolitics in benign terms as an effect of labour-power.[28] However, as we have seen with Foucault, biopolitics – which is only the other side of biopower – has a somewhat different connotation, referring to a mode of power which *makes live and allows to die*, and which, as Agamben shows, is always attached to a sovereign relation that rules over 'bare life' through the state of exception. So there is a certain danger in turning this concept around and seeing it as a fundamentally productive, creative and emancipative concept opposed to sovereignty. It is not at all clear that 'biopolitical production' escapes the hold of sovereign power and creates new possibilities for emancipation, as Hardt and Negri imagine. Again we see here an attempt to use the language of the dominant structure rather than trying to explore a space outside it, and this, as Badiou would maintain, only gets caught up in its processes.

However, where I would disagree with Badiou is in his characterisation of the whole anti-globalisation movement in this way – as being somehow the spectacular underside or 'wild operator'[29] of capitalist globalisation itself. What I have been trying to do is construct another way of looking at this movement – one that departs from the 'movementism' and economism of Hardt and Negri, and which emphasises the *political* moment of invention, articulation and disidentification. In other words, I would argue that anti-globalisation politics can be seen in terms of a radical break or separation from the system of global capitalism, and the attempt to define an autonomous space beyond it in which new modes of living are possible. Indeed, it is ironic here that a number of examples that Badiou uses of a genuine emancipative politics – particularly the Zapatista movement in Chiapas and the landless movement in Brazil – could also be seen as aspects of the very anti-globalisation politics he dismisses. As I have shown, anti-globalisation politics does not just refer to the spectacular demonstrations outside the WTO and G8 summits, but also to the daily experiments around the world in new ways of living and new forms of community that characterise movements like the Zapatistas. Indeed, when Badiou talks about the function of radical politics being to 'place the state at a distance', he is referring precisely to movements such as these in which there is the attempt to construct a new autonomous space which is outside the control of the state.

What is also interesting is that Badiou, in other places, has been less dismissive of the anti-globalisation movement. However, here he comments on the need to construct greater transnational and cross-class alliances, particularly between people in the First World – those who conduct an intellectual revolt against globalisation – and poor people in the Third World. Moreover, he argues for a new kind of movement and a new kind of internationalism which is based on an affirmation of something positive, rather than simply being negative and reactive – being *for* something rather than simply against something:

> In the international field we have to find something new which is a relation with the large masses of people in the South. And for some time, the question will be: what is the new form of internationalism? Affirmative internationalism, new organization, not only protestation against globalization, but affirmation of a common political will.[30]

Here I would agree with Badiou: what is needed is for something new to be constructed out of the current struggles against globalisation – a new form of collective action and a new mass movement which brings together different people and which forms durable alliances between people in the North and those in the South. What is needed, then, is a new International – a mass political movement which cuts across the divisions created by global capitalism and brings together people from around the world.[31] Moreover, as Badiou argues, this movement can no longer simply be a movement *against* something but must become affirmative – affirming, for instance, the idea of *a world without money*. In other words, there is a need for a global project involving the construction of a common political imaginary, a common vision of what the world should be. I would suggest that the basis for this new International might be found in the existing anti-globalisation movement, although it obviously requires much greater political elaboration and organisation.

The notion of organisation might appear, at first, to go against the very nature of anti-globalisation politics: have we not stressed the decentralised and anti-institutional character of the movement, and the way that it is made up of autonomous affinity groups rather than formal political organisations? Here, however, we must differentiate the concept of organisation from political parties and formal representative institutions. What is needed here is a completely new understanding of political organisation – something which is different from a political party and which avoids party structures and centralised forms of power. This would be an organisation that, as Badiou insists, is close to the people and in which there is no longer the monopoly on political knowledge and direction that characterised the old Marxist parties.[32] In other words, this new mass organisation would no longer be dominated by a Party vanguard claiming to be the only body capable of understanding the correct 'line of march'. To emphasise organisation and unity here does not mean that the differences which make up anti-globalisation politics are swallowed up – rather they are articulated in a new way, as I have indicated. Nor does it mean that the movement would loose its spontaneity. Indeed, the ability to organise is, paradoxically, the precondition for spontaneous, yet coordinated, political action. Indeed anti-globalisation activists today already place a great deal of importance on organisation.

However, in trying to define a new radical political movement and organisation, we have to avoid returning to the old authoritarian form of politics which the movements on the Left often succumbed to in the past. The iron discipline of the Party, the cult of the leader and the ruthless and violent exertion of power are the seductive lures and potential pitfalls of any radical politics. Yet, this is exactly the trap that someone like Žižek falls into. In his desire to formulate a radical political position that goes beyond the limits of what he sees as liberal-capitalist multiculturalism – in which he includes, rather unfairly, post-Marxist approaches – he ends up valorising a kind of authoritarian Leninist-style politics. What is interesting about Žižek is that while he claims to be a Marxist committed to restoring the economic realm and the figure of the proletariat to the centre of political debates and struggles, he is more concerned with asserting a purely political stance – one which is not determined by economic processes but, rather, by a contingent act or decision. I have discussed Žižek's ethics of the act, which he derives from the psychoanalytic ethics of Lacan: implied here is the notion of a genuine ethical and, indeed, political act which retroactively constitutes its own foundations and which, moreover, changes the ideological coordinates of a given situation – making possible what was hitherto considered impossible. It is clear that such 'miraculous' acts do take place in the political field: indeed, the emergence of the anti-globalisation movement during the Seattle demonstrations was genuine political innovation which dramatically changed the terms of reference for capitalist globalisation itself, showing that it was a fundamentally contested process.

Moreover, bound up in this politico-ethical act, for Žižek, is a kind of subjec-tification through a moment of self-sacrifice. While Žižek takes this concept of sacrifice to extremes, seeing moments of total abjection – what he calls, follow-ing Lacan, 'subjective destitution' – as the ultimate condition for freedom, there is no doubt that radical politics does involve an degree of sacrifice and self-disci-pline, or at least a strong commitment to a certain cause often at great personal risk. For Žižek, then, the politico-ethical act involves a courageous and partisan position that is taken against often difficult odds, against public opinion, against the prevailing consensus about what is possible and impossible. Again, we could point to the anti-globalisation struggle here, which has refused to be deterred by overwhelming state security measures, by the political sensitivity of the post-September 11 climate, and by the constant chant of disapproval from the media and from neo-liberal economists and policy makers who proclaim the 'indu-bitable' truth of the free market. Against this political and economic consensus there is the assertion of a political singularity, a partisan position through which a more universal truth emerges. However, it is here that the figure of Lenin is a central for Žižek: Lenin's principled opposition to war in 1914 and his revolu-tionary seizure in 1917 in the most unlikely of conditions, symbolise, for Žižek, a kind of singular political will and decisiveness, and a courageous act, which, in going against prevailing political wisdom and the dictates of theory, produced a reconfiguration of both politics and theory. For Žižek, then, Lenin is a kind of signifier that has a strong political resonance for us today: '"Lenin" stands for the compelling FREEDOM to suspend the stale existing (post)ideological coor-dinates, the debilitating Denkverbot in which we live – it simply means that we are allowed to think again.'[33]

However, while I fully accept the need to break with the dominant liberal and capitalist ideological order that constrains our thinking today, and while I am prepared even to recognise the uniqueness of Lenin's political intervention, it seems to me that Lenin's moment has passed, and that the old Leninist style of politics – the seizure of power by a small revolutionary vanguard party – is no longer a relevant model for radical politics today. Indeed, today this authoritar-ian style of politics goes against the very ideas of emancipation and universality. The limits of this approach to radical politics are perhaps exposed in Žižek's fetishisation of its ruthlessness: for Žižek, what becomes important here is the idea of *authenticity* – the willingness to assume responsibility for the act. In Lenin's case, his authoritarianism and his readiness to exercise power ruthlessly against his opponents is seen by Žižek as a sign of authenticity – of the ability to 'get one's hands dirty'. Here Žižek seems to celebrate revolutionary violence and terror simply for its own sake – as a sign of one's willingness to 'go to the end'.[34] However, when the revolutionary will becomes caught up in the lures of the death drive in this way, it can only lead to catastrophe – one need only reflect on the horrors of Stalinism to see the pitfalls of such an approach.

The anarchist tradition

It is clear, then, that radical politics today can no longer conform to the model of the revolutionary vanguard party. Instead, the new radical politics – that which is symbolised by the anti-globalisation movement – no longer aims at the seizure of state power but, rather, at its dismantling. In this sense, it is an anti-authoritarian or even *anarchist* politics.

Why is it necessary to invoke the anarchist tradition here? There are a number of parallels and points of convergence between anarchism and contemporary anti-globalisation politics. Many have commented on the 'unconscious' anarchism of the movement. Apart from the fact that many anarchist affinity groups are involved, the movement itself seems to embody certain anarchist political principles: it is, as I have shown, a politics without a leader, without a centralised political party or bureaucratic apparatus; as well as a politics which, for the most part, works outside the state and fundamentally challenges its hegemony and legitimacy. Furthermore, at a time marked by the decline of Marxism and Leninism and the exhaustion of identity politics, and when we see the upsurge of new libertarian and emancipative forms of politics in their wake, it does not seem too far fetched to talk about the anarchist 'moment' in contemporary politics. Perhaps anarchism, which for so long has been overshadowed by Marxism, is becoming the new 'paradigm' for radical politics today. Whatever the case, the parallels with contemporary anti-globalisation politics are sufficient to warrant at least a reconsideration of anarchism as a political philosophy.

However, an examination of the entire anarchist tradition would be impossible here and would require another book. While anarchism encompasses many different voices and perspectives, I will largely focus on nineteenth-century anarchist-communist thinkers like Mikhail Bakunin and Peter Kropotkin. While this form of anarchist thought had much in common with Marxism, it also radically departed from Marxism on a number of important points, both theoretical and strategic – indeed, it was the dispute between Marx and Bakunin that led to the eventual collapse of the First International in 1878. This dispute is of more than just historical interest, though: it highlights perhaps the central question confronted by radical Left politics – the function and role of the state and its place in revolutionary theory. As we have seen, the structure of the state remains a significant obstacle for radical politics: it acts as a struc-

[*191*]

tural support for global capitalism, but at the same time exercises its own mode of domination which can no longer be reduced to the workings of the global economy.

Indeed, it is the extent to which the state could be seen as an specific instance of domination, or simply as an effect of the capitalist economy, that formed the basis for the disagreement between Marx and the anarchists: generally speaking, for Marx, the state was an expression of economic and class domination; while, for anarchists, the state had to be seen as an autonomous institution – or series of institutions – which had its own logic of domination. As Bakunin put it: 'They (Marxists) do not know that despotism resides not so much in the form of the State but in the very principle of the State and political power.'[35] In other words, despite the various ideological guises which the state may assume – monarchical, parliamentary, socialist – and despite which class controls its apparatus – the bourgeoisie or even the proletariat – the state will always be the same; it is always conditioned by the principle of sovereignty which is ultimately absolutist and oppressive. Indeed, today we see this naked sovereign power being asserted in an ever more blatant fashion, stripped of any semblance of accountability or legitimacy, and functioning under the increasingly dubious banner of 'security'. The anarchist critique of the state implied, then, a completely different relationship between the political and economic realms: for Marx, the political was generally determined by the economic; whereas for anarchists like Bakunin and Kropotkin, the relationship is much more ambiguous – the political realm, embodied in the state and its institutions, is largely autonomous from the economic, and even has, in some cases, a determining effect on the economic and social life, creating its own sites of domination and antagonism. Indeed, institutional domination, economic exploitation, religious obfuscation, patriarchal relations and even class oppression itself are all made possible in part by the structural determinations of the state, rather than simply by the workings of the capitalist economy.[36]

Furthermore, because of the way that this structural determination leads to a 'corruption' of the subjectivity of those who control the state, the state can never be trusted as a tool of revolution: the Marxist workers' state and the dictatorship of the proletariat will simply perpetuate state power, serving as its latest guise. Therefore, it was argued that any revolution which is aimed at the *seizure* of power rather than its abolition, will simply lead to another form of oppression: the Marxist revolutionary programme, rather than leading to the 'withering away of the state', would produce new relations of domination and even new class divisions. In the words of Kropotkin, then: 'there are those who, like us, see in the State, not only its actual form and in all forms of domination that it might assume, but in its very essence, an obstacle to the social revolution'.[37] Communism would not come about through the socialist state or the dictatorship of the proletariat, but rather through the interaction of free, autonomous communes which would emerge out of the revolution.

It is for these reasons, then, that the anarchists believed that the revolution must be libertarian in its forms as well as its aims: it must not seek to use state power as a tool of revolution, but rather dismantle it as the first revolutionary act. Moreover, the revolution must be a mass uprising against the state which is not directed by a centralised vanguard party. This was another major difference between Marx and the anarchists: for anarchists, the revolutionary party was an inherently conservative institution which was always tied to the state; it sought to 'represent' the masses by claiming to have a monopoly on revolutionary knowledge, thus channelling the collective will into hierarchical structures. Moreover, the party – with its centralised apparatuses and bureaucracies – was already a kind of microcosm of the state, a future 'state in waiting'. Even the Marxist concept of class was questioned in this critique: Bakunin claimed that class was itself an authoritarian and exclusivist concept, representing only the upper echelons of the industrial working class and neglecting other social identities such as the peasantry and *lumpenproletariat*. For this reason, he preferred the word 'mass' to class – the former expressing the heterogeneity of revolutionary identities and struggles.[38] Indeed, we could say that the attempts today on the part of contemporary thinkers like Rancière, Laclau, Badiou, and even Hardt and Negri, to formulate some concept of a non-class, non-Marxist radical subjectivity, were all foreshadowed, well over a century ago, by Bakunin's notion of the revolutionary mass.

The central contribution of anarchism to radical political thought therefore lies in its rejection of the state and all authoritarian forms of politics, its critique of Marxism, and its commitment to a libertarian and egalitarian ethos. In particular, the innovativeness of anarchism lies in its theorisation of political power – namely the power of the state – as an autonomous field of political struggles and antagonisms that was not determined by the capitalist economy or class relations. Therefore, in breaking the absolute structural link that Marxism had established between the political and the economic, anarchism performed a vital theoretical operation – highlighting what might be termed the *autonomy of the political*. It is in this sense that anarchism is of great importance to contemporary radical politics – a politics which, as we have seen, can no longer be defined in strictly economic terms or through class subjectivities; and which, while it challenges a particular economic system, does so on the terrain of politics – seeing global state capitalism in terms of the more general problematic of political, economic, social and cultural domination, rather than in the more narrow terms of economic exploitation.

Moreover, even though anarchists stressed the libertarian and spontaneous character of the revolution – in opposition to the Marxist and Leninist vanguard model – thinkers like Bakunin still emphasised the need for political organisation. Indeed, he talked of a Secret Society of anarchist revolutionaries whose role would be not to lead the masses in a revolutionary upsurge, but rather to act as a link between 'people's instincts and revolutionary thought'. While some might argue that this is simply another kind of revolutionary vanguard, Bakunin himself makes it quite clear that the Society

> does not impose any new resolutions, regulations or ways of living on the people, and only unleashes their will and gives a wider opportunity for their self-determination and their social-economic organizations, which should be created by them alone from the bottom up ... [39]

The Secret Society is not a revolutionary vanguard, or even a separate political entity, but simply a way of articulating the desires of the people into a common political will. In other words, it might be seen as the *name of a contingent link* that is constructed between the people and revolutionary ideas. It refers, then, to the actual moment of political articulation. The revolutionary mass cannot emerge completely spontaneously – some sort of common position needs to be constructed amongst the multiplicity of particular wills. Therefore, even though the anarchist revolution against capital and the state would be a *social* one, made by the people themselves, Bakunin recognised the need for some sort of *political* intervention, some form of synthetic articulation that would unite the people. In this sense, the Secret Society is a mediating link between everyday social relations and revolutionary political will, between which there is no necessary or organic connection. This suggests, once again, that radical struggles cannot be seen as immanent to social and economic relations but, rather, rely on a political moment of articulation.

In stressing this moment of political articulation, and in pointing to the autonomy of the political field more broadly, anarchist theory also converges, in crucial respects, with poststructuralism. Indeed, the two theoretical traditions could be characterised by a general anti-authoritarian *ethos* – a desire, in other words, to interrogate political and social authority in all its forms, as well as to unmask its ideological pretences. Both perspectives engage in a kind of 'genealogical' project of undermining authority – of exposing the violence and domination behind every institution's claims to inevitability and naturalness. Whether it be the 'social contract' or the 'reason of state'; whether it be the metaphysical authority of the god or the 'iron law' of markets – all such claims are stripped of their legitimacy, morality or rationality. We also find, in these two traditions, a critique of representative political structures, a move beyond Marxist economism and classism, and a strong commitment to libertarian and egalitarian ideals notwithstanding. Poststructuralism can be seen, I would argue, as a kind of anarchism.[40]

Conclusion: postanarchism, universality and radical politics today

In exploring this link between poststructuralism and anarchism, I have else-where spoken of *postanarchism* – signifying a theoretical move away from many of the essentialist-humanist premises of classical anarchism.[41] If the emancipa-tive potential of anarchism – inherent in its anti-authoritarian politics and its commitment to an unconditional liberty and equality – is to be taken seriously today, and if anarchism is to continue to remain relevant to contemporary polit-ical struggles, it can no longer rely on the foundations of rationalism, humanism and the dialectic. However, in talking about a politics of postanarchism, I am suggesting that anarchism can be seen as the hidden referent or 'missing link' that informs poststructuralist and even post-Marxist lines of enquiry.[42] Therefore, post-anarchism should *not* be taken to imply a theoretical move beyond anarchism or as saying that the anarchist moment has passed. On the contrary, after the theoretical and political decline of Marxism, and at a time when we see unprecedented struggles against global capitalism and state author-ity, we can talk about the anarchist moment finally arriving. Postanarchism is simply the attempt to renew anarchist theory and politics through a decon-struction of its original foundations in the rationalist and humanist paradigms of the Enlightenment.

Postanarchism therefore asserts the contingency of the political, without relying on a notion of rational social objectivity that is outside discursive artic-ulation or guided by rational processes. The unpredictability of the event and instability of social identity replaces the dialectic and the idea of the rational social order as anarchism's new ontology. In seeing these theoretical categories as central to a new anti-authoritarian politics, I have drawn a parallel between postanarchism and a certain post-Marxist and post-Althusserian approach in particular – that which is associated primarily with Laclau and Mouffe, but also in different senses, with Rancière. Indeed, there are many points of convergence here: apart from the anti-essentialist and non-dialectical ontology that they both share, postanarchism and post-Marxism are both committed to a form of eman-cipative and radically democratic politics which can no longer be reduced to a purely economic logic. Both strategies emphasise the heterogeneity of social struggles and identities today, and the sense in which they elude the traditional Marxist category of class struggle. We should note here that this does not mean that the struggles of workers are no longer important today or would no longer be included amongst these new social and political struggles. However, instead of seeing the proletariat as the central revolutionary identity, perhaps we can speak here of a global *lumpenproletariat* whose position is defined by a common experience of marginalisation and domination rather than by its place in the productive process. Here Rancière talks about a class which is at the same time not a class: the proletariat is not a distinct economic category but rather a subjective articulation of a wrong, an injustice – thus embodying, through its position of exclusion, the very universality of equality.[43]

What postanarchism also shares with post-Marxism is the idea that a particular situation of oppression, marginalisation or inequality must become politicised before it can become a struggle. That is to say, there is nothing organic or inevitable about social struggles – there are many situations in which an overwhelming experience of subordination remains mute and incommunicable, or is perhaps even seen by those who suffer it as natural or inevitable. There must be some sort of political articulation which links a particular situation to a broader problematic and to a demand for liberty and equality. Indeed, what is primary for Laclau is the socio-political *demand* rather than some pregiven identity: the demand is the moment of articulation which retroactively bestows intelligibility upon the identity who makes it.[44] However, this approach has been criticised in a recent work on contemporary anarchist politics by Richard Day, who argues that the act of making demands only empowers the state, which simply responds to such demands in a reformist manner; therefore, a form of politics based on the logic of demand ends up in a liberal pluralism which does nothing to question the existing state capitalist order.[45] Here, though, I think Day neglects the way in which demands – and in particular the demand for rights – can at times fundamentally disturb the dominant order. Rancière gives an example here of the claim of women during the French Revolution to be included in political processes: they did this by pointing to the gap that existed between the formal universality of the Declaration of the Rights of Man – which guaranteed equal political rights to all, including women – and the reality of the political situation founded on these ideals, from which women were excluded. By pointing to the formal inscription of universal rights and equality, they could highlight the inconsistency of a situation in which they were deprived of their rights: 'They acted as subjects that did not have the rights that they had and had the rights that they had not.'[46] In other words, the simple demand to be included can at times throw into question an entire political and symbolic order based on a particular instance of exclusion.

A postanarchist approach sees a constellation of struggles emerging around certain key demands which would be *impossible* for the state to fulfil without creating major dislocations in the existing power structure. To fight for the rights of 'illegal' immigrant workers, or for asylum seekers in detention, for instance, or to demand an end to draconian border control measures – are demands that cannot be fulfilled without destabilising and limiting, at least to some extent, the very principle of nation state sovereignty. Indeed, the specific situation of asylum seekers and 'illegal' immigrants has become one of the major issues of concern for many anti-globalisation activists.[47] This is not just because of the barbarity and racism of existing border control policies, but also because this situation embodies the general problematic of global capitalism itself: the contradictory nature of a system which, on the one hand, claims to encourage the free circulation of people (and capital, technology, etc) across national borders, and on the other hand leads to the aggressive reassertion of borders and imposes severe limitations on movement; the economic, social and political dislocations wrought by global capitalism, which are forcing people to seek refuge in the wealthy West; the way that refugee camps and detention centres springing up everywhere are *liminal* spaces of exception created by global capitalism – political 'no man's lands' in which power is exercised over people who have no rights. The demand to recognise the rights of 'illegal' migrants and asylum seekers and to not subject them to humiliating and draconian detention and surveillance measures is therefore also a demand directed ultimately at the entire state capitalist system. Another example might be the demands of the anti-war movement, with which the anti-globalisation movement has largely intersected. Here the millions who turned out across the world to demonstrate against the impending Iraq war in 2003, were not simply demanding a halt to the war machine but, through this specific issue, were also calling into question the whole convergence between global capitalism and war – the way that global capitalism increasingly articulates itself through a situation of permanent warfare in which the whole of humanity is caught up. In other words, in the logic of the demand and the language of rights there is always the potential for dislocation and subversion which goes beyond their specific setting. There is always the potential for a certain demand to open onto a radical universality.

However, where postanarchism differs from these post-Marxist/post-Althusserian approaches – apart from its emerging from a different political and theoretical tradition – is in its more specific focus on the state and the problem of political sovereignty. Laclau and Mouffe, and Rancière, are strangely silent on this question: Rancière does not speak in terms of the state, but rather of a 'police' order – a certain logic of ordering or *counting,* to which 'the people' form an uncounted surplus; whereas Laclau and Mouffe's analysis focuses on the logic of political articulation, in which 'the people' is constituted through its opposition to a common, yet shifting, frontier. In the case of the anti-globalisation movement, this common frontier would of course be globalised capitalism, understood in its various dimensions – corporate greed, environmental destruction, dispossession of indigenous people etc. However, what is increasingly emerging today is the problem of the sovereign state itself – a problem which, while it is part of the broader dynamic of global capitalism, also goes beyond it and constitutes its own arena of domination and antagonism. For instance, while the state acts to sustain and protect the economic structures of capital, at the same time it articulates itself through a logic of securitisation and war which has the potential to destabilise global capitalism. The emergence of the security state can only partly be understood in terms of the economic exigencies of global capitalism; it also has its own specific logic of emergency or 'exception' which to some extent goes beyond this. Indeed, I would argue that we are increasingly faced with what can only be described as a global 'state of emergency' in which people everywhere are finding themselves in opposition to the state. Agamben contends that 'the novelty of coming politics is that it will no longer be a struggle for the conquest or control of the State, but a struggle between the State and the non-State (humanity) …'[48] Whether through the imposition of military force, or the subjection of people to unprecedented measures of control, detention and surveillance, it would seem that state power is being asserted in increasingly oppressive ways, and that this power is becoming less accountable. Perhaps it would be more precise to say that the ideological masks of democratic accountability and liberal legitimacy have fallen away to reveal sovereignty in all its nakedness and brutality. The invasion of Iraq, despite the protests of millions, shows that the state today acts with total impunity. Increasingly, then, the state itself is coming to be seen as the main obstacle to radical politics today. We therefore find that whether it is through making demands upon the state, or building new organisations, communities and relationships that exist outside the state, state power is everywhere being called into question. Postanarchism might be seen, in this sense, as a new internationalist politics which, through different strategies, opposes the hegemony of the state.

The main threat to any internationalist politics today, however, is the situation of global civil war which we seem to be inexorably heading towards. The terrain of globalisation is increasingly being defined by a permanent and escalating violence, and a relationship of mutual incitement and provocation between terrorism and the state. Yet, we have to see these two forces as linked in an almost structural sense, terrorism emerging as the shadowy underside of a security state apparatus which increasingly relies on the existence of a permanent terrorist threat for its legitimation.[49] Terrorism provokes counter-terrorism, which becomes simply another form of terrorism: the tortures and humiliations of Abu Ghraib, the shooting of an innocent commuter in a London underground station, the massacre of unarmed civilians by US marines in Haditha, the killing by a robotic 'Predator' drone of eighteen tribal members on the Afghan–Pakistan border, and so on. The invasion of Iraq seems to have – perhaps deliberately? – manufactured a situation in which terrorism threatens to destabilise the entire Middle East. The made-for-TV wars that the democratic West launches on the Islamic world in the name of defeating terrorism, seem to find their ultimate answer in the grotesque terrorist home videos of beheadings and of suicide bombers strapping on explosive vests; violence becomes a strange simulacrum of itself. As Baudrillard suggests: 'There is a fierce irony here: the irony of an anti-terrorist world system that ends up internalising terror, inflicting it on itself and emptying itself of any political substance – and going so far as to turn on its own population.'[50] On this global terrain which is quickly becoming consumed by nihilistic violence and terror, and characterised by the uncanny reappearance of religious fundamentalism and neo-conservative paranoia, the space for emancipative politics would appear to be shrinking. Indeed, a situation in which the only choice that seems to be available is between the totalitarian 'security' state and Islamist terrorism, would appear to portend the very eclipse of politics.

However, while I agree with Baudrillard that globalisation and universality are two different things and, indeed, are in many ways opposed – globalisation creating fragmentation, division and violent hatred and delirium everywhere – at the same time, I would argue that globalisation is also, paradoxically, creating new possibilities for universality. And the only way out of this situation of global civil war – with all its violence, oppression, inequality and obscurantism – is through the assertion of a new universal political project, and a radical politics whose time has come.

Notes

1 Many activists are uncomfortable with this label, claiming that they are not against globalisation itself – indeed they form a global movement with transnational alliances and use globalising technologies such as the internet to mobilise – but rather against a particular form or vision of globalisation that is predominant: that of *neo-liberal capitalist* globalisation. In other words, they are working towards a different vision of globalisation – one that is more just, democratic and egalitarian. For this reason, they often prefer labels such as 'alterglobalisation', 'anti-capitalism', 'global justice movement,' 'the global movement for democracy', etc. However, while I fully acknowledge the inadequacies of the term 'anti-globalisation', I will, for reasons of convenience and recognition, continue to use it.

2 See for example: M. Mayo, *Global Citizens: Social Movements and the Challenge of Globalization* (London: Zed Books, 2005); S. Tarrow, *The New Transnational Activism* (New York: Cambridge University Press, 2005); and G. Baker and D. Chandler (eds) *Global Civil Society* (Abingdon, Oxford: Routledge, 2005).

3 See K. Marx, 'The Manifesto of the Communist Party', *The Marx-Engels Reader*, ed. Robert Tucker (New York: W.W. Norton & Co, 1978), pp. 473–500, p. 476.

4 See Deleuze and Guattari, *Anti-Oedipus*, p. 34.

5 See S. Tormey, *Anti-Capitalism: A Beginner's Guide* (Oxford: Oneworld, 2004), pp. 38–61.

6 One of the ways of symbolising this new democratic space was through a 'People's Assembly' which was set up during the demonstrations, and which was designed to parallel the official deliberations at the WTO, creating an alternative and more democratic forum in which alternative concerns could be discussed. See J. Smith, 'Globalizing resistance: the Battle of Seattle and the future of social movements', in Jackie Smith and Hank Johnston (eds), *Globalization and Resistance: Transnational Dimensions of Social Movements* (Lanham, MD: Rowman & Littlefield, 2002), pp. 207–228, p. 219.

7 See D. Graeber, 'The new anarchists', *New Left Review*, 13 (Jan/Feb 2002): 61–73. However, direct democracy does not always apply in every case, and indeed there has been much debate amongst activists and commentators about the leadership role played by certain self-appointed 'representatives' and 'non-violence' facilitators in protest actions, as well as the undemocratic nature of major NGOs like Greenpeace.

Also, I think that Žižek's critique of consensus building techniques used by certain activist groups is at least worth considering in this context. In claiming to speak from personal experience with activist circles, Žižek's said in an interview: 'all the time, beneath the mask of this consensus, there was one person accepted by some unwritten rules as the secret master. The totalitarianism was absolute in the sense that people pretended that they were equal, but they all obeyed him. The catch was that it was prohibited to state clearly that he was the boss. You had to fake some kind of equality. The real state of affairs couldn't be articulated.' See Žižek, 'I am a Fighting Atheist: Interview with Slavoj Žižek' (interview by Doug Henwood), *Bad subjects* (February 2002): <http://bad.eserver.org/issues/2002/59/zizek.html>.

8 Coalitions such as the PGA, for instance, have a website but no central political apparatus or headquarters, and are composed of activists from around the world, including in the global South. See PGA website: <www.nadir.org/nadir/initiativ/agp/>.

9 See Smith, 'Globalizing resistance', p. 212.

10 See Graeber, 'The new anarchists'.

11 Of particular interest here is the Surveillance Camera Players (SCP) who perform live plays – such as scenes from Big Brother – in front of surveillance cameras, as an ironic attempt to draw attention to the growing surveillance society. See R.J.F. Day, *Gramsci is Dead: Anarchist Currents in the Newest Social Movements* (London: Pluto Press, 2005), p. 23.

12 See E. Larana, H. Johnston and J.R. Gusfield, *New Social Movements: From Ideology to Identity* (Philadelphia: Temple University Press), pp. 3–35.

13 See Žižek, *The Ticklish Subject*, pp. 215–221.

14 Žižek and Daly, *Conversations with Žižek*, p. 149.

15 This is not to ignore, of course, the major difficulties that continue to exist in building a common project out of such a diverse series of groups, issues and identities: the anti-globalisation movement still lacks a sense of a coherent, unified purpose, and there are significant disagreements between activists about aims and tactics. What I *am* suggesting here is that the potential at least exists for a new collective and affirmative political project to develop from this.

16 M. Foucault, 'For an ethic of discomfort', *Essential Works*, pp. 443–448.

17 For Badiou, for instance, May '68 was a moment of rupture with existing modes of politics, out of which emerged new forms of militant subjectivity – and indeed a new political and intellectual configuration which was no longer defined through the old Marxist class historicist paradigm. See *Metapolitics*, p. 27.

18 See Laclau, *On Populist Reason*, p. 223.

19 See Lacan's discussion of the operation of the 'Name of the Father' as a master signifier in the understanding of psychosis, in *The Seminar of Jacques Lacan. Book III: The Psychoses 1955–1956*, trans. R. Grigg (New York and London: W.W. Norton & Co., 1997), p. 102.

20 Žižek, *The Sublime Object of Ideology*, p. 87–88.

21 See Jacques Rancière in 'Peuple ou multitude: question d'Eric Alliez a Jacques Rancière', *Multitudes*, 9 (May–June, 2002): 95–100.

22 Hardt and Negri, *Multitude*, p. 101.

23 This query has also been raised by Jason Read in his review of Hardt and Negri's *Multitude*, 'From the Proletariat to the Multitude: *Multitude* and Political Subjectivity', *Postmodern Culture* 15:2 (2005): <http://muse.edu/journals/postmodern_culture/v015/15.2read.html>. See also Malcolm Bull, 'The limits of the multitude', *New Left Review*, 35 (Sept–Oct 2005): 19–39.

24 Laclau, *On Populist Reason*, p. 242.

25 Here we should recognise not only that many of these demands and identities would have little in common outside the anti-globalisation movement, and that therefore the unity that is achieved is only temporary and contingent, but also that many of the demands involved here – particularly those which relate to concerns about the activities of multinational companies, labour outsourcing and privatisation – might also, in other circumstances, overlap with forms of right-wing populism. Of course, there are major ideological differences between the anti-globalisation movement and the right-wing populisms of Le Pen in France and Buchanan in the US – the latter does not call into question capitalism, per se; champions national preference and strong state sovereignty at the expense of internationalism; and targets immigrants and refugees as part of its anti-globalisation rhetoric. However, we nevertheless have to accept, if we are to take Laclau's analysis of populism seriously, that the social logics that the anti-globalisation movement draws upon – those that are based around the figure of 'the people' – are also those that are drawn upon by anti-globalist conservative forces. 'The people' is not, in other words, a coherent political identity but can be articulated in different ways by different ideological and political forces.

26 Laclau, *On Populist Reason*, p. 232.

27 See Badiou, 'Beyond formalisation', p. 121.

28 See Virgon, 'General intellect, exodus, multitude: interview with Paolo Virno', *Archipélago* 54: <www.generation-online.org/p/fpvirno2.htm>.

29 Badiou, 'Beyond formalisation', p. 125.

30 See Badiou, 'Interview with Alain Badiou', *The Ashville Global Review* (April 2005): <www.lacan.com/badash.htm>.

31 Derrida also recognises the need for such an international organisation, and characterises it in the following: 'I believe in an often silent, but more and more effective global solidarity. It is no longer defined as an organisation of International Socialists (but I keep the old name of an "International" to recall something of the spirit of revolution and of justice which ought to reunite the workers and the oppressed beyond national frontiers). It does not recognise itself in the states or the international agencies that are dominated by certain stately powers. It is closer to non-governmental organisations, certain humanitarian projects, but it transgresses them as well and appeals to a profound change in international law ...' Derrida, 'Intellectual courage: an interview' (with Thomas Assheuer, *Die Zeit* 11, March 5, 1998): <http://culturemachine.tees.ac.uk/Cmach/Backissues/j002/articles/art_derr.htm>.

32 See Badiou, 'Interview', *The Ashville Global Review.*

33 See Žižek, 'Repeating Lenin'.

34 See Žižek, *The Ticklish Subject*, p. 236

35 Bakunin, *Political Philosophy*, p. 221.

36 Kropotkin also attributes the rise of the state to non-economic factors such as the historical dominance of Roman law, the rise of feudal law, the growing authoritarianism of the Church, as well as the endemic desire for authority. See P. Kropotkin, *The State: Its Historic Role* (London: Freedom Press, 1943).

37 Kropotkin, *The State*, p. 9.

38 Mikhail Bakunin, *Marxism, Freedom and the State*, trans. K. J. Kenafick (London: Freedom Press, 1950), p. 47.

39 See Bakunin, 'Revolutionary Organization and the Secret Society', in *Mikhail Bakunin: Selected Writings*, ed. A. Lehning, trans. S. Cox (London: Jonathan Cape, 1973), pp. 178–194, p. 190.

40 Some of the links between anarchism and poststructuralist theory have also been explored by Todd May in *The Political Philosophy of Poststructuralist Anarchism*

(University Park, PA: Pennsylvania State University Press, 1994). See also A. Koch, 'Poststructuralism and the epistemological basis of anarchism', *Philosophy of the Social Sciences*, 23:3 (September 1993): 327–352.

41 See S. Newman, 'The politics of postanarchism', Institute for Anarchist Studies (23 July 2003): <www.anarchist-studies.org/article/articleprint/1/-1/1/>.

42 This convergence between poststructuralist and anarchism should be rigorously distinguished from the so-called 'New Philosophers' like André Glucksmann and Bernard-Henri Lévy who drew on elements of classical anarchism, as well as poststructuralism, in order to criticise not only Marxism but the whole socialist tradition, thus playing into the hands of the neo-liberal Right. Indeed, Lévy's support in recent years for NATO and US military interventions around the world, particularly in Afghanistan, are testimony to this. By contrast, postanarchism – like classical anarchism – has to be seen as part of the radical socialist tradition of unconditional liberty and equality, and has nothing to do with this anaemic liberal humanism. See G.C. Spivak and M. Ryan, 'Anarchism revisited: a new philosophy', *Diacritics* (June 1978): 66–79.

43 See Rancière, *Disagreement*, p. 37–39

44 Laclau, *On Populist Reason*, p. 224.

45 Day, *Gramsci is Dead*, p. 80.

46 See Rancière, 'Who Is the subject of the Rights of Man?'

47 For example the 'No Border' network is a loose coalition of affinity groups and grass roots organisations in Europe who are opposed to state border controls and restrictions on human migration, and who organise demonstrations, direct actions and anti-deportation campaigns. In particular they are opposed to the Schengen Information System which is a government database used for information gathering and border security purposes. In targeting this sort of surveillance technology, the 'No Border' network is drawing attention to the contradictions not only of globalisation itself, but, more specifically, the way that the EU – for all its talk of the free movement of people and the respect for human rights – is policing its borders more ruthlessly and extensively than ever (see <www.noborder.org/>). Also here, in reference to activism on behalf of the *sans-papiers* or workers 'without papers' in France, Badiou talks about the relevance of making *prescriptions against the state*: 'This is not to say we participate in the state. We remain outside the electoral system, outside any party representation. But we include the state within our political field, to the extent that, on a number of essential points, we have to work more through prescriptions against the state than in any radical exteriority to the state.' See 'Politics and philosophy: an interview with Alain Badiou' (with Peter Hallward) in *Ethics*, p. 98.

48 G. Agamben, *The Coming Community,* trans. M. Hardt (Minneapolis: University of Minnesota Press, 1993), p. 84.

49 See Agamben, 'Security and terror'.

50 J. Baudrillard, 'Virtuality and events: the Hell of power', *International Journal of Baudrillard Studies*, 3/2 (July 2006): <www/ubishops.ca/baudrillardstudies/vol3_2/jb_virtpf.htm>.

Bibliography

Agamben, G. *The Coming Community*, trans. M. Hardt (Minneapolis: University of Minnesota Press, 1993).

____ *Homo Sacer: Sovereign Power and Bare Life*, trans. D. Heller-Roazen (Stanford, CA: Stanford University Press, 1998).

____ *Remnants of Auschwitz: The Witness and the Archive*, trans. D. Heller-Roazen (New York: Zone Books, 2002).

____ 'Security and terror', trans. Carolin Emcke, *Theory and Event* 5 (2002): <http://muse.jhu.edu/journals/theory_and_event/v0005/5.4agamben.html>.

Althusser, L. *Lenin and Philosophy, and other essays*, trans. B. Brewster (New York: Monthly Review Press, 1977).

Badiou, A. *Manifesto for Philosophy*, trans. and ed. N. Madarasz (Albany, NY: State University of New York Press, 1999).

____ *Ethics: An Essay on the Understanding of Evil*, trans. P. Hallward (London: Verso, 2001).

____ 'Beyond formalisation: an interview', with P. Hallward, *Angelaki* 8:2 (2003).

____ *Saint Paul: The Foundation of Universalism*, trans. R. Brassier (Stanford, CA: Stanford University Press, 2003).

____ 'A Conversation with Alain Badiou' (interview with Mario Goldenberg, 2004): <www.lacan.com/lacinkXXIII6.htm>.

____ 'Democratic materialism and the materialist dialectic', *Radical Philosophy* 130 (March/April 2005).

____ 'Interview with Alain Badiou', *The Ashville Global Review* (April 2005): <www.lacan.com/badash.htm>.

____ *Metapolitics*, trans. J. Barker (London: Verso, 2005).

Baker, G. and Chandler, D. (eds) *Global Civil Society* (Abingdon, Oxford: Routledge, 2005).

Bakunin, M. *Marxism, Freedom and the State*, trans. K.J. Kenafick (London: Freedom Press, 1950).

____ *Mikhail Bakunin: Selected Writings*, ed. A. Lehning, trans. S. Cox (London: Jonathan Cape, 1973).

____ *Political Philosophy: Scientific Anarchism*, ed. G. P. Maximoff (London: Free Press of Glencoe, 1984).

Balibar, E. 'Ambiguous universality', *Differences: A Journal of Feminist Cultural Studies*, 7:1 (1995).

____ 'Is there a 'Neo-Racism?', in E. Balibar and I. Wallerstein (eds), *Race, Nation, Class: Ambiguous Identities* (London: Verso, 2002).

____ *Politics and the Other Scene*, trans., C. Jones et al. (London: Verso, 2002).

Bibliography

Baudrillard, J. *The Spirit of Terrorism*, trans. C. Turner (London: Verso, 2002).

_____ 'War porn' ('Pornographie de la guerre'), *International Journal of Baudrillard Studies*, 2:5 (2005): <www.ubishops.ca/baudrillardstudies/vol2_1/taylor.htm#_edn1.>.

_____ 'Virtuality and events: the Hell of power', *International Journal of Baudrillard Studies*, 3/2 (July 2006): <www/ubishops.ca/baudrillardstudies/vol3_2/jb_virtpf.htm>.

Benhabib, S. (ed.) *Democracy and Difference: Contesting the Boundaries of the Political* (Princeton, New Jersey: Princeton University Press, 1996).

Borradori, G. *Philosophy in a Time of Terror: Dialogues with Jürgen Habermas and Jacques Derrida* (Chicago: University of Chicago Press, 2004).

Brasset, J. and Merke, F. 'Just deconstruction? Derrida and global ethics', in P. Hayden and C. el-Ojeili (eds), *Confronting Globalization: Humanity, Justice and the Renewal of Politics* (New York: Palgrave, 2005).

Bull, M. 'The limits of the multitude', *New Left Review*, 35 (Sept–Oct 2005).

Bulter, J. *The Psychic Life of Power: Theories in Subjection* (Stanford, CA: Stanford University Press, 1997).

_____ *Precarious Life: The Powers of Mourning and Violence* (London: Verso, 2004).

Butler, R. and Stephens, S. 'Slavoj Žižek's Third Way': <www.lacan.com/zizway.htm>.

Callinicos, A. *An Anti-Capitalist Manifesto* (Oxford: Polity Press, 2003).

Caputo, J. 'Beyond aestheticism: Derrida's responsible anarchy', *Research in Phenomenology*, 19 (1988).

_____ 'Without sovereignty, without being: unconditionality, the coming God and Derrida's democracy to come', *Journal for Cultural and Religious Theory*, 4:3 (August 2003).

Connolly, W.E. *Identity/Difference: Democratic Negotiations of the Political Paradox* (Ithaca: Cornell University Press, 1991).

Coole, D. 'Master narratives and feminist subversions', in J. Good and I. Velody (eds), *The Politics of Postmodernity* (Cambridge: Cambridge University Press, 1998).

Critchley, S. *The Ethics of Deconstruction: Derrida and Levinas* (Oxford: Blackwell, 1992).

Day, R.J.F. *Gramsci is Dead: Anarchist Currents in the Newest Social Movements* (London: Pluto Press, 2005).

Deleuze, G. *Nietzsche and Philosophy*, trans. H. Tomlinson (London: Athlone Press, 1983).

_____ 'Postscript on the societies of control', *October*, 59 (Winter 1992).

Deleuze, G. and Parnet, C. *Dialogues*, trans. H. Tomlinson and B. Habberjam (New York: Columbia University Press, 1987).

Deleuze, G. and Guattari, F. *Anti-Oedipus: Capitalism and Schizophrenia* (New York: Viking Press, 1972).

_____ *A Thousand Plateaus: Capitalism and Schizophrenia,* trans. Brian Massumi (Minneapolis: University of Minnesota Press, 1987).

Derrida, J. *Dissemination,* trans. B. Johnson (Chicago: University of Chicago Press, 1981).

_____ *Margins of Philosophy,* trans. A. Bass (Chicago: University of Chicago Press, 1982).

_____ 'Force of law: the mystical foundation of authority', in D. Cornell (ed.), *Deconstruction & the Possibility of Justice* (New York: Routledge, 1992).

_____ *Deconstruction in a Nutshell: A Conversation with Jacques Derrida,* ed. J. Caputo (New York: Fordham University Press, 1997).

_____ 'Intellectual courage: an interview' (with Thomas Assheuer, *Die Zeit* 11, 5 March 1998): <http://culturemachine.tees.ac.uk/Cmach/Backissues/j002 /articles/art_derr.htm>.

_____ 'Hostipitality', trans. B. Stocker, *Angelaki,* 5:2 (December 2000).

_____ *On Cosmopolitanism and Forgiveness,* trans. M. Dooley and M. Hughes (London: Routledge, 2001).

_____ *Negotiations: Interventions and Interviews, 1971–2001,* ed. and trans. E. Rottenburg (Stanford: Stanford University Press, 2002).

_____ *Rogues: Two Essays on Reason,* trans. Pascale-Anne Brault and Michel Naas (Stanford, CA: Stanford University Press, 2005).

Dershowitz, A. *Why Terrorism Works* (Melbourne: Scribe Publications, 2003).

_____ 'Rules of war enable terror' (6 June 2004): <www.aish.com/jewishissues/ middleeast/Rules_of_War_Enable_Terror.asp>.

_____ 'Tortured reasoning', in S. Levinson (ed.), *Torture: A Collection* (USA: Oxford University Press, 2004).

Downs, A. *An Economic Theory of Democracy* (New York: Harper & Row, 1957).

Eagleton, T. *After Theory* (London: Allen Lane, 2003).

Foucault, M. 'War in the filigree of peace: course summary', trans. I. Mcleod, *Oxford Literary Review,* 4:2 (1976).

_____ *The History of Sexuality VI: Introduction,* trans. R. Hunter (New York: Vintage Books, 1978).

_____ 'Truth and power', *Power/Knowledge: Selected Interviews and Other Writings 1972–77,* ed. Colin Gordon (New York: Harvester Press, 1980).

_____ 'Nietzsche, Genealogy, History', in P. Rabinow (ed.), *The Foucault Reader* (New York: Pantheon Books, 1984).

_____ 'What is Enlightenment?', in P. Rabinow (ed.), *The Foucault Reader* (New York: Pantheon, 1984).

_____ *The Use of Pleasure, Vol. 2 of The History of Sexuality,* trans. R. Hurley (New York: Pantheon Books, 1985).

_____ *Discipline and Punish: The Birth of the Prison,* trans. A. Sheridan (Penguin: London, 1991).

_____ 'Governmentality', in C. Gordon (ed.), *The Foucault Effect: Studies in*

Governmentality (Chicago: University of Chicago Press, 1991).

_____ *Michel Foucault: Essential Works 1954–1984, Volume Three: Power* (London: Penguin, 2002).

_____ *Society Must Be Defended: Lectures at the Collège De France 1975–76*, trans. D. Macey (London: Allen Lane, 2003).

_____ *The Order of Things: an Archaeology of the Human Sciences* (London: Routledge, 2003).

Freud, S. *The Standard Edition of the Complete Psychological Works of Sigmund Freud*, trans. James Strachey (London: Hogarth Press, 1953–1975).

_____ *The Freud Reader*, ed. P. Gay (London: Vintage, 1995).

Graeber, D. 'The new anarchists', *New Left Review*, 13 (Jan/Feb 2002).

Gray, J. *Heresies: Against Progress and Other Illusions* (London: Granta Books, 2004).

Habermas, J. *The Theory of Communicative Action: vols I–II* (Cambridge: Polity Press, 1984–1987).

_____ *Moral Consciousness and Communicative Action*, trans. C. Lenhardt and S. Weber Nicholsen (Cambridge, MA: MIT Press, 1990).

_____ *The Philosophical Discourse of Modernity: Twelve Lectures*, trans. F. Lawrence (Cambridge, MA: MIT Press, 1990).

_____ 'Three normative models of democracy', in S. Benhabib (ed.), *Democracy and Difference: Contesting the Boundaries of the Political* (Princeton New Jersey: Princeton University Press, 1996).

Haraway, D. 'A cyborg manifesto: science, technology, and socialist-feminism in the late twentieth century', in *Simians, Cyborgs and Women: The Reinvention of Nature* (New York: Routledge, 1991).

Hardt, M. and Negri, A. *Empire* (Cambridge, MA: Harvard University Press, 2000).

_____ *Multitude: War and Democracy in the Age of Empire* (New York: Penguin, 2004).

Heller, A. and Feher, F. *The Postmodern Political Condition* (Cambridge: Polity Press, 1988).

Jameson, F. *Postmodernism, Or the Cultural Logic of Late Capitalism* (London: Verso, 1991).

Kant, I. *Critique of Practical Reason*, trans. T. Kingsmill Abbot (London: Longmans 1963).

Kearney, R. 'Derrida's ethical re-turn', in G.B. Madison (ed.), *Working Through Derrida* (Illinois: Northwestern University Press, 1993).

Koch, A. 'Poststructuralism and the epistemological basis of anarchism', *Philosophy of the Social Sciences*, 23:3 (September 1993).

Kropotkin, P. *The State: Its Historic Role* (London: Freedom Press, 1943).

La Boetie, E. de *The Politics of Obedience: The Discourse of Voluntary Servitude*, trans. H. Kurz (New York: Free Life Editions, 1975).

Lacan, J. *Ecrits: A Selection*, trans. A. Sheridan (London: Tavistok, 1977).

_____ 'Kant with Sade', *October*, 51 (1989).

_____ *The Ethics of Psychoanalysis 1959–1960: The Seminar of Jacques Lacan, Book VII*, ed. J.-A. Miller, trans. D. Porter (London: Routledge, 1992).

_____ 'A theoretical introduction to the functions of psychoanalysis in criminology', *JPCS: Journal for the Psychoanalysis of Culture and Society*, 1:2 (1996).

_____ *The Seminar of Jacques Lacan: Book III: The Psychoses 1955–1956*, trans. R. Grigg (New York and London: W.W. Norton & Co., 1997).

_____ *The Four Fundamental Concepts of Psychoanalysis: The Seminar of Jacques Lacan, Book XI*, ed. J.-A. Miller and trans. A. Sheridan (London: W.W. Norton & Co., 1998).

Laclau, E. and Mouffe, C. *Hegemony and Socialist Strategy: Towards a Radical Democratic Politics*, 2nd edn (London: Verso, 2001).

Laclau, E., Butler, J. and Žižek, S. *Contingency, Hegemony, Universality: Contemporary Dialogues on the Left* (London: Verso, 2000).

Laclau, E. *Emancipation(s)* (London: Verso, 1996).

_____ *On Populist Reason* (London: Verso, 2005).

Larana, E., Johnston, H. and Gusfield, J.R. *New Social Movements: From Ideology to Identity* (Philadelphia: Temple University Press).

Lefort, C. *Democracy and Political Theory*, trans. D. Macey (Cambridge: Polity Press, 1988).

Lefort, C. *The Political Forms of Modern Society: Bureaucracy, Democracy, Totalitarianism* (Cambridge: Polity Press, 1986).

Levinas, E. *Totality and Infinity: An Essay on Exteriority*, trans. A. Lingis (Pittsburgh: Duquesne University Press, 1969).

_____ *Otherwise than Being or Beyond Essence*, trans. A. Lingis (The Hague: Martinus Nijhoff Publishers, 1981).

Lummis, C.D. *Radical Democracy* (Ithaca: Cornell University Press, 1996).

Lyotard, J.-F. and Thebaud, J.-L. *Just Gaming*, trans. W. Godzich (Minneapolis: University of Minnesota Press, 1985).

Lyotard, J.-F. *The Differend: Phrases in Dispute*, trans. G. Van Den Abeele (Manchester: Manchester University Press, 1988).

_____ *Otherwise than Being or Beyond Essence*, trans. A. Lingis (The Hague: Martinus Nijhoff Publishers, 1981).

The Postmodern Condition: a Report on Knowledge, trans. G. Bennington and B. Massumi (Manchester: Manchester University Press, 1991).

Marx, K. 'The Manifesto of the Communist Party', *The Marx-Engels Reader*, ed. R. Tucker (New York: W.W. Norton & Co., 1978).

May, T. *The Political Philosophy of Poststructuralist Anarchism* (University Park, PA: Pennsylvania State University Press, 1994).

Mayo, M. *Global Citizens: Social Movements and the Challenge of Globalization*, (London: Zed Books, 2005).

Mouffe, C. (ed.) *Dimensions of Radical Democracy: Pluralism, Citizenship, Community* (London: Verso, 1992).

_____ *The Democratic Paradox* (London: Verso, 2000).

Newman, S. *From Bakunin to Lacan: Anti-authoritarianism and the Dislocation of Power* (Lanham, MD: Lexington Books, 2001).

_____ 'Interrogating the master: Lacan and radical politics', *Psychoanalysis, Culture and Society*, 9 (2004).

_____ 'The politics of postanarchism', Institute for Anarchist Studies (23 July 2003): <www.anarchist-studies.org/article/articleprint/1/-1/1/>.

Nietzsche, F. *The Gay Science*, trans. W. Kaufmann (New York: Vintage Books, 1974).

Noys, B. *The Culture of Death* (New York: Berg, 2005).

Pangle, T.L. *The Ennobling of Democracy: The Challenge of the Postmodern Age* (Baltimore: The Johns Hopkins University Press, 1992).

Peters, M. 'What is poststructuralism? The French reception of Nietzsche', *Political Theory Newsletter*, 8:2 (1997).

Rancière, J. *Disagreement: Politics and Philosophy*, trans. J. Rose (Minneapolis: University of Minnesota Press, 1999).

_____ 'Peuple ou multitude: question d'Eric Alliez a Jacques Rancière', *Multitudes*, 9 (May–June, 2002).

_____ 'Who is the subject of the Rights of Man?', *South Atlantic Quarterly*, 103.2/3 (2004).

Read, J. 'From the proletariat to the multitude: *Multitude* and political Subjectivity', *Postmodern Culture*, 15:2 (2005): <http://muse.edu/journals/postmodern_culture/v015/15.2read.html>.

Rorty, R. *Contingency, Irony and Solidarity* (Cambridge: Cambridge University Press, 1989).

Schmitt, C. *Political Theology: Four Chapters on the Concept of Sovereignty*, trans. G. Schwab (Cambridge, MA: MIT Press, 1985).

Simons, J. *Contemporary Critical Theorists: From Lacan to Said*, ed. J. Simons (Edinburgh: Edinburgh University Press, 2005).

Smith, J. 'Globalizing resistance: the Battle of Seattle and the future of social movements', in J. Smith and H. Johnston (eds), *Globalization and Resistance: Transnational Dimensions of Social Movements* (Lanham, MD: Rowman & Littlefield, 2002).

Spivak, G.C. and Ryan, M. 'Anarchism revisited: a new philosophy', *Diacritics* (June 1978).

Stavrakakis, Y. *Lacan and the Political*, London: Routledge, 1999.

_____ 'Re-activating the democratic revolution: the politics of transformation beyond reoccupation and conformism', *Parallax*, 9:2 (2003).

_____ 'The lure of Antigone: aporias of the ethics of the political', *UMBR(a)*, 1 (2003).

Stirner, M. *The Ego and Its Own*, ed. D. Leopold (Cambridge: Cambridge University Press, 1995).

Tarrow, S. *The New Transnational Activism* (New York: Cambridge University Press, 2005).

Torfing, J. *New Theories of Discourse: Laclau, Mouffe and Žižek* (Oxford: Blackwell, 1999).

Tormey, S. *Anti-Capitalism: A Beginner's Guide* (Oxford: Oneworld, 2004).

Virilio, P. 'From sexual perversion to sexual diversion', *The Paul Virilio Reader*, ed. S. Redhead (Edinburgh: Edinburgh University Press, 2004).

Virno, P. 'General intellect, exodus, multitude: interview with Paolo Virno', *Archipélago*, 54: <www.generation-online.org/p/fpvirno2.htm>.

Žižek, S. 'Repeating Lenin': <www.lacan.com/replenin.htm>.

_____ *The Sublime Object of Ideology* (London: Verso, 1989).

_____ *The Indivisible Remainder: An Essay on Schelling and Related Matters* (London: Verso, 1996).

_____ 'For a leftist reappropriation of the European legacy', *Journal of Political Ideologies*, 3/1 (1998).

_____ 'The spectre of ideology', in E. Wright and E. Wright (eds), *The Žižek Reader* (Blackwell: Oxford, 1999).

_____ 'You may', *London Review of Books* 18 March 1999: <www.lacan.com /zizek-youmay.htm>.

_____ *The Ticklish Subject: the Absent Centre of Political Ontology* (London: Verso, 2000).

_____ 'I am a fighting atheist: interview with Slavoj Žižek' (interview by Doug Henwood) *Bad subjects* (February 2002): <http://bad.eserver.org/issues/2002 /59/zizek.html>.

_____ *Welcome to the Desert of the Real: Five Essays on September 11 and Related Dates* (London: Verso, 2002).

_____ '"What some would call ...": a response to Yannis Stavrakakis', *UMBR(a)*, 1 (2003).

Žižek, S and Daly, G. *Conversations with Žižek* (Cambridge: Polity Press, 2004).

Zupančič, A. *Ethics of the Real: Kant, Lacan* (London: Verso, 2000).

Index

Note: 'n' after a page reference indicates the number of a note on that page.

Index